AN INTRODU
MEDIEVAL PHILOSOPHY

AN INTRODUCTION TO MEDIEVAL PHILOSOPHY

Basic Concepts

Joseph W. Koterski, S.J.

WILEY-BLACKWELL

A John Wiley & Sons, Ltd., Publication

This edition first published 2009
© 2009 Joseph W. Koterski, S.J.

Blackwell Publishing was acquired by John Wiley & Sons in February 2007. Blackwell's publishing program has been merged with Wiley's global Scientific, Technical, and Medical business to form Wiley-Blackwell.

Registered Office
John Wiley & Sons Ltd, The Atrium, Southern Gate, Chichester, West Sussex, PO19 8SQ, United Kingdom

Editorial Offices
350 Main Street, Malden, MA 02148-5020, USA
9600 Garsington Road, Oxford, OX4 2DQ, UK
The Atrium, Southern Gate, Chichester, West Sussex, PO19 8SQ, UK

For details of our global editorial offices, for customer services, and for information about how to apply for permission to reuse the copyright material in this book, please see our website at www.wiley.com/wiley-blackwell.

The right of Joseph W. Koterski, S.J. to be identified as the author of this work has been asserted in accordance with the Copyright, Designs and Patents Act 1988.

Library of Congress Cataloging-in-Publication Data
Koterski, Joseph W.
   An introduction to medieval philosophy : basic concepts /
Joseph W. Koterski.
       p. cm.
   Includes bibliographical references and index.
   ISBN 978-1-4051-0677-1 (hardcover : alk. paper) – ISBN 978-1-4051-0678-8
(pbk. : alk. paper)
   1. Philosophy, Medieval. I. Title.
   B721.K68 2009
   189–dc22

                                        2008018528

A catalogue record for this book is available from the British Library.

Set in 10.5/13pt Sabon by SNP Best-set Typesetter Ltd., Hong Kong
Printed and bound in Singapore
by Fabulous Printers Pte Ltd
02   2010

CONTENTS

PREFACE

There is a long list of individuals to whom I owe thanks for their assistance with the composition of this book. It was Professor Greg Reichberg who first suggested the project, and I am grateful to him for placing me in touch with the wonderfully patient staff at Blackwell, especially Jeff Dean with his constant and gentle encouragements to finish, and to Sarah Dancy for her help in the editorial process. Let me also express my deep appreciation to two anonymous referees for Blackwell, and two anonymous Jesuits who read the manuscript on behalf of the New York Provincial of the Society of Jesus. The helpful comments that all four of these individuals provided were invaluable.

My colleagues at Fordham over the years have been of great assistance and encouragement, in particular Prof. Susanna Barsella, Fr. W. Norris Clarke, S.J., Fr. John J. Conley, S.J., Fr. Christopher Cullen, S.J., Fr. Brian Davies, O.P., His Eminence Cardinal Avery Dulles, S.J., Prof. Gyula Klima, Fr. Joseph Lienhard, S.J., the late Fr. Gerald McCool, S.J., Prof. Dana Miller, Fr. Louis Pascoe, S.J., Prof. Giorgio Pini, and Prof. Daryl Tress, with each of whom I have discussed one or another of the ideas that have come into this volume. I owe a debt of gratitude to friends and colleagues elsewhere, including Prof. Ed Peters, Sr. Thomas Augustine, O.P., and Prof. Wayne Storey. I am also grateful to my students over the years, students whose questions and conversations have often helped me to clarify my ideas. In particular, let me record my debt of gratitude to a number of current or recent graduate students here at Fordham who have commented on various portions of this book: Prof. James Jacobs, Prof. Siobhan Nash-Marshall as well as Paul

Kucharski, Brendan Palla, and Br. Charles-Benoît Reche, C.F.R. And let me not leave out offering my thanks as well to the other members of the Philosophy Department and to my brother Jesuits in the Fordham Jesuit community for their support over the years.

Joseph W. Koterski, S.J.

INTRODUCTION

The period of European history that we call the Middle Ages was profoundly religious. But our appreciation of that aspect of medieval culture should not obscure our awareness of the vibrancy of its philosophical currents. For its intellectual heritage, the era of the Middle Ages was deeply indebted to the literature and learning of the ancient world as to the traditions of reason and revelation that came from nascent Christianity and its roots in Judaism.

This volume is intended as an introduction to medieval philosophy. For a comprehensive approach to the subject, a good history of medieval philosophy will also be indispensable reading, but this book is not intended to be that history. Rather, it is intended to offer an overview of philosophy in the Middle Ages by considering the range of positions and arguments that were taken on a select set of philosophical problems by various figures in the world of Latin Christianity from the patristic age until the dawn of the Renaissance. While mindful of the rich history of Islamic and Jewish thought in the Middle Ages as well as that of Byzantine Christianity, this study is principally concerned with the Latin-speaking authors of Christian Europe. While a good case could be made for putting the start of the Middle Ages at some point after authority of the Roman Empire definitively broke down in the West, considerations of medieval philosophy have to begin somewhat earlier, given the vast influence of Augustine of Hippo throughout the period. Likewise, there are legitimate disputes about the proper demarcation point between the Middle Ages and the Renaissance that it would be more important to debate if this book aimed to recount the history of medieval philosophy chronologically.

But in order to fill what seems to be a lacuna within the literature, this volume will not be organized historically by a review of the leading philosophers and theologians, but rather will proceed by considering a select number of themes that are treated again and again in the course of the medieval period without trying to be encyclopedic. The hope here is to provide readers with little or no previous experience of this period of philosophy with a suitable preparation for their further study. If it is necessary to err in one direction or the other, this study will err on the side of presenting more rather than less of the theological context of the period in an effort to make the context for medieval philosophy more readily intelligible.

The goal of this volume is thus to provide an introduction to medieval philosophy by presenting a certain number of fundamental concepts within their historical context. There has been need, of course, to choose from among the many issues that medieval philosophers treated a representative set of topics without any pretense of providing a comprehensive survey.[1] To make the sampling as representative and helpful as possible, I have concentrated on certain problems that persistently fascinated medieval philosophers and I have tried to give special attention to some of the assumptions that were operative during the period, especially when those assumptions are not our typical assumptions. Typically, they had an earth-centered view of the cosmos, for instance, rather than our current understanding of the planet earth as orbiting a central star, the Sun, which is but one of millions of stars within the Milky Way galaxy, which in turn is just one galaxy among countless others. In a sense, the project here includes giving attention not just to those topics that contemporary philosophers think of as philosophical problems, but also to the background assumptions that one needs to know in order to read texts in medieval philosophy well. This will mean paying attention to the way in which medieval thinkers posed the problems on which they worked and the framework within which they thought. Doing so can help to bring into focus a period of philosophy that seems very distant from our own and yet one that in many ways is decisive for the subsequent history of philosophy.

There are many fine books on the history of medieval philosophy, both general histories[2] and specialized studies of various kinds, including critical editions and translations, intellectual biographies, books and articles on individual thinkers and schools of thought, and countless studies on specific philosophical problems. To organize an introduction to medieval philosophy around certain basic concepts in historical context is quite different from structuring such a work directly as a history. While attention to the places and dates and figures always remains an indispensable component, the focus here is not just on recounting the routes of transmission or outlining the paths of influence or on contextualizing the great individuals of a given period, but on making appropriate philosophical use of these and similar perspectives by discussing in somewhat greater detail a select number of the topics and problems addressed by medieval thinkers that have proven to be of abiding interest. To help with understanding the chronological relationships of one individual to another, I have also included within this volume an appendix on Historical Figures, with their dates.

Care and precision in the use of language must always be an aim of philosophers, and so a part of this study will be the identification and explanation of the specific terms that have been used to express these concepts. Our concern here is not just a matter of studying the history of a given term's usage, but of trying to appreciate the concepts that these terms were used to express, the better to philosophize along with the medieval thinkers who used them. The meaning of words, including technical terms, can change significantly over time, and at any one moment a given term can have a range of meanings.

The very notion of a concept and the philosophical problem of understanding how the words in any given language are able to carry the meanings that they are intended to signify were frequently the subject of philosophical reflection in the medieval period. While this topic is not among those chosen for separate treatment in this book, perhaps a short account of it will be helpful here for introducing the topics that have been chosen for more detailed consideration. In the parlance of medieval philosophy, a word can be used univocally (with precisely the same meaning), equivocally (with different meanings), or analogously (with meanings that are different in certain respects but in some identifiable respects the same). The sameness of meaning involved in univocal usage is crucial to the project of proving or demonstrating anything in a rigorous way. A valid syllogism, for instance, needs to have three and only three terms, each used with precisely the same meaning twice within the syllogism; by contrast, an equivocal use of any one term within a syllogism would render the reasoning immediately invalid because it would break the connection that the syllogism is trying to establish. But because terms used in philosophical and theological treatises are often used analogously, careful scrutiny of the range of meanings given for any particular term can help us to understand the contours of a given concept as well as to understand more deeply the arguments and the positions that medieval philosophers offered on the problems related to these concepts.

Each of the chapters below will explore the set of terms and concepts used for the analysis of various problems. In addition, the book contains a glossary at the end, for the sake of having easy access to a succinct account of these important terms and concepts. Because the class of objects and relationships to which a given term refers can be easier to know in some cases than in others, the precise reference of some concepts or ideas will be easier to identify in these cases than in some others, and this will affect the effort to grasp the essence of some reality in an appropriately defined and delimited concept. The concepts in question are no less important when the terms are being used somewhat flexibly over different but related spheres of inquiry.

Consider, for example, the perennial philosophical quest to understand the realities that are intended by such common terms as "person" and "matter" (to be discussed in greater detail below in the chapter on the concept of the soul). At one level, it might seem relatively easy to gain agreement about the set of entities intended by "person," and yet there remain problems aplenty – not just the contemporary moral problems associated with ascertaining the proper definition of the term and the corresponding inclusion or exclusion of such groups as the unborn, the senile, and the mentally defective, but also the theological problems about God and the angels that were of tremendous interest in the Middle Ages. Grasping the personal character of God and the angels can help to make us mindful that the concept designated by the term "person" must have a different definition from, say, "rational animal" and that it has a broader reference than to just the set of human beings. In fact, it was a set of theological problems pertaining to the Christian doctrine of the Trinity of Divine Persons and the two natures of Christ that prompted considerable philosophical creativity in this area. The philosophical distinctions needed for generating an appropriate definition for "person" then allowed some further progress on the theological problems.[3]

The concept of matter is equally complicated. Presumably a suitable account of matter would somehow have to take stock of everything in the physical universe. In our own day, we would need to consider things like the notion of extension and the distinction between matter and mass that have been so important to recent science. Within medieval philosophy, one of the crucial aspects to consider is the idea of something's ability to receive form and to experience changes of structure and appearance. When undertaking a study of certain basic concepts of medieval philosophy, the crucial factor is not that the same term was always used by all the philosophers of the period, or that the same term always had a univocal meaning during this era. Rather, the important thing is to appreciate the conceptual continuity in the problem being discussed by appreciating the analogous use of a given term. With regard to the question about the medieval understanding of matter, this concept is recurrently a part of philosophical discussions about change and continuity and about the inner constitution of things. Matter was often understood as the substrate that remains the same during a change, whether this is a change in the dominant organizational principle of an entity or some alteration of its quality or its quantity or its relationships to other things. This concept came to play an important role in discussions about individuation (how different entities of the same type are distinct from one another); it also entered into the investigation about how one whole order of beings (the physical) can be distinguished from another whole order (the immaterial or spiritual). Despite the obvious differences of focus from one discussion to the next, the recurrent use of the same term in their reflections on these questions gives evidence of a common concept that we need to understand in order to enter into medieval philosophy. We will see that sometimes one school of thought stretched the usage of a given term beyond its usual range. The Franciscans who wrote in the tradition of Augustine, for instance, often spoke about "spiritual matter" in ways that seemed almost unintelligible to Dominicans in the Aristotelian tradition.

In its aim to serve as an introduction to medieval philosophy, this study has required the selection of a certain number of concepts while subordinating others and entirely skipping over still others with regret. We begin with the pair of concepts that probably sums up the entire period of medieval philosophy better than any other – faith and reason. After examining the range of meanings associated with *fides* and with *ratio*, the chapter takes up several related pairs of terms that are crucial for seeing the complexity of faith and reason in the Middle Ages, including *scientia* ("science," "demonstrative knowledge") and *sapientia* ("wisdom") as well as the notions of philosophy and theology considered as disciplines.

Given the vast amount of thinking about God that occurred within medieval philosophy, it seemed only right to devote part of this book to the concept of God and to provide special consideration for such questions as proofs for the existence of God, the problems involved in trying to knowing the essence of something infinite within the finite categories of human thought, and the relationship of the creator to the creation. While we might be inclined to reserve some of these topics for theology rather than philosophy, it would give a false portrait of medieval philosophy to think that the philosophers of that period did their work without these ideas in the background, any more than philosophers today could do their work without the background picture that included such notions as evolution, galaxies, and theory of relativity.

Medieval thinking about the relation between God and the cosmos involves an extremely creative medieval development of a central aspect of Plato's philosophy. His solution for the metaphysical problem of differentiating the kinds of things and the epistemological problem of knowing these kinds involves his famous theory of the Ideas or Forms. For medieval thinkers, the Platonic doctrine of the Ideas becomes a doctrine of the Divine Ideas within the mind of God, considered as the exemplary causes for all created beings. This doctrine helped to provide an understanding of why the various kinds of creatures have the natures they do and how these creatures are related to God.

In medieval reflection on how we human beings know the natures of anything and on how we are to explain the common structures of individuals that belong to the same kind, the concept of a "universal" was crucial. The medieval problem of how best to understand universals emerged from their study of Aristotle's logical works and proved one of the most fruitful inquiries of the entire period. This book devotes a chapter to the range of opinions and arguments that characterized various schools of thought on this problem. It also devotes a chapter to the related topic of the transcendentals. These are the properties of being as being that cross over all the categories of beings – properties such as unity, truth, goodness, beauty, and being itself. Jan Aertsen, a distinguished historian of medieval philosophy in our own day, has called the doctrine of the transcendentals the defining trait of medieval thought,[4] not only for the pervasive attention to these concepts but also for the creative medieval development of certain notions that first arose in antiquity, e.g., in Plato's concentration on the Good or Plotinus' focus on the One.

The final two chapters of this volume treat yet other fruitful problem areas that came within the ken of medieval philosophers. Operating as they did within the religious conviction that everything that the omnibenevolent Creator made was good, they asked questions about the goodness of the world and the goodness of human beings. Because the world-picture they used differed considerably from the models prevalent today, it is crucial to understand their fundamental assumptions in regard to the cosmos as a whole as well as their understanding of nature as an internal principle for the operations and activities typical of things according to their kind. Within the chapter devoted to this area of thought there is also a section on human goodness and the idea of a natural moral law. Cosmology and nature might seem to be entirely separate from ethics, but for medieval philosophers and theologians, discussions of ethics made sense only in relation to the God who made these creatures in his own image. While some theorists preferred to articulate morality purely in terms of the will of God, others saw creation as a source for knowledge of the divine will and developed an ethical theory about the role of reason in discerning the pathways to happiness and virtue by reflecting on our natural inclinations in light of our end as human beings. Seeing how medieval philosophers thought about morality may well help to understand the subject more deeply and thereby to develop our own positions in some better way.

The final topic chosen for consideration in this volume concentrates on the concept of the soul. As has been the case in the other topics discussed, there are considerable differences of opinion in the medieval period over what a soul is and how it operates. But there is also a common concept here that is crucial for understanding medieval philosophy, a notion that has not only religious roots but also roots in ancient Greek philosophy. The medieval developments of this idea that we will consider in this chapter provide a helpful way to deepen the notion of nature discussed in the previous chapter, especially in examining the considerations offered by those scholastic philosophers who took the idea of soul as the substantial form for living beings and posed their own questions about topics such as immortality and the nature of knowledge.

The articulation of these concepts in their medieval locations necessarily involves a certain lumping together and a certain splitting. It will be necessary to group together many thinkers from across the centuries so as to bring out what they held in common and sometimes what they seem merely to have assumed without demonstrating. There will also be a need to spell out the differences among them as well as to explore some of the ways in which the medieval concepts are different from our modern views. Admittedly, some of the figures covered in this book might not even have considered themselves philosophers, or at least not primarily philosophers – we will see this to be the case with Bonaventure, for instance – and yet they employed the resources of philosophy very skillfully when doing their theological work and other scholarly endeavors, and they remain of great philosophical interest to us today. It is my hope that this volume will be of assistance in appreciating their labors.

NOTES

1   A wonderful new volume in this respect is Brown (2007).
2   The following items may be of special interest: Gilson (1955), Armstrong (1967), Sirat (1985), Kretzmann (1988), and Marenbon (2003b).
3   See Koterski (2004).
4   See Aertsen (1996), pp. 19–23.

1

FAITH AND REASON

For medieval philosophers, faith and reason were both regarded as possible sources for genuine wisdom and knowledge. The contributions that each of them could make to the understanding of reality were regarded as different but complementary. Both played important roles in the eventual emergence of philosophy and theology as formal academic disciplines. Although philosophy and theology were recognized as distinct from one another in their goals and methods, the subject-matter proper to each of them had a certain overlap with the other. One could thus legitimately pursue such things as the truth about God, the nature of the world, the demands of morality, and many other topics from both perspectives.

This chapter will employ three interrelated pairs of terms in its effort to provide an overview of the medieval intellectual landscape in this sphere: faith and reason, wisdom and science, theology and philosophy. As with the other concepts treated in this book, there were differences of opinion among the various schools of thought as well as among the individuals within a given school on how best to make the necessary distinctions and how best to group things together. Further, there were significant shifts of opinion over the course of time, especially once the texts of Aristotle were rediscovered. But the fundamental orientation provided by these important pairs of ideas provides much that is crucial for understanding medieval philosophy.

We begin with the consideration of *fides* and *ratio* ("faith" and "reason"). The classic phrase *fides quaerens intellectum* ("faith seeking understanding") can readily serve as a kind of motto for the whole medieval period, for it indicates not only the correlation of faith and reason, but also the relative priority of faith for medieval thinkers. In the second portion of the chapter we take up the relation of *scientia* and *sapientia* ("science" and "wisdom") as distinct ways in which to identify and pursue the goals of intellectual activity. From its origins in Greece, philosophy (a term that means "love of wisdom" in Greek) has had a sapiential orientation, and philosophers have continually worked at distinguishing knowledge that is well grounded by an understanding of the causes of things (in Greek *episteme*, in Latin *scientia*) from mere opinion (in Greek *doxa*, in Latin *sententia*). The idea of *scientia* continued to animate philosophical thinking throughout the entire Middle Ages, but the scholastic period of medieval philosophy in particular was marked by a new effort to identify and employ rigorous standards for what is to count as scientific knowledge. The third section will treat *philosophia* and *theologia* in tandem by considering the formal disciplines designated by these terms as they emerged with the rise of university culture in the high Middle Ages.

1   *FIDES QUAERENS INTELLECTUM*

For philosophers throughout the Middle Ages, faith (*fides*) and reason (*ratio*) were usually regarded as allies rather than adversaries. The voices of fideists like Tertullian with his pervasive skepticism about the usefulness of philosophy to the faith ("What has Athens to do with Jerusalem?"[1]) are relatively rare. Rare too are medieval thinkers who are skeptical about faith as a source of knowledge – at least until after the translation of various texts of Greek philosophy into Latin in the thirteenth century. One then begins to find figures like Siger of Brabant and Boethius of Dacia, who read Aristotle as offering access to knowledge that was not just independent of Christianity, but to be preferred where the two were in contradiction. Much more common throughout the period was the sentiment expressed in the pair of phrases that shaped Augustine's attitude on this point: *credo ut intellegam* ("I believe so that I may understand") and *intelligo ut credam* ("I understand so that I may believe"). We see the confluence of these ideas in Anselm's formulation *fides quaerens intellectum* ("faith seeking understanding"). In this first part of the chapter we will consider the meaning of the terms faith and reason, certain

decisions made early on within Christianity's history about the importance of making use of philosophy rather than ignoring or even
scorning such pagan learning, and some representative treatments of
belief and unbelief by medieval philosophers.

The term *fides* clearly has a range of meanings across the medieval
period. It includes trust and belief (especially belief in God), specific
acts of giving one's assent to something or someone, the habitual
state of having trust and belief, the body of beliefs held by believers,
the grace of a divine light that illumines the mind about certain truths,
and the gift of God by which one is able and ready to give God one's
assent, love, and trust. In reading any medieval philosophical text on
faith, it will always be helpful to ask which senses of "faith" are
operative.

Similarly, the term *ratio* has a range of meanings that include a
reason or a cause, a line of reasoning, and an act of discursive reasoning, but also the mind in general and the faculty or power by which
one thinks and knows. The term can equally designate the basic
mental capacity or the use of that capacity. Often *ratio* is used to
refer specifically to thinking through an issue discursively (that is, in
step-by-step fashion), and in this usage it stands in contrast to *intellectus*, which is the term that tends to be used in the sense of intellectual insight or intuition, that is, the grasp of some point without
any apparent mental process. Once one has mastered an art or a
science, such as geometry, or plumbing, or astronomy, one has an
understanding of these bodies of knowledge and can use that knowledge on any number of questions without having to rethink the
process by which the knowledge was acquired. To know something
"by reason" can also refer to an explicitly philosophical use of the
mind (e.g., by logical reasoning), and then by extension it can also
refer to the body of truths known by the use of our intellectual
powers without the light of any special divine grace. The range of
meanings possible for these terms should make us alert to the complexity of the subject and hence the variety of opinions on it that one
encounters during the medieval period.

In standard Latin usage *fides* primarily designates "good faith."
By delivering whatever one promised, one shows fidelity and is worthy
of trust. Readiness to believe (*credere*) someone is *fides* in the derived
sense. One can use these terms to describe a single occasion or an
ongoing relationship like a friendship, which presupposes mutual

fidelity. The Scriptures recount numerous dramatic cases of the making, keeping, and breaking of promises,[2] and even God is said to be one who keeps faith by fulfilling promises – not in the sense that God was ever in debt to human beings, but in the sense that God is always faithful to his people by his fidelity to his own nature.

Formal declarations of faith came to have special prominence in Christian liturgical practice, especially in the baptismal promises that were an important part of the sacramental rites of initiation for new Christians, and also in the community's worship of God at each Sunday Eucharist.[3] Not all religions, of course, have required an explicit profession of faith in this sense (that is, a creed). The pagan religions of ancient Rome, for example, concentrated on the precise execution of rituals, without apparent regard for what one personally believed.[4] Even religions like Judaism that did expect faith in God and that had a strong sense of the divine deeds that created and preserved Israel as God's "chosen people" did not demand the profession of a creed. The religion of Judaism centered upon the performance of certain actions required by *torah*.[5] But Christian religious practice from early on also demanded the profession of a creed, that is, an explicit statement of faith in God as deeply involved in human history and at the same time as beyond the sensible order, eternal and transcendent.

From the point of view of ancient philosophy, Christian claims about a God who is always unseen and yet who commissioned his only Son to take on human nature and to redeem humanity by his suffering, death, and resurrection involved a leap of faith far beyond what could be empirically shown or logically proven. Where Greek philosophy had reacted to the mythological presentation of deities as charming but often willful personalities and had progressively come to see God more and more as an impersonal force,[6] even the most philosophical presentations of Christian doctrine always insisted on the personal nature of God. The stories of God's creation of the world, the choice of Israel as God's people and its divine guidance through history, and then the incarnation and mission of Christ as the ultimate fulfillment of God's promises were central to Christian evangelizing. But concurrently with the presentation of these stories about God's interventions into history, apologists[7] for the Christian faith from the beginning saw the need to include a philosophical dimension in their work to distinguish it from the mythic religions of antiquity.[8] These apologists employed philosophical demonstrations to show that this religion included not just claims to truth about certain historical facts but also claims of universal validity that are accessible to anyone (e.g., that there necessarily has to be a supreme being). In part, they introduced these philosophical distinctions to make clear what Christian belief did and did not entail (e.g., that Christianity held Christ to be a divine person who came to assume a human nature, not some hybrid being inferior to God and yet superior to human beings). In part, they brought philosophical definitions to bear, the more clearly to outline the paradoxes entailed in Christian belief (e.g., that Christian belief in the Trinity of divine persons is not a polytheism with three gods but a monotheism in which each of the three divine persons within the unity of God should be defined as a subsistent relation with the other persons).[9]

Accordingly, philosophically inclined Christian apologists in the early centuries struggled with the problem of how best to articulate Christianity's beliefs in lands and cultures outside those of their origination (Palestine and Judaism). What could be explained in categories recognizable to Jews, such as the fulfillment of promises recorded in the Hebrew prophets, had to be explained to Gentiles in terms intelligible for them, yet without compromising the particularities of the new Christian faith. In particular, there were profound questions about whether their explanations and defenses of their religion ought to employ philosophical terminology at all. To do so risked inadvertently altering the truths that were disclosed by revelation in the very effort to render them more intelligible to other cultures. Restating these truths in the more *universal* fashion demanded by the canons of philosophical reason (whether the specific philosophical approach being used was Platonic or Aristotelian, Stoic or Neoplatonic) could somehow distort the *particularity* of the historical claims about God's interventions into history. But the alternative to embracing some philosophical approach presumably meant confining the presentation of this religion to the form of narrative and story. The advantage of that approach would have been to keep the focus on the events of the history of Israel and the events of the life, death, and resurrection of Jesus. But such an approach risked allowing the claims being made by the Christian story simply to appear on a par with those of other religions that conveyed their messages by stories and myths. Recourse to the philosophical forms of reasoning that were so highly developed in Hellenistic civilization reflected a certain confidence about being able to express adequately what the Christian religion meant in these new forms. The apologists also wanted to show that sound reasoning could disclose by means of reasoning the cogency of at least some portions of what they had been given to know by faith.[10] Later generations of Christian thinkers took philosophy to be useful for generating the precise definitions and distinctions that were needed to articulate and defend the biblical faith against what were judged to be false interpretations.

A classic example of this somewhat reluctant admission of the need for a resort to philosophical terms to explain and preserve biblical beliefs occurs in the creed that was adopted at the Council of Nicaea in 325 and then slightly modified in 381 at the Council of Constantinople. Despite a strong desire to use only biblical words in this account of Christian faith, the Council ultimately chose to include within this creed one non-biblical phrase of philosophical provenance (the assertion that the Son of God is "of the same substance" as the Father – in Greek *homoousios*, in Latin *consubstantialis*) in order to protect biblical faith about the divine nature of the second member of the Trinity from those interpretations of biblical passages about Christ that would have been at variance with their understanding of the tradition on this question.

Christian thinkers, almost without exception, embraced some use of philosophical approaches within their theological work, both as appropriate for the purposes of evangelization and apologetics and as helpful for the technical articulation of religious doctrines. But they also frequently voiced their sense of the need to be vigilant against trading away any of what they considered to be the non-negotiable elements of revelation and tradition for what might seem more philosophically attractive but might unwittingly threaten to alter what had been received as the deposit of faith. Much could thus be *adopted* directly from pagan philosophers, but there was also reason to *reject* certain otherwise attractive philosophical ideas in the interests of religious orthodoxy, and to be ready to *adapt* other concepts in significant ways that might have surprised their originators. The early scripture-scholar Origen is an interesting case in point. Origen had founded a catechetical school at Alexandria, where he combined scriptural exegesis and research on the Christian interpretation of the Old Testament with the training of teachers in Christian doctrine. In his more speculative writings, Origen explored the appropriation of certain ideas drawn from what is now called "Middle Platonism."[11] His effort to explain the Trinity as a hierarchy of principles descending from "the One" (God the Father) to the *Logos* (the Divine Word) to the *Pneuma* (the Holy Spirit) along the general lines taken by his slightly younger contemporary Plotinus were ultimately judged unsuccessful by Christian evaluation. His use of these philosophical notions appeared to place the members of the Divine Trinity in an order of subordination rather than to preserve their equality with one another. But even in its failure, his effort serves as evidence of the general willingness of theologians to think philosophically and as a lesson in the need to reflect on whether any given philosophical perspective could be adopted straightforwardly or only with certain adaptations. Only a handful of theologians, often arguing from texts such as 1 Corinthians 2: 1–5, where St Paul insists that he relies on no human wisdom when preaching the wisdom of Christ, tried to resist any use of philosophical ideas or methods at all.

One particularly important instance of the theological adaptation of a philosophical notion (discussed at greater length below in the chapter on divine ideas) is the transformation of the Platonic theory of Ideas or Forms.[12] During the patristic period we find the relocation of the Ideas from the place in a separate world that Plato had envisioned for them in the *Timaeus*: Christian Platonists think of these Ideas as residing in the mind of God. This doctrine had sustained importance as a crucial philosophical component of the medieval understanding of creation. The philosophical fruitfulness of the concept of divine ideas extends very broadly, especially for philosophical theories of morality.

Christian thinkers thus tended to use philosophical approaches to various questions with considerable enthusiasm, but they generally resisted the inclination to start thinking of Christianity as wholly or even primarily a new philosophy among others. It is vital to keep in mind here that many ancient philosophies were seen not merely as dispassionate bodies of knowledge but as holistic ways of living, and often as ascetical disciplines.[13] In its self-understanding, Christianity shared this sense of offering a way of life, but it did not regard itself as something that could be known by reason alone independently of revelation. Even in asserting the fundamental harmony of faith and reason, Christian theorists resisted the notion that one could ever reduce the truths of the Christian faith to a set of conclusions attainable through reasoning about human experience.

What began to be worked out regarding the relations between faith and reason within the patristic era developed further during the Middle Ages. The philosophers of this period did not tend to pose questions about, say, the relations between science and religion with the assumption of their incompatibility that is sometimes found today, but with the conviction that faith was a higher source than reason.[14] The philosophers of the period did deal frequently with questions of unbelief and with difficulties in belief. In Augustine's account of a preliminary stage of his conversion, for instance, he records his difficulties with three interrelated problems that constituted intellectual impediments that he needed to resolve before he could give his free assent to faith. Until he learned from the Neoplatonists that God must be understood as spiritual rather than material in nature, he was troubled by the corruptibility inherent in all the images of God that he had ever considered. He did not feel that he could offer his faith to a supreme being who was not incorruptible.[15] Likewise, he felt perplexed by the reality of evil in the world. He could not reconcile the claim of an all-good God who was the creator of everything in the universe with the reality of pain, suffering, and wickedness until he came to understand the privative character of evil and the genuine freedom possible in human choices. Release from this set of stumbling-blocks on the road to faith came with the philosophical insight that evil is not a being in its own right but the absence of the goodness that ought to be present in a given being. Finally, deeper understanding about the causal connectedness of the material cosmos and about the root of free choice in the spiritual nature of the will allowed Augustine to rid himself of worries about astrological fatalism and to repudiate the superstitions of Manicheism to which he had been attracted. Yet in Augustine's own judgment, none of these philosophical clarifications enabled him to make an act of faith in the God of the Bible. The resolution of these problems only cleared away what were intellectual roadblocks for him. He tells us that faith came to him as an impulse of grace while he wrestled with the demands of chastity that conversion would require.[16]

Precisely because Augustine was an adult convert to the Christian faith, the issue of unbelief has a deeply personal dimension for him.

Making a commitment meant a drastic change in his life. Most medieval philosophers, by contrast, grew up within a culture already Christian, and so the question of unbelief tended to have a rather different cast for them. In his *Proslogion*, for instance, Anselm makes his opening gambit a line from Psalm 13(14) "The fool says in his heart, 'There is no God.'" The connotations of the word "fool" here could cause his point to be misunderstood. Although the sentence in question clearly implies a warning about the misconduct that one might be tempted to justify on the basis of denying God's existence, there is nothing of condescension or contempt in Anselm's use of the term "fool" within his philosophical treatment of the question about the existence of God. Quite the opposite: Anselm's argument (discussed in its own right in the chapter below on God) uses for its starting point the case of a person who denies the existence of God in order to show the need for sound reasoning about this most important of topics. That Anselm takes very seriously what the "fool" has to say is evident from the sustained treatment that he gives to the position. In fact, most editors of the *Proslogion* have respected Anselm's own wish that future editions of his work always contain as a companion piece an extensive set of objections to his arguments by Gaunilo, a monk of the Marmoutier, "on behalf of the fool,"[17] as well as Anselm's judicious replies to these objections.

As R. W. Southern argues in his intellectual biography of Anselm,[18] what Anselm accomplishes here is not only the give-and-take of good argument but also a new use for philosophical reasoning. In preceding centuries philosophical reason had often been instrumental for progress in clarifying the exposition of Christian faith, especially by drawing distinctions, making analogies, or providing explanations of the paradoxes involved in beliefs such as the unity of persons in the Trinity or the unity of human and divine natures in Christ. But now philosophical reason is being used for examining faith itself. Anselm does so by considering the topic of unbelief. It would not just be a matter of asking what someone of this faith should believe on specific questions, but of asking philosophical questions about belief itself. It is not Anselm's position that reason can decide what the content of faith should be, but simply that good reasoning can provide a special kind of security for faith. What is believed on the basis of faith need not be thought to be destroyed when submitted to natural reason. Rather, there is a complementarity. Belief grounded on divine authority will tend to come first in the order of time. But faith is being taken as an acceptance of something not yet clearly seen in all respects and it ought to lead toward understanding as its fulfillment.[19]

The style of philosophizing most often at work in the first half of the Middle Ages was often more meditative than dialectical. It tended to be done by bishops and monks and commentators on Scripture. In the later periods of medieval philosophy it more often bears the marks of the classroom. There are advantages and disadvantages that come with philosophizing within an institutional setting like the university, including a tendency that arises from professional specialization to set faith and reason on different but complementary tracks, if not to make them actually opposed to one another. These aspects of the relation of faith and reason can be considered by reflecting on the relations between wisdom and understanding and between theology and philosophy.

2   *SCIENTIA* AND *SAPIENTIA*

Histories of philosophy that pass quickly over medieval thought as predominantly theological and insufficiently philosophical risk missing not only the richness of medieval philosophizing but also the relative novelty of theology as a distinct academic discipline that formally emerged in the scholastic era. For all of the spiritual writing done during the Middle Ages, there was no separate discipline called theology for much of that period. If anything, authors preferred to speak of the *philosophia Christi* ("the philosophy of Christ"). Many of the works that we might be inclined to see as theological tended to take the form of moral exhortations or reflections on the Scriptures.[20] Even the term "theology," for instance, is a somewhat alien term for Augustine. In the *City of God*, he contrasts the *philosophia Christi* with the three spheres of pagan "theology" identified by the Roman philosopher Varro: (1) civil theology, which was focused on the cultic activities of various civic and ethnic groups; (2) mythical theology, which contains the myths about the gods found in the likes of Homer and Hesiod; and (3) natural theology, which considers the arguments of philosophers for the existence and nature of the gods.[21]

The philosophical arguments typical of natural theology provided material that could find a place within Christian thought, but Augustine takes it as unlikely that they will have as much prominence among adherents of revealed wisdom as they did for pagan philosophers. Such arguments at best, he thinks, might be helpful in an auxiliary way to support and elucidate the Scriptures.

For the long period of Augustinian dominance within medieval thought, there is greater attention given to the themes of *sapientia* ("wisdom") and *scientia* ("science") than to reflection on theology and philosophy as distinct disciplines.[22] It may prove helpful here to consider the place that a thinker like Augustine accorded to divine wisdom in ordering our thoughts about the structure of reality, and then to turn to the type of differences that he envisioned to stand between wisdom and science. Many of the distinctions that he employed on this question persisted long into the scholastic period.

While Augustine wrote no metaphysics in the formal Aristotelian sense of a treatise on being, his works nevertheless contain a metaphysics that is a scripturally informed version of Neoplatonism. At the peak of the hierarchy is God the Creator. The middle range is the sphere of angelic spirits and souls, including the human mind. At the base is the vast world of bodies, lowest in the hierarchy but still good precisely because created by God who is good.[23] To each of these three levels corresponds a *ratio*, a principle that accounts for the structure of the being and its intelligibility.[24] At the level of the elements, for instance, there are the "seed-principles" (*rationes seminales*) that God planted in the created world and that direct the development of material bodies. Within the mind of God, Augustine locates the divine ideas (*rationes aeternae*, "eternal reasons") that are his version of the Platonic Forms; these are the prototypes for everything that God creates.[25] As thoughts in the mind of God, they are unchangeable, necessary, and eternal, the exemplary causes of all creatures. In between the lowest and highest levels of reality is the sphere of angelic intelligences and spiritual souls, including the *ratio hominis*, the human rational soul.[26] The possession of a rational soul not only accounts for the distinctive human essence and for the intelligibility of human nature, but also makes human minds capable of understanding other things above and below them within the hierarchy. By virtue of its intermediate position, human reason is able to consider material creatures through the *ratio inferior* ("lower reason" or "reason directed to lower things") as well as to contemplate the eternal reasons through the *ratio superior* ("higher reason" or "reason directed to higher things").[27]

Higher and lower reason have different ends or goals.[28] The goal of higher reason is the wisdom (*sapientia*) achievable through contemplation, while the goal of lower reason is the knowledge of things in the changeable world of time (*scientia*). This sort of knowledge is more restricted than *sapientia* and subject to error, but extremely valuable in the practical order.[29] Augustine believes wisdom to be constituted by knowledge of the eternal and immutable truths in the mind of God:

> Action, by which we use temporal things well, differs from contemplation of eternal things; and the latter is reckoned to wisdom [*sapientia*], the former to knowledge [*scientia*]. . . . When a discourse relates to [temporal] things, I hold it to be a discourse belonging to knowledge [*scientia*], and to be distinguished from a discourse belonging to wisdom, to which those things belong which neither have been nor shall be, but are; and on account of that eternity which they are, are said to have been, and to be, and to be about to be, without any changeableness of times. . . . And they abide, but not as if fixed in some place as are bodies; but as intelligible things in incorporeal nature, they are so at hand to the glance of the mind, as things visible or tangible in place are to the sense of the body. . . . If this is the right distinction between wisdom and knowledge, that the intellectual cognizance of eternal things belongs to wisdom, but the rational cognizance of temporal things to knowledge, it is not difficult to judge which is to be preferred.[30]

For Augustine, the divine ideas play a crucial role in human knowledge. Human minds need to be in accord with the eternal ideas in order to know any necessary truths. *Scientia* is a methodical knowledge about the truth of things in this world and their mundane causes, whereas *sapientia* is a knowledge of Truth itself. For this reason, the contemplative life is higher than the active life. Although Augustine sometimes warns against allowing excessive curiosity about worldly concerns,[31] lest one be distracted from higher things and thereby fail to establish the right order of loves in one's life, he clearly holds *scientia* in high regard. The superiority of *sapientia* to *scientia* comes from the greater importance of a goal than the means to that goal.

In the distinctions that Augustine articulates here one can discern the influence of his respect for revelation as more certain and more insightful than anything that could ever be attained by natural reason. Charles Norris Cochrane argues that the wisdom accessible through the Scriptures seemed to Augustine to offer a way to escape from "the insoluble riddles of classicism" about the identity of the supreme good in a universe conceived to be endless. This new source of wisdom pointed the way to a new synthesis, a vision of the final order and goal toward which change and history are directed.[32] Augustine's subordination of reason to faith and of *scientia* to *sapientia* thus does not mean a repudiation of reason in favor of impulse or emotion, but a route by which one could hope actually to reach the certitude about the meaning of life that classical reason always desired but could never seem to achieve. The approach of *fides quaerens intellectum* does place faith as prior to reason. But rather than treating them as antithetical, it sees a deeper understanding of reality as one of the fruits that faith will provide.

In the sapiential books of the Old Testament[33] medieval exegetes in the tradition of Augustine found considerable support for this position.[34] The *Wisdom of Solomon* is frequency cited in this regard, and especially the passage (7: 17f) in which Solomon, who is taken as the epitome of a wise king, testifies to his fellow rulers that wisdom (*sapientia*) had come to him as a grace from above, and with it learning (*doctrina*) and understanding (*scientia*) in the various disciplines, practical and speculative. Yet it was not simply in isolated passages that medieval thought found a connection between *sapientia* and *scientia*. Medieval exegesis found this relationship to be pervasive, especially because of the complementary roles played by faith and reason in what they considered to be the most crucial aspect of proper biblical interpretation, namely, ascertaining the four senses of scripture.[35]

The Scriptures were understood to have four "senses" or levels of meaning. At the heart of this approach to interpretation is a distinction between the literal level and the three spiritual levels. Contrary to what the term might lead one to expect, the "literal level" does not mean that everything in the Scriptures is to be read as if a simple historical account. The literal level includes not only straightforward narrative but metaphor and simile and a variety of other rhetorical devices too. The *sensus ad litteram* consists of whatever is intended by the human author, whether the authorial intention is historical (such as the Gospel narratives about Jesus' life or the record of Israel's exile in Egypt and wanderings in the desert), figures of speech (such as the use of metaphor in Psalm 18: 2, "The Lord is my rock"), or even wisdom stories and tales such as Job and Jonah. The three spiritual senses – the "allegorical" (perhaps better called the "typological"), the "moral," and the "anagogical" – are designated as "spiritual" because of their source. They are said to come from the Holy Spirit, but they can only be properly discerned within the text once its literal sense is understood. The medieval exegete is thus concerned to apply reason (*ratio*) and learning (*scientia*) to the text in order to discover the wisdom (*sapientia*) awaiting there in the spiritual levels of meaning that were implanted by the divine author.

While most medieval interpreters employed the discernment of these various levels of meaning in the Scriptures creatively but cautiously, there were some whose practice has given allegory a bad name through the excessively imaginative connections they made. But the more disciplined masters of the art used it responsibly and by the later portion of the Middle Ages the method could even be applied to non-biblical texts. Dante's famous letter to Can Grande della Scala, for instance, explains that the *Commedia* employs a four-level structure of meaning, like that found in the Bible.[36]

In order to appreciate the medieval use of what today we might call hermeneutics, it may be helpful here to consider briefly the philosophically informed distinctions at work in this four-level structure of interpretation. The first of the three spiritual levels is usually called the "allegorical sense" in the Middle Ages, but recent scholarship has more appropriately entitled it the "typological" level.[37] The central idea here is that the life of Christ as recounted in the Gospels provides the proper guide for understanding the whole of the Old Testament according to the rule of recapitulation: at each stage of his life Christ "recapitulates" the life of the people of Israel, which is to be taken as if it were a single lifetime. Each of the figures from the Old Testament is called a "type," and the corresponding moment from the life of Christ is called the "anti-type." At each stage Christ completes what is incomplete, perfects what is imperfect, and sanctifies what is sinful in the type. Seen in this way, Christ is thought of as the new Adam, who repairs what Adam's fall damaged. He is the new Isaac, who actually suffers what the original Isaac did not have to suffer when God sent Abraham a lamb to replace the son he was about to sacrifice. He is the new Moses who in his own person delivers commandments of love (see Matthew 22: 37–9) that perfect the understanding of the commandments that Moses delivered to the people at Sinai (see Exodus 20: 1–17 and Deuteronomy 5: 6–21).

Reason's role in ascertaining the typological meaning is to elucidate the truths that are present in revelation but often hidden under shadows and figures. It would not be possible even to begin to grasp the spiritual senses without a thorough penetration of the literal sense, and it is for this reason that we see throughout the Middle Ages so many efforts to better appreciate the literal sense. Augustine's *De Genesi ad litteram*,[38] for example, is only one of the four commentaries that he wrote on Genesis. Yet the literal sense, that is, the understanding of what the human authors intended, can never be the end of the matter. It is simply the privileged point of access for reason's search for the higher and deeper truths of divine wisdom.

The second of the spiritual levels is the moral sense. In the course of exhortatory treatises on virtue and vice, one sees in a particularly strong way the medieval sense of the collaboration expected between reason and faith. One finds this moral level of meaning not only in those passages concerned with the commandments and beatitudes, various exhortations to virtue and admonitions against vice, prophetic invectives against idolatry, and morality tales like the stories of Noah and Job; this level is also evident in the moral lessons that can be drawn from the stories about the sinful habits and practices of even some of the Bible's greatest heroes, such as Abraham's readiness at one point to sell his wife Sarah in order to make his own escape, the account of David's adultery with Bathsheba, and the betrayal of Jesus by Peter. And in texts such as the first chapter of Paul's letter to the Romans, scholastic authors of the twelfth and thirteen centuries found biblical warrant for the philosophical theory of the natural law that they were developing (a point to be considered in more detail in chapter 6 below).

To use the categories of later scholastic philosophy, we see in the reasoning being employed in this type of scriptural exegesis a concern

with both divine commands and with appeals to reason in the exegeti-
cal effort to understand biblical texts about right and wrong, goodness and wickedness, virtue and vice. Ultimately, the truth of the
moral lessons is guaranteed by faith, but it is always a faith seeking
understanding by the vigorous use of reason. One makes progress in
this sphere not only by considering how human life prospers when
lived in accord with divine commands and falters under disobedience,
but also by noting how deeply reasonable biblical morality is when
the text is understood more fully. Medieval commentaries on the
Gospels, for instance, take note of those passages in which Jesus
deepens some of the commandments of the Decalogue by explaining
that the prohibition on murder extends not just to killing but to
holding someone in contempt, or when he takes the commandment
on adultery to include lustful looks. In noting how deeply insightful
the commandments are for human well-being,[39] the commentators
trace the suitability of these moral truths back to God's plan for
humanity at the creation described in Genesis and note how accessible many of these points are to human reasoning even apart from
their mention in the Bible. In the judgment of these medieval authors,
even after the loss of likeness to God brought about by Adam's fall,
human beings remain creatures who are made in God's image even
though that image has been disfigured by the fall. For this reason they
possess a dignity superior to that of any other creature, and they
ought to seek the recovery of that likeness by works of moral
reform.[40]

The third of the spiritual senses is the "anagogical" level. Reason's
task was to discern in certain scriptural texts important signs about
the way to return to God (in Greek, *anagoge* means "a going back
up" or "a return"). At this level of the text's meaning, medieval
commentators found in the images and symbols of scriptural stories
anticipations of the sacraments (the escape of the people of Israel
from Egypt through the crossing of the Red Sea, for instance, is
taken to anticipate the escape of a person from sin and death
through baptism). Philosophical consideration of the pervasive use
of signs and symbols in the Bible led them to think about the part
of philosophy that is today called semiotics. Augustine's work *De
Doctrina Christiana*,[41] for instance, is not only philosophically interesting for its sophisticated theory of signs,[42] but for its contribution
thereby to a philosophically informed Christian ethics. At one point,

for instance, Augustine brings up his philosophical perplexity about rightly ordering our love for other people. Only God is to be loved purely for himself, and to love a person like that would be idolatrous. But it does not strike Augustine as right to say that we should then only love other people the way we love other things, namely, as objects of use and as the means to some end.[43] Augustine's solution, that human beings should be loved not "as God" but "in God," depends on appreciating that all human beings are made in the image of God. Even when that likeness to God has been defaced by sin, it is never entirely blotted out and should always serve for us as a sign of the way in which God loves us and thus as an indication of how we ought to bear love for each other out of love for the God who made us.

Over the course of the Middle Ages these reflections on the anagogical and moral senses of the Scriptures progressively involves the philosophical articulation of more and more distinctions, both to resolve questions that arose from biblical texts and to find practical answers to problems encountered in life. Medieval treatises on the *scientia* of morals differentiate, for instance, among types of killing – from the inexcusable and intolerable form that is murder, through those forms that are justifiable, such as self-defense,[44] to those killings thought to be required, such as the killing involved in capital punishment and just war. The reasoning that develops to handle questions like these shows great philosophical sophistication when trying to resolve apparent conflicts, such as the biblical injunction against killing in general (for the fifth commandment itself makes no further distinctions) when considered in light of the need for those charged with care of the community to defend the innocent and to protect the peace of the community. The work of reason involves making the necessary distinctions, identifying the conditions for a lawful resort to arms, and devising a set of steps through which one must pass before claiming the right to the use of force.

Although there was agreement about the relative priority of faith to reason, there were sometimes disagreements about how just reason ought to be used, and one can see this tension in the area of ethics. For instance, Abelard, a philosophically inclined theologian of the early twelfth century, has a voluntarist dimension to his moral theory that can be seen in his inclination to ground moral obligation on decisions by the will (divine or human) rather than on an intellectual recognition of what human nature requires for its flourishing. This voluntaristic approach is later taken up and developed further by various fourteenth-century nominalists. In stressing that morality does not consist in external observances but in rightness of mind and heart, Abelard's teachings in this area clearly spring from the Gospels, but they emphasize practical reason almost to the exclusion of speculative reason. His attempt at a morality of pure intention risks neglecting such other crucial aspects of morality as the nature of the action under consideration and the way in which circumstances can affect one's obligations. To argue, for instance, that what is wrong with murder or lying or breaking of vows is the contradiction of one's latest choice with one's earlier efforts at a previous life-determining choice does put emphasis on the important aspects of conscience, personal intention, and the consent that flows from a free choice. But to limit one's argument, at least for practical purposes, to these considerations is to sideline speculative reason by minimizing the value of reflecting on the nature of things and even to miss the universal scope of certain negative moral precepts that forbid intrinsically evil actions (e.g., that one may never deliberately take innocent life). Abelard eventually aroused the wrath of the authorities not only because of his affair with Héloïse, a young woman for whom he served as a tutor, but because of certain worrisome implications that figures like the Cistercian abbot Bernard of Clairvaux saw in his ethics.[45]

Bernard tended to distrust not just Abelard but the entire movement toward dialectical philosophizing, then still new, that later came to flourish with the rise of scholasticism. But despite Bernard's efforts, the general movement in this direction proved unstoppable. The rise of the universities encouraged the responsible use of the new methods of reasoning. With the renewal of appreciation for Aristotle's theory of science (especially as articulated in the *Posterior Analytics*) after the recovery of his texts in natural philosophy, scholastic philosophers worked to provide a *scientia* of ethics, and thinkers like Thomas Aquinas developed an ethics that balanced respect for the sovereign will of God with a vigorous naturalism that combines both the virtue ethics that medieval thinkers saw with fresh eyes in the *Nicomachean Ethics*[46] and the incipient form of natural law theory (discussed at greater length in chapter 6 on cosmos and nature) that Christian asceticism had received from ancient Stoicism.

The same trend that is evident in this example from the area of ethics was pervasive in the philosophy faculties of the new medieval universities. The *scientia* that was their goal was not limited to empirical "science" in our modern sense of the word, but could be found in any area of knowledge. The scholars worked at organizing knowledge by the articulation of the foundational principles of each discipline and the elaboration of conclusions that could be demonstrated to follow by the rigorous application of logic.

3 PHILOSOPHY AND THEOLOGY

The scholastic period of the Middle Ages saw the professionalization of philosophy and theology as university disciplines. Often their subject-matter overlapped, but there remained a crucial distinction in their methods and sources.

Tempting as it might be simply to associate faith with theology and reason with philosophy, it would be a mistake to try to differentiate them from one another in this way. As we have just seen, there are tremendous demands on the theologian for the use of reason to ascertain the proper interpretation of scriptural texts. Further, scholastic theologians received considerable impetus for the development of their discipline from the application of questions in logic, natural philosophy, and metaphysics to the mysteries of the faith; and, in turn, the interest in resolving these theological questions prompted further philosophical work.[47] The controversies over the nature of Christ's presence in the Eucharist emerged in part by asking questions derived from the distinctions about substance and accident in twelfth-century treatises on grammar and logic. Thirteenth-century treatises on the nature of Christ profited greatly from the new level of sophistication achieved in natural philosophy after the recovery of Aristotle's texts in that area. Likewise, theological attention to questions about the very knowability of God benefited from metaphysical consideration of the transcendental properties of being and of the debate on the question whether "being" can rightly be predicated analogously or must be predicated univocally.

It is not just that theology as well as philosophy is dependent on a highly disciplined use of reason. It is also the case that faith played a crucial role in philosophy as well as in theology. In the case of medieval theology, the type of faith in question is technically called "divine faith," that is, the trust (made possible by God's grace) that one places in God's self-revelation and the church's fidelity in handing down the tradition received from Christ. From the point of view of method, scholastic theologians considered premises known by divine faith to have special warrant for the definitions, distinctions, and demonstrations on which they labored. Even when dealing with precisely the same topics, philosophers of the scholastic period sought to make their arguments without the aid of premises guaranteed by divine faith.[48] They were often guided in their choice of problems by their understanding of theological positions and concerns, and in this sense even philosophy received a certain direction from faith. But in the course of its growth as an academic discipline within the medieval university, philosophical method was progressively restricted to demonstrations attainable without invoking revealed premises.[49]

In addition to these connections to divine faith, medieval philosophers also operated with a kind of philosophical faith, that is, a systematic trust in certain fundamental principles of being and of reason. In the systematization of the many fields of learning that emerged during the rise of universities, there was considerable reflection on the presuppositions and methods of scientific disciplines and of philosophy itself. One sees, for instance, in the commentaries on Aristotle's *Prior* and *Posterior Analytics*[50] a sustained interest in the very notion of the *principia* ("principles") of a *scientia* ("science" or "discipline"), for instance, in the realization that the principles or starting points of a given discipline could not be proven within that discipline but needed to be assumed for the work of defining, distinguishing, and demonstrating within that sphere. Optics, for instance, depended on physics, and physics in turn depended on metaphysics. But the principles of metaphysics, as Aristotle had taught, were as indemonstrable in principle as they were crucial for any meaningful discourse at all, let alone for the rigorous work in the specialized areas of learning. In a sense, then, medieval philosophers recognized in these indemonstrable first principles of being and of reasoning a set of commitments in which they needed to put their trust as the presuppositions of realism.

Among the first principles explicitly discussed by medieval philosophers are the principles of non-contradiction, identity, and excluded middle. Both as a principle of logic and of metaphysics, the principle of non-contradiction has a certain primacy among the rest, and a validity for every order of being as well as of knowledge: *nothing can belong to a given thing and simultaneously not belong to it in the same respect*. Whether the insight is expressed in this way in terms of being and non-being, or put in terms of assertion and denial (e.g., *the same attribute cannot be simultaneously affirmed and denied of the same subject in the same respect*), this principle provides a norm and basis for every affirmation and yet is itself indemonstrable. Aware of Aristotle's comment that the principle cannot be proven but only defended indirectly,[51] medieval philosophers treat it as a lynch-pin for everything else, as the following quotation from Aquinas suggests:

> For that which first falls under apprehension is being, the understanding of which is included in all things whatsoever a man apprehends. Therefore, the first undemonstrable principle is that the same thing cannot be affirmed and denied at the same time, which is based on the notions of being and non-being, and on this principle all others depend.[52]

Correlative with the principle of non-contradiction is the principle of identity (*a being is identical to itself and is one in itself*), which is once again not just a logical principle for our thinking but a metaphysical principle of reality.[53] The insight here, whatever the precise formula used, is that there is an ontological structure in things by virtue of which things that are different in number can be recognized to be the same in form and come under one species or genus. This principle can also be understood in reference to any one being when considered over time and recognized as the same being. A given horse, for instance, is the same organism when a colt or when full grown; its unity as a substance comes from its form and abides the same over the course of many changes in quality, quantity, and relationships.

Closely connected to both of the above principles is the principle of excluded middle. As stated by Aristotle, "There cannot be an intermediate between contradictions, but of one subject we must either affirm or deny any one predicate."[54] In both ancient and medieval sources this principle tends to be formulated for the sake of explaining how demonstrations in a science work, but its basis is once again in being and in a certain insight about how one must speak of being. It is true to say of what is, that it is, and of what is not, that it is not, whereas it is false to say of what is, that it is not, and of what is not, that it is. But to say that anything is, one must either say something true or something false. Either the affirmation or the negation will be true, and there is no middle ground (hence, the name of this principle).[55] Anyone who tries to hold to some intermediate between contradictory opposites is failing to recognize that one must say of a given being that it is or that it is not.

The confidence that medieval philosophers generally show in putting their faith in principles like these is an aspect of their philosophical realism.[56] In later scholasticism one finds some philosophical worry over whether these principles are perhaps innate or whether they might be constructions of the human mind, but this tendency seems generally correlated with a subordination of metaphysics to logic. The mainstream tradition generally held these principles[57] to be human realizations about the nature of being itself, and took these metaphysical principles naturally to have correlates in logic, for logic was regarded as an art in service of philosophy proper.

4 OVERVIEW

Difficult as it is to discern the precise beginning or ending dates for medieval philosophy, the typical attitude of thinkers from this entire period on the topics under discussion in this chapter constitute a distinctive philosophical stance. The quest for understanding by means of reason in ancient philosophy brought figures like Plato to rank *pistis* ("faith") along with *doxa* ("opinion") as different in kind and far below the levels of *episteme* ("scientific knowledge") and *nous* ("intellectual insight") in his Divided Line.[58] Even in the occasional dialogue in which claims to divine inspiration are discussed, such as the *Ion* or the *Phaedrus*, there is much reason to suppose that Plato is arguing for the superiority of reason by virtue of philosophy's ability to explain what the artist or the prophet can only recount but not explain. Aristotle shows the same general tendency to place faith in the general region of opinion.[59] They understand that faith is a human act of belief that is useful in the process of learning and discovery and that the value of this act depends on the trustworthiness of the source that one is choosing to believe. But their focus is on reaching higher levels of cognition by coming to know a thing's causes (*episteme*) and eventually achieving understanding by intellectual intuition (*nous*). In certain important respects the entire project of ancient philosophy is an effort to break away from the brand of trust given to the stories of mythology, so as to find compelling and cogent reasons of a universal character.[60]

Likewise, thinkers from the period of classical modern philosophy as well as many contemporary philosophers have taken the problem of faith and reason very seriously.[61] For various reasons that include scholarly conviction about the autonomy proper to natural reason, skepticism over the scandal of the sixteenth-century wars of religion, weariness with the interest in minutia of logic and with the fideism that tended to accompany late medieval nominalism, and the optimism of the Renaissance and the Enlightenment that human reason could solve new problems through empirical research, philosophers of the modern period tend to separate faith and reason rather sharply.[62] It is not that every philosopher of the modern period was hostile to religion, but the preponderance of views antithetical toward revelation and institutional religion typical of the Enlightenment made the very term *philosophy* suggest a split between faith and reason into different intellectual spheres that was reinforced politically and socially by new demarcations of what was properly public and what should be considered private.[63]

Philosophers of the medieval period give clear evidence of respecting the difference between faith and reason as sources of knowledge and wisdom, but they also stressed a deep connection between them. Ultimately, their juncture is rooted in their convictions that religious faith as they knew it was truly a gift from God that elicited a human response of trustworthy belief, that human reason is a creaturely participation in divine reason, and that this participation means that there must be in principle a fundamental harmony between what faith and what reason each show. Admittedly, some medieval thinkers were fideists who either distrusted reason altogether or thought the spheres of reason to be separate and distinct. But the majority worried that asserting too great a difference between faith and reason would risk making belief seem unreasonable or arbitrary. Without presuming to claim that faith could be reduced to reason or reason to faith, most medieval philosophers were inclined instead to see them as complementary. Their religious conviction that divine intelligence had created an orderly world of creatures gave them a certain confidence with which to pursue philosophical wisdom in the ordering of human affairs and the scientific understanding of the natural world, especially in the period of scholasticism that emerged with the rediscovery of Aristotelian natural philosophy in the twelfth century, a topic to which we will return in a number of the chapters that follow.

NOTES

1 *De Praescripto*, ch. 7 in Tertullian (1994). For an overview of Tertullian, see Dunn (2004).
2 For instance, the promises that Moses and the people make in response to God's gift of the covenant (e.g., Deuteronomy 23: 21–3); the promises that God makes to his people in the course of establishing his covenants (summarized in Hebrews 6); or Jephthah's rash vow in Judges 11–12. For a fine review of the entire topic of promising, see Mansini (2005).
3 See Kelly (1981) and Pelikan (2003).
4 See Ando (2003).
5 There are certain expressions within Jewish religious practice that can function as something comparable to a creed, such as the *Shema*: "Hear, Israel, the Lord is our God, the Lord is one" (Deuteronomy 6: 4); see also its context, Deuteronomy 6: 4–9.
6 I have developed this theme at greater length in chapter 2 on God. See also Gerson (1990).
7 "Apologists" in the sense of "defenders," much as Socrates' *Apology* was his defense speech, not an admission of wrong-doing.
8 See Ratzinger (1990), esp. part I, ch. 3: "The God of Faith and the God of the Philosophers," pp. 94–137.
9 See Koterski (2004).
10 See Danielou (1973) and Ratzinger (1990), esp. pp. 46ff. For a discussion of a similar strategy used by scholastic philosophers such as Thomas Aquinas in their discussion of the "preambles of the faith," see McInerny (2006), esp. pp. 159–306.
11 See Dillon (1990), Dillon (1996), and Rist (1985).

12 One of the central features of Platonic philosophy is the notion that there are archetypal Forms or Ideas for every kind of thing. The use of Form and Idea as synonyms for these archetypes serves both metaphysically as a way to unify the multiplicity of instances within a kind by their "participation" in a common Form, and epistemologically as a way by which we can recognize in an Idea what is common to these many instances.

13 See Hadot (2002).

14 For an overview on this question, see Cochrane (2003), esp. chs. 11 and 12.

15 For the problem of God's incorruptibility as a roadblock on Augustine's way to faith, see *Confessions* VII.1–4, in Augustine (1991b). The problem of evil is discussed at VII.5, and the problem of the free choice of the will at VII.6; see also his classical treatment of this problem in *On Free Choice of the Will* in Augustine (1982b). In the remainder of the *Confessions* (esp. VII.7–17) Augustine recounts how what he learned, particularly from the Neoplatonists, emancipated him from an overly corporeal way of thinking. In the final section within the same book (VII.18–21) he describes his need for Christ's grace to liberate him from his sinfulness and the emotional chains that kept him from faith. In book VIII we read the story of his conversion experience.

16 The story of Augustine's conversion is recounted in book eight of the *Confessions*, culminating in the voice he heard calling out *tolle, lege* ("take up and read") that moved him to imitate the example of St. Anthony and read a passage chosen at random from the Scripture. When he read from Romans 13: 13–14, he saw no need to read any further: "At once, with the last words of this sentence, it was as if a light of relief from all anxiety flooded into my heart. All the shadows of doubt were dispelled."

17 Gaunilo of Marmoutiers, *Pro Insipiente* ("On Behalf of the Fool") in Anselm (1998), pp. 105–10. Anselm's reply to Gaunilo can be found on pp. 111–22.

18 See Southern (1990).

19 *Fides quaerens intellectum* is the subtitle of Anselm's *Proslogion*. See Anselm (1998), p. 83. In this respect Anselm is following closely on Augustine's lead. See also *On Order* II.16.26–7, in Augustine (2007); *Against the Academicians* III.43, in Augustine (1995b); and *Soliloquies* I.12–14.23, in Augustine (1990).

20 See Wilken (2003).

21 *The City of God* VI.5, in Augustine (1984). See Gerson (1990), pp. 1–5.

22 See Gilson (1969).

23 In chapter 5 on the transcendentals, I discuss in further detail the commitment found throughout the Middle Ages to the thesis that all beings as beings are good, in the sense of possessing various inherent perfections that can be the object of desire of a being with appetitive drives. As a philosophical position, the doctrine of transcendental goodness reaches back at least as far as Plato's *Republic*. For the Middle Ages, it was also a religious doctrine stemming from the account of creation in Genesis.

24 For a collection of Augustine's texts on this subject, see Bourke (1978), pp. 43–66. For example, *Letter 18* to Coelestinus: "There is a nature which is susceptible of change with respect to both place and time, namely, the corporeal. There is another nature which is in no way susceptible of change with respect to place, but only with respect to time, namely, the spiritual. And there is a third Nature which can be changed neither in respect to time, that is, God."

25 See, for instance, *Eighty-Three Different Questions*, q. 46.1–2, in Augustine (1982c).

26 See Burnell (2005), esp. pp. 18–53.

27 See, for instance, *The Trinity* XIII.1.1–2, XIV.1.3, and XIV.6.11, in Augustine (1991a). See also *The Literal Meaning of Genesis* in Augustine (1982a).

28 See Nash (1969).

29 See *Enchiridion*, ch. 17 in Augustine (1961).

30 *The Trinity* XII.14.21–15.25, in Augustine (1991a).

31 For instance, *Confessions* X.34.54, in Augustine (1991b).

32 Cochrane (2003), pp. 399–400. Cochrane explains the problem as Augustine saw it to be a kind of stalemate between the Apollonian quest for a principle of an abiding order vis-à-vis the Dionysian recognition of the inevitability of process and change.

33 Included in this set are the books of Proverbs, Job, Qoheleth (known in the Middle Ages as Ecclesiastes), Sirach (called Ecclesiasticus in the Middle Ages), Canticle of Canticles, Wisdom of Solomon, and some of the psalms.

34 For a more detailed discussion of other sapiential books (e.g., Proverbs, Job, Qoheleth, Sirach, and Canticles), see Koterski (2003).

35 See the English translations of vols. I and II of de Lubac (1959).

36 "Letter to Can Grande della Scalla" in Alighieri (1318).

37 For a fine discussion of the merits of this term and a detailed account of how the entire method worked, see Quay (1995).

38 *The Literal Meaning of Genesis* in Augustine (1982a).

39 This is true not only of the natural law tradition of thinkers like Aquinas, but even of voluntarists like Duns Scotus, who emphasizes

that morality is necessarily geared to the nature that God has chosen for us. See Ingham and Dreyer (2004), esp. pp. 173–85.

40 See Ladner (1959).

41 *On Christian Doctrine* in Augustine (1995a).

42 See Deely (2001), esp. pp. 220–2.

43 In Augustine's language, to love something for its own sake is called *frui* ("to delight in"), whereas to love something as a means to something else is *uti* ("to make use of"). With his penchant for clever use of words, he puts the issue in terms of the rhetorical choice between *uti* and *frui*. See *On Christian Doctrine* I.73ff, in Augustine (1995a).

44 The principle of double effect, so important to later medieval casuistry, seems to have been developed primarily to handle questions about killing in self-defense.

45 For the lives of Abelard, Héloïse, and Bernard of Clairvaux, see Clanchy (1997), Mews (2005), and Evans (2000).

46 See Kent (1995).

47 Commenting, for instance, on the work of Aquinas, J.-P. Torrell explains: "Contrary to a deductive method that is sometimes attributed to him but which is not his, Thomas does not want to prove the truths of the faith, nor to demonstrate other truths from those that he holds in faith. He simply wants to bring to the fore the connections that bind together the truths that we do hold and to show how all of this is explained as coming from God." Torrell (2005), pp. 50–1.

48 See Dulles (1994), especially on the medieval understanding of divine faith.

49 Some scholars, however, have argued that this progressive restriction of philosophical method to naturalistic reasoning was a contributory cause to the eventual rise of secularism. See Buckley (1987).

50 See McKirahan (1992). There were various such commentaries, including some by Averroes, whose translation into Latin assisted the composition of yet others such as Robert Grosseteste, Walter Burleigh, and Thomas Aquinas. See DiLascia et al. (1997).

51 See *Metaphysics* 1006b8–10, in Aristotle (1984): "If words have no meaning, our reasoning with one another, and indeed with ourselves, has been annihilated; for it is impossible to think of anything if we do not think of one thing."

52 *Summa of theology* I–II 94.2, in Aquinas (1945). See also *Metaphysics* 1005b32–4, in Aristotle (1984).

53 See, for instance, *Metaphysics* 1015b17–1017a7, in Aristotle (1984), and the comments on this text at *Commentary on Aristotle's Metaphysics* V.8–9, in Aquinas (1995), and *Summa of Theology* I.11.1 ad 2, in Aquinas (1945).

54 *Metaphysics* 1011b23–4, in Aristotle (1984).

55 Aristotle himself recognized that future contingents present a special problem. See *On Interpretation* 18a28–19b4, in Aristotle (1984). His medieval commentators show their respect for the difficulty of the problem by the number and the length of their treatments of this issue. For them, the problem is further complicated by the omniscience of God and their commitment to human free will.

56 It should be noticed here, of course, that there are also medieval thinkers who do not share or at least question these realist assumptions. Bonaventure, Meister Eckhart, and Nicholas of Cusanus, for instance, accept in one way or another the "coincidence of opposites," which puts in question the principle of non-contradiction. See Cousins (1978), Casarella (2006), and McGinn (2001).

57 In the history of philosophy, perhaps the most controversial of these first principles is one that the medieval period often used but rarely formulated as such, namely, the principle of sufficient reason (*that for anything, there must be a sufficient reason for its existence, either in itself or in another*). Correlative with this principle is that of causality (*for anything whose sufficient reason does not reside in itself, the sufficient reason must reside in another*). The principle of sufficient reason is controversial especially because of Leibniz's formulation of the principle, a formulation that Kant and others considered excessively strong. See Pruss (2006) and Gurr (1959).

58 *Republic* VI.509d1–511e3, in Plato (1997).

59 See, for instance, *On the Soul* III.3.428a20–b9, in Aristotle (1984).

60 For a cross-cultural comparison between the relation of mythological and philosophical thinking in ancient Egypt, Persia, Israel, and Greece, see Frankfort (1977).

61 For an overview of this topic, see Koterski (1998), pp. 12–21. See also Collins (1978, 1984).

62 Russman (1987) provides a sophisticated account of the context for the change in attitude on the question of faith and reason.

63 On this subject, see Weiss (1983) and Ariès and Duby (1987), esp. vol. II: *Revelations of the Medieval World*. Political philosophy is beyond the scope of this book, but one can readily see the difference on this question between, say, the medieval tendency to unite the orders of religion and politics in the legal arrangements of Christendom as a juridical order and the modern tendency to require the separation of church and state.

2

GOD

———

Schooled as they were in biblical exegesis and interpretation,[1] many medieval thinkers also exhibit considerable philosophical sophistication in handling the concept of God. They devoted themselves to such problems as proving God's existence, assessing the possibilities for knowing God's nature and of describing it adequately in human language, discerning God's relation to the world, and handling the problem of evil.

Most of the philosophical considerations of God during the Middle Ages were developed as part of the general quest of *fides quaerens intellectum* ("faith seeking understanding," discussed in chapter 1). Some fruitful approaches to this topic arose precisely from the personal situations of individual thinkers – the tempestuous anguish of the young Augustine, for instance, when he was seeking the truth about God prior to his conversion, or the enforced solitude of monastic life that turned Anselm to compose works that alternate between prayer and philosophical argument. Unsurprisingly, the differences of situation and temperament among these thinkers is matched by a considerable difference in the resulting approaches. For the worldly-wise but inwardly unsettled Augustine, assurance about God gradually emerged with his resolution of various related problems, such as how to avoid confining the infinite and omnipotent God within the limited forms that his imagination could devise. Likewise, he needed to determine how to think of evil as real without implicating a supposedly all-good God in its creation. By contrast, the more settled tranquility of a monastery allowed Anselm to devise a new kind of demonstration for God's existence that was based solely on thinking about what the term "god" entails.

The lively forum of university disputations enabled thinkers of the scholastic period to generate a series of formal proofs of the existence of God that were rooted in the principle of sufficient reason. The insight fundamental to this principle is that everything whatsoever must have, either in itself or in another, an adequate explanation for its existence. If something does not have a sufficient ground entirely within itself, then one must look to some cause that is other than that being. Tracking the causal chain may require looking to yet other causes that explain the cause that is immediately responsible for the data with which one starts. Arguments like these begin from some observable facts that do not have an adequate explanation entirely within themselves and then work backwards. Proofs of this sort trace back the lines of causality that produced whatever items or events one takes as evident in the present situation and in need of explanation. On the assumption that an infinite regress is impossible, medieval philosophers held that arguments of this sort could warrant the conclusion that something uncreated and eternal must exist as the first cause in order to provide a sufficient explanation for the observable facts about the cosmos with which the argument began. These arguments depend in various ways on evidence about the nature of things and the nature of the cosmos, which will be the focus of chapter 6.

Other scholastic arguments concentrate on the notion of God as the goal of all things, and especially on union with God as the fulfillment of human life. Yet other arguments are more strictly metaphysical in their focus on questions about necessary and contingent being and on the distinction between essence and existence. Yet, for all the abstractness typical of these proofs, the scholastic philosophers who proposed these arguments regularly insisted that the supreme being whose existence was shown by their proofs was the personal God whom they knew through biblical revelation.

Our study of the concept of God in medieval philosophy will consider first the ways in which these thinkers as religious believers used philosophy to consider the relation between God and the world. We will then consider some of the main forms of arguments that they advanced for the existence of God, and finally some questions about the divine nature and divine attributes as well as some reflections on the limits of human language in speaking about God. It is helpful to bear in mind that not all the theological discourse of this highly religious age was strictly philosophical in character. But there were some highly philosophical forms of theology that we need to consider in order to appreciate the philosophy that this age produced.

1   THE IMMANENCE AND TRANSCENDENCE OF GOD

One of the recurrent problems in any philosophical approach to God concerns the relation of the deity to the world. The three religions that were most culturally influential for medieval philosophy were Judaism, Christianity, and Islam. Each had a strong sense of the transcendence of God, and in Judaism and Christianity there was also a vivid recognition of God's immanence.[2] In the philosophizing done about the concept of God within these religious traditions there is a contrast not only with the understanding of the gods of Greek and Roman mythology, but also with the philosophical notions of divinity in ancient philosophy.[3] Following in the tradition of such thinkers as Xenophanes, the major schools of ancient thought tried to purify the concept of God from anthropomorphism by progressively eliminating not just the willful and idiosyncratic aspects, but anything of a personal sort. Invariably, however, they still viewed the gods or first principles as beings within the universe – that is, as perfect but finite. Ancient philosophers applied the term "divine" to things as diverse as the Olympian deities, the heavenly spheres, the First Mover, the Ideal Forms, and the intellect. None of them ever seems to have written a separate treatise on either the existence or the nature of God.[4] As a general rule, the philosophers of antiquity tended to deny the personal character of God as a way to point toward divine transcendence. Aristotle, for instance, sometimes envisioned God as a perfect sphere and at other times as thought thinking itself. Plotinus regarded God as the One, beyond being.[5]

In trying to appreciate what is at play in the notions of God's relationship to the world that were current among medieval philosophers, it is crucial to remember that they inherited from ancient philosophy a deep respect for arguments about various natural necessities – that is, the specific ways in which the members of a certain kind of being are found and the ways in which these things necessarily have to operate because of their natures. The novelty that medieval philosophers introduced into the situation came from their commitment to the biblical idea of God's freedom. In freely creating the world, God's choices were seen as responsible for what the ancients had taken as the natural necessities within the cosmos. That God freely chose to create the universe *ex nihilo* ("out of nothing") – an idea that medieval thinkers received from their reading of *Genesis* – implied that it was possible that the world might never have existed or might have been different if God had acted differently. God alone could have been all that there ever was, without in any way diminishing God's goodness.

The very things that struck ancient thinkers as natural necessities, intrinsic to the eternal essences of every species, came to be seen in the eyes of Christian philosophers as regularities that would be unexplainable except as the result of the intelligent design of these natures by God.[6] For thinkers philosophizing within the context of religious faith, there is then a deep-seated contingency to the world as a whole as well as to any given object and event within it. Once things have come into being, they exhibit a certain natural necessity according to their kind. But they need not have come into existence at all. The natures of things could have been different from how we find them to be.

To hold a view like this is still to have full respect for all causal factors operative within the world. Medieval thinkers tend to call these factors "secondary causes," while the "first cause" of all things is taken to be God's action in creating and preserving the world.[7] The dependence of all things on God, from this point of view, does not remove the relative autonomy of things as independent substances that have come to exist *in se* ("in their own right"), even though in their created existence they are ultimately *ab alio* ("from another," that is, caused), rather than *a se* ("from itself," uncaused), as God is.

The distinction between God as creator and the world as created is absolutely fundamental to the distinctive way in which medieval philosophers regularly thought of God. They want to maintain both that God is utterly different from creation and yet that creatures are in some important ways like the God who made them. Although God is "always greater" (*semper maior*) than we could ever imagine, it is nevertheless by thinking about creatures as effects of divine causality that one can gain at least some purchase on the nature of God, even if one can never fully comprehend the infinite perfection of God.

But there is a considerable range of views on this topic, and some deep disagreement. Thinkers like Nicholas of Cusa stress the difference between creator and creatures virtually to the point of denying that anything can truly be said of God in a positive way. Others such as John Scotus Eriugena and Meister Eckhart show pantheistic tendencies in practically identifying creator and creatures. Most, however, try to distinguish between creator and creature in such a way as to uphold both divine immanence and transcendence. They stress God's omnipresence throughout the world, for God is pure spirit. The purely spiritual (that is, non-material) nature of God is entirely different from the nature of anything found in the physical world of our experience. In their view, God encompasses the universe as a whole, but this is not because God is somehow "larger" than the world. It is because the relation of God to the world is not spatial at all, but rather a relation of causal dependence.

The philosophers who make these highly abstract metaphysical claims also show themselves mindful of the concreteness of expression that is typical of the Scriptures in their own religious traditions. The sacred texts of Judaism, Christianity, and Islam can easily give the impression that God is a vastly powerful but nonetheless finite being who does particular things to and for the world. These texts often use quite ordinary language to describe how God acts. Perhaps God has much greater power than human beings possess, but nonetheless God seems to act in much the same way that any other agent would tend to do. The philosophical theologians in each of these traditions repeatedly point out that God is not just another being (however much more powerful) in the same order as other beings within the world. Rather, God's being transcends all finite being.[8] In order to be understood in a way that is suitable to genuine divinity, God must be regarded as omniscient (all-knowing), omnipotent (all-powerful), omnibenevolent (all-good), and in fact the very source of the being of all limited beings. Ancient philosophers worried that anything infinite must not yet have achieved the completeness of perfection. But the religious philosophers of the medieval period came to see perfection precisely in terms of infinity. Rather than taking the notion of infinity as implying any defect on God's part, they came to recognize it as the best that human thought can manage in trying to express what surpasses human imagination, let alone human comprehension.

Precisely because they regard God as real and as the ultimate cause that sustains all the rest of reality, medieval philosophers often speak of God as a being and the supreme being. But when attempting to speak with greater precision, these philosophers tend to insist that one may only call God "a being" in the same way that one would call anything else "a being" if one also acknowledges that divine being is not constrained by any sort of limitation. All the objects of our normal experience are what they are by the forms that organize but also delimit their existence. A dog is a dog, precisely by having the sort of form that makes the dog this individual canine and not anything else. So too for human beings, and plants, and anything else in the physical world. By contrast, God is divine, not by having a limiting form, but by being infinite, by possessing all perfections without limitation. When dealing with countless theological questions, medieval thinkers wrestled with how to preserve the difference between infinite being and any form of finite being. It is with this highly philosophical consideration in mind that Christian theologians, for instance, undertook to think about the doctrine of the Incarnation (the belief that the second member of the Trinity took on human nature as Jesus Christ).[9]

In all three of these traditions there is a strong sense of the personal nature of God that needs to be accounted for, even while recognizing that divine transcendence will always exceed the categories that our imagination-rooted intellects risk imposing on God. Likewise, the forms of prayer by which believers address God and the forms of action by which they worship God invariably imply a sense of God as both transcendent and immanent, that is, both as hidden or absent from the normal world of experience and as providentially caring for and pervasively present to that world.

Throughout the Augustinian tradition one can easily sense the paradox involved in wanting to have it both ways. Anselm of Canterbury, for instance, prays in the opening chapter of his *Proslogion*:

Come then, Lord my God, teach my heart where and how to seek You, where and how to find You. Lord, if You are not present here, then where, since You are absent, shall I look for You? On the other hand, if You are everywhere, why then, since You are present, do I not see you?[10]

Anselm's spatial adverbs and metaphors of place cannot rightly be interpreted as trying to confine God to the dimensions of our world. They must be understood as signs that he is thinking about the paradox involved in trying to think and talk about a God who is both immanent and transcendent. Anselm's diction and the prayerful form of his reflections echo the opening book of the *Confessions*, where Augustine likewise modulates between the immanence and the transcendence of God:

> How shall I call upon my God, my God and Lord? Surely when I call on him, I am calling on him to come into me. But what place is there in me where my God can enter into me? "God made heaven and earth" [Gen. 1: 1]. Where may he come to me? Lord my God, is there any room in me which can contain you? Can heaven and earth, which you have made and in which you have made me, contain you? Without you, whatever exists would not exist. Then can what exists contain you? I also have being. So why do I request you to come to me when, unless you were within me, I would have no being at all?[11]

For Augustine, it is the light of the transcendent God's presence within the human mind that allows us to recognize eternal truths.[12] Even thinkers like Thomas Aquinas, who rejected Augustine's doctrine of illumination, maintain the same paradoxical stance on God's simultaneous immanence and transcendence, as when he notes:

> God is in all things, not, indeed, as part of their essence, nor as an accident, but as an agent is present to that upon which it acts. . . . Since God is being itself by His own essence, created being must be His proper effect. . . . But God causes this effect in things not only when they first begin to be, but as long as they are preserved in being. . . . Therefore, as long as a thing has being, so long must God be present to it, according to its mode of being. But being is innermost in each thing and most fundamentally present within all things, since it is formal in respect of everything found in a thing. . . . Hence it must be that God is in all things, and innermostly.[13]

In sounding the theme of the ongoing dependence of everything on the creator as both the cause of its coming to be in the first place and of its perseverance in being, Aquinas explains his sense of divine immanence and transcendence. Late medieval mystics express a comparable point when they speak of the transcendent God as the "ground" of the soul.[14]

Another important aspect of the general problem of the relation between God and the world is captured by the notion that God is the world's creator. By asserting that God created the world *ex nihilo*, medieval thinkers mean not just to assert the world's dependence on God. They also intend to exclude two of the explanations that they find among the ancient philosophers, namely, the view that the universe comes to be as a necessary emanation from God's own nature (a view held by Plotinus and many Neoplatonists) and the notion that the universe always somehow existed (a position held by Aristotle). Although there was considerable dispute about whether one could prove by natural reason alone whether the act of creation took place in time or not,[15] there was great consensus that God is the first cause in regard to the existence of all beings. Medieval philosophers regularly hold that it is an entirely free act by which God brings the whole universe, including all matter, into existence by his own choice. God is not compelled or constrained by anything outside his own nature. Further, God's action in creation is gratuitous. God's nature is in no way incomplete or in need of anything that he creates for his own completion or perfection.

Throughout the medieval period one finds discussions of the difference between necessary being and contingent being as one way to explain the difference between creator and creature. By definition, a necessary being is one that cannot not be. A contingent being is one that is, but could never have been. When this distinction is applied to questions about God, the argumentation usually runs from the fact of contingency among creatures to the need for a necessary being, and thus there is a claim that necessity must be regarded as a mark of God's being. God's being is not contingent, not causally dependent on anything else. It is not that God has a cause, but that God is the one being that is not in need of a cause. While the creatures of our experience have specific causes within the universe that have directly or indirectly produced them,[16] the causal lines that generated them could always have been altered or prevented. Hence, the being of these creatures is contingent rather than necessary. It is dependent on the causality exercised by beings outside themselves that might never have been activated. When we turn below to consideration of proofs for the existence of God, we will have the opportunity to consider the reasoning involved. But for the moment it suffices to note that medieval philosophers often saw that the presence of creatures whose being is contingent requires that the presence of a being whose existence is necessary in the sense that the primal being that is God could never not be. For creatures to owe their existence to God, God must exist necessarily. Medieval thinkers did not mean by this assertion that something other than God caused God to be, but rather that God as the source of all beings exists uncaused and uncreated *a se* ("from himself").

2 ARGUMENTS FOR THE EXISTENCE OF GOD

Neither the pervasive presence of religious faith in medieval culture nor the personal religious convictions of these philosophers dampened their enthusiasm for asking whether there could be a satisfying proof of God's existence. One might well wonder why believers would even try to prove God's existence by rational means if the truth of this claim were already a matter of their faith. With rare exception, it is not so much that those who offered proofs were doubtful about God's existence and felt some need to reassure themselves by philosophical arguments. Rather, the effort was part of the project of *fides quaerens intellectum* ("faith seeking understanding"). The confidence brought by faith in God's existence struck many of them as a sufficiently reasonable point for beginning other intellectual inquiry, especially about the nature of God and the conduct that faith required. But to put these advanced questions on sound footing as questions on which philosophical reasoning might have some bearing, it was important for them to begin treatises about God by asking whether natural reason by its own resources could show that God exists.

Aquinas, for example, counts a set of proofs for the existence of God (the famous "five ways") among the "preambles of the faith."[17] These preambles constitute a set of claims that he thinks can equally well be known by reason as by faith. The purpose of his listing these preambles is to show how reasonable it is to hold certain other doctrines that are accessible only by faith. To the extent that a compelling case from reason can be made for some of the claims that faith also makes, there is increased reason to trust other truth-claims that are not demonstrable by reason, but accessible only on the basis of faith in the trustworthiness of divine revelation. The point is that some (but not all) claims made by the Christian faith in its creeds can also be established by philosophical argument. On this model, belief in God's providential care for the universe is within the set of things known by faith, but the fact of God's existence is something that reason can demonstrate.

The proofs that Aquinas offers have often been called "cosmological" in that they start from certain aspects of the cosmos as data. They work toward showing that these data must have as an ultimate source the sort of thing that we call God. By contrast, Augustine and Anselm use what has come to be called an "ontological" approach, one that proceeds not from data about the world but from an analysis of the very idea of God.[18] One can learn much about how a given medieval figure thought that philosophical reason works by considering the patterns of reasoning used in their demonstrations. In general, those more sympathetic to Platonism show a greater willingness to turn to ontological arguments and to rely upon the respect accorded to essences in that tradition. Those more inclined to Aristotelianism tend to prefer cosmological arguments that trace observable data back to first principles through causal chains.

Near the beginning of the *Proslogion*, Anselm offers a rather sophisticated version of a line of reasoning that Augustine had used long before in such early works as *On Free Choice of the Will* and that Boethius also emplyed in his *Consolation*.[19] Anyone, even the proverbial "fool" mentioned in the Psalms who says that there is no God,[20] can understand the definition of the term "God," especially when it is presented with some precision. In Anselm's famous phrasing, God is *aliquid quo nihil maius cogitari possit* ("that than which nothing greater can be conceived"). This is not merely to assert, Anselm insists, that God is simply the greatest being within a series of beings, for by definition there has to be some greatest member within any limited series. If this notion only meant the greatest member of a series, one could always imagine something still greater in some respect or other. Rather, this formulation of the definition of God turns on the use of a formula that can go beyond any such focus on the greatest within a given series. The intended focus is on the notion of something that in principle cannot be exceeded. It is not that we have a positive understanding of what this being is, but simply that we are able to have a kind of placeholder: the ideas of that than which nothing greater can be conceived.

The reason for this starting-point is that the argument requires the definition of God to signify a being, regardless of whether such a being exists, that is "greater than" anything that could ever in principle be thought or imagined. Anselm admits that he himself believes in God, and his argument is sometimes accused of begging the question by assuming the very point that needs to be proven. But merely to articulate the definition of something as a way to get started on trying to determine whether the thing exists or not is not to beg the question. There is no denying that the religious character of his culture allows Anselm to propose a definition like this as a way to identify that sort of thing whose existence he wants to prove. Anselm's defense against this objection is that his argument, considered *as an argument*, does not begin by assuming the correctness of a belief that he personally holds. Rather, the argument starts by inquiring whether one who disbelieves in God understands the definition, for he wants the argument to have as its starting-point a common definition.

If one will assent to the use of this definition, the move to demonstrate the necessary existence of what is being defined here is swift. Anselm directs us to consider which is greater, the essence of any given thing as it is in our minds or that same essence as actually existing independently of our minds. Just as a real apple is greater than merely the thought of that same apple, or a real book is greater than the book one merely wants to write, so too a God who truly exists would be greater than the mere concept of such a God. But if one has agreed to the definition of God as that than which nothing greater can be conceived, God must (Anselm argues) necessarily exist. Otherwise we would not have been thinking about that than which nothing greater can be conceived, but about something else.

The soundness of Anselm's reasoning was debated in his own time and has remained a subject of great interest ever since. Aquinas, for instance, takes him to task for confusing the existence of the concept of God with the God that the concept is intended to signify, and thus for indeed begging the question.[21] In Anselm's own time, the monk Gaunilo attacked the argument as proving too much. If the argument were valid, then we could presumably hold that there must exist a greatest conceivable instance of anything – a beautiful island, for instance, than which none more lovely could ever be conceived. This objection provoked a fruitful reply by Anselm. He distinguished between things that are contingent, for they can be conceived not to exist, and something truly necessary, that which cannot be conceived not to exist. The discussion of this point between Anselm and Gaunilo tends to presume that existence (whether of the contingent or the necessary type) is a kind of property that an essence can have or lack. Debate over whether existence is a property at all, such that one could have it or lack it, continues to engage contemporary philosophers as much as the ontological argument itself.[22]

Cosmological arguments for the existence of God are numerous in Jewish, Christian, and Islamic philosophy during the Middle Ages. The first three of Aquinas' famous "Five Ways"[23] are clearly of this sort, for these arguments of his begin, respectively, from the fact of change or motion, the fact of causes and effects, and the fact of contingency in the world. The phenomena immediately under observation in each case can be traced to their direct causes, and the causes of those causes can in turn be traced to other causes. Whether one is working backwards in time or doing one's analysis of causal dependence diachronically,[24] one must in principle reach something that does not need a causal explanation. Otherwise one will only have attained part of the explanation that one was seeking. Even more important philosophically than how many steps there are in the chain and how far back one can trace the specific lines is the need to find something that can serve as a sort of philosophical bedrock for the whole explanation. By appealing to the impossibility of an infinite regress (that is, a chain of other movers or causes or contingent or perishable beings) in order to provide an ultimate explanation for present phenomena, these first three arguments lead one to admit that there had to be a first mover, a first efficient cause, a necessary being. Like Maimonides[25] and Averroes,[26] Aquinas borrows heavily from Aristotle (especially from *Physics* VIII) in constructing these arguments.

Much of the reaction to this type of reasoning in the Middle Ages and since has focused on the validity of an appeal to the thesis that an infinite regress is impossible. As arguments that are structured so as to move from an observed effect back to a sufficiently powerful cause that one must postulate even when it is not directly observed, these arguments do not claim to bring one to know everything that one might like to know about the causal source, but only to the admission that there must have been a cause of this effect, and that it must have been the sort that can produce this type of effect, whatever other properties or qualities that cause may have. Arguments of this type only reach back to the fact that something ultimate exists and serves as the unmoved mover, the uncaused cause, the necessary being that makes possible all contingent beings. Further investigation will be needed to determine what else, if anything, can be said about the nature of this causal source. But the arguments will have done their intended work if one can reach the conclusion that this source necessarily exists. At the conclusion of each of his arguments, Aquinas comments ". . . and this we call God" – not in the sense that he has said all that he can say or all that he wants to say, but simply in the sense that God, whatever else he is or does, must be admitted to exist.

The fourth and fifth of Aquinas' "Five Ways" take up other approaches to showing the need to admit God's existence. In the fourth way he considers the degrees of perfection in the objects of our experience as leading to the need to posit a source in which these perfections are at their maximum. In the fifth way he offers an argument from the regularity that can be observed in the goal-directed ways in which natural things that do not themselves have any intelligence do operate always or for the most part. This approach leads him to the conclusion that these cases of the regular attainment of ends by beings that do not themselves have the intelligence to design the ways by which they achieve their own ends must be governed by a supreme intelligence.[27] Otherwise one could not adequately explain the regularity in which things that do not have the cognitive ability to choose the means by which to reach their goals so regularly do reach them. This type of argument thus depends entirely on the principle of sufficient reason.

3   THE DIVINE ATTRIBUTES

Throughout the Middle Ages the recurrent quest to understand God better through extensive discussion of the attributes of divinity invariably involves reflection on language. One needs to consider both the power and the limit of human language with regard to expressing a reality that touches but also transcends human experience. We will explore some of these limits in chapter 3 below in our consideration of the possibilities of super-eminent predication opened up by Dionysian *negative theology*.

There is something paradoxical involved in claiming that creatures are in some way like God because they are dependent on his causal activity, and that God's own nature is utterly unlike creatures. Despite this paradox, many medieval philosophers regularly insist that the ongoing dependence of creation on God and God's own complete self-sufficiency mean that it must be possible to gain some knowledge of God from creatures.[28] In his *De Trinitate* ("On the Trinity"), for example, Augustine provides extensive philosophical development of a scriptural point favored by many medieval thinkers in their reflections on human nature. While all creatures show forth something about their maker as effects display something of their cause, Genesis (1: 27) reveals that only human beings are made in the image of God.[29] For Augustine, the direction of the likeness between human beings and God (that we are made in God's image, and not the reverse) has enormous significance. Although the nature of God is infinitely greater than our own, it is less known to us. If one proceeds with proper humility and caution,[30] one can discern many things about the nature of God. One can even discover some things about the Trinity of divine persons by reflecting on our own minds and on the triads one can discover in the soul, such as memory, understanding, and will. Augustinians of the scholastic period, such as Bonaventure in *The Mind's Journey to God*,[31] take up this theme.

Modestly confident, then, that it is at least possible in principle to speak about God's nature, medieval thinkers regularly cite two main sources as their justification for specific claims about the divine attributes: positive divine revelation and the philosophical discernment of the suitability of a given attribute for God. The respect of religious philosophers of the Middle Ages for revelation provided them with ample data for philosophical reflection about the nature and qualities of God. This is especially the case when scriptural revelation is taken in tandem with philosophical considerations about the propriety of any suggested attribute, that is, the suitability or fittingness of a given quality for attribution to God. Philosophically, the criterion of suitability (whether a proposed attribute is fitting to be ascribed to the divine nature or not) often has a kind of regulatory function that soberly serves to temper claims to know more than one can know about God. As we noted in chapter 1 on faith and reason, the application of philosophical tests for the suitability of religious language gave a certain credibility to the presentations of the Christian religion; without such cautions, the stories told in the Scriptures might have seemed formally indistinguishable from the stories told in pagan mythology.[32] But if medieval philosophers had not been willing to credit revelation as a genuine source of knowledge, the philosophical criterion of suitability might well have promoted a theology of silence and iconoclasm rather than a disciplined effort to provide a philosophical discussion of the attributes of divinity. Used in tandem, these two sources permitted medieval thinkers to articulate a considerable body of material about the characteristics of God, but also to have a sense of what should not be said (e.g., one should not think of God as really having arms or legs even when the stories about God in the third chapter of Genesis talk of God as walking in the Garden with Adam and Eve).

Although individuals and schools of thought offer different lists of divine attributes and give different emphases, there is considerable overlap about many of the properties that may legitimately be predicated of God, including such attributes as eternity (that God is not within time), perfection (that God lacks nothing), unity (that there is only one God), simplicity (that God is undivided and indivisible, without constituent parts), incorporeality (that God has no body), immutability (that God is unchanging), impassibility (that God does not suffer), omniscience (that there is nothing that God does not know), and omnipotence (that there is nothing that God cannot do). There is biblical warrant for asserting some of these items, but the justification for others comes from philosophical reflection on what we must say about a perfect being. Even for those terms whose meaning seems quite plain and straightforward, it became clear over time that asserting any one of them about God had implications for other philosophical problems (and sometimes for other parts of philosophical theology) whose solution called for considerable dexterity.

Biblical assertions about God's eternity, for instance, can often seem as if they refer to everlasting endurance throughout time, but thinkers as early as Augustine and Boethius came to distinguish the "eternity" of God (an everlasting "now" – the simultaneous presence of God to all moments of time) from, say, the "everlasting" life of the saints in heaven (an ongoing succession of time without end). They do so for philosophical reasons, such as trying to resolve the problem constituted by the human freedom of choice in relation to God's omniscience. If God's eternity were an endless passage through time comparable to our own passage through time, the claim of divine omniscience at any one point within this flow of time would seem incompatible with the claim of human freedom. For if God truly knew "in advance" what we were going to do at some point prior to our decision, then it would appear impossible also to claim that we are really free in our choices. For anyone genuinely to know something and not merely to be guessing, there has to be something definite to know. But if something has to be determinate already in order to become known, then our apparently free choices would not really be free but already determined (even if unknown to us). On the other hand, if our free choices only come to be determined by our own decision at the moment of choice and are not determined ahead of time, then there is nothing available "in advance" for God (or anyone else) to know. Unless there is something definite to know, God's knowledge would be akin to merely making good guesses. But guessing would be something "unfitting" to say of God, for it would render God imperfect in an important respect. The conundrum here is something like the problem one encounters with the string on a parka: if one pulls too hard in either direction, the other side disappears. Hence, the solution often preferred by medieval thinkers is to envision God as outside of time, for even time is something that God created. By thinking of God in this way, God is no more determining any free choice that is being made by human beings than any human onlooker is determining it. The difference in the case of God is that God's position outside the flow of time makes it possible for God to see the entire flow of time and all the choices made by free creatures within that flow.

While there remain certain important problems in this sort of solution, there are some obvious advantages as well. Medieval philosophers gained a way to defend the reality of freedom even if it meant that we cannot fully comprehend how divine knowing works. At best, we can only point toward an answer that is beyond human experience by understanding eternity as the "complete and perfect possession of endless life all at once."[33] In his application of the definition of eternity to the question at hand, Boethius envisions God as a timeless observer of all time as it unfolds. God is thus no more the cause of specific acts of free human choice than any human observers would be of, say, the action of another person under their observation. Such a solution makes us stretch our imaginations with regard to the way in which God knows. It makes us restrain any inclination to presume that God's life is a succession of moments like our own. The apparent success of this solution at accommodating divine omniscience and human freedom served as an invitation for subsequent generations of thinkers to elucidate a variety of important problems latent in this conception. One of these problems concerns the way in which this resolution of the difficulty still seems to make God's knowledge of creatures and their choices dependent on creatures, for it still requires that God watch what those creatures do. Later scholastic thinkers, for instance, wrestled with this notion by devising a whole new category for handling the problem of God's knowledge called "middle knowledge." In addition to the possibility of knowledge of the past and knowledge of the future, they postulated a knowledge of all the possible states of future affairs that could arise in the future from a human being's free choice on any given question. By this intermediate or middle way of knowing, they hoped to escape the dilemma of either making God's knowledge dependent on his creatures or making free choice impossible. This third option seemed to some thinkers a good way to explain divine omniscience as the knowledge God has of all the possible implications of any given free choice.[34] Yet, this sort of solution received much criticism as being still subject to the dilemma that God either does or does not know which of these possibilities will be realized in fact. According to this line of criticism, this resolution simply pushes the same basic problem to another level without really resolving it.

Among the other recurrent topics of philosophical discussion was the question of divine unity. Jewish and Muslim philosophers of the

Middle Ages generally had less difficulty than Christians in defending the unity of God. Israel's affirmation of radical monotheism ("Hear O Israel, the Lord our God is one Lord"[35]), like Islamic insistence on the tenet that "there is no god but God,"[36] left no questions about the matter. Christian belief in a Divine Trinity (God the Father, God the Son, and God the Holy Spirit) generated much discussion about how to differentiate one from another without dividing the single *ousia* ("being" or "substance") of God into three separate beings and to the development of the very concept of the person. The recurrent attention in all these traditions to philosophical arguments for the unity that must be attributed to God tends to be associated with reflection on divine perfection. If there were two (or any greater number), one would possess what the other lacked and thus would not be absolutely perfect.[37]

Related to the attribute of unity is divine simplicity (the absence of component parts). Medieval thinkers usually treated simplicity not as a separate and distinct attribute, but more as a rule for their own theological discourse. Asserting divine simplicity was a way by which to rein in the understandable inclination to suppose that anything that we need to distinguish in order to understand is actually separate in reality.[38] While each of the divine attributes that are named separately are distinct from one another in meaning, each one must also be thought to express the whole of God, even if the precise manner of their unity as attributes of the one God transcends our imagination.

By contrast with divine simplicity, every creature whatsoever is composite. All physical beings are obviously composite by virtue of their materiality, whether their parts are homogeneous (like the matter that makes up a rock) or heterogeneous (like the various kinds of tissue in an animal). But even immaterial beings like angels[39] or souls once separated from their bodies by death[40] are composed of essence and existence. They are composite precisely by virtue of being members of a kind and having potentialities that are actualized in one way or another and in some specific degree at any given time. Another way to put this point is to say that God is purely actual. God is thus not a fit subject for the substantial changes that creatures undergo when they are generated or destroyed. Nor can God be subject to accidental changes, the modifications of quality, quantity, or relation that creatures constantly experience even while remaining the same basic individual within the same species. In the technical language of scholasticism, essence (what a thing is) and existence (that it is) are the same only in God, and this identity of essence and existence is the meaning of divine simplicity. Everything else is composed of essence and existence. An individual is a member of the kind that is characterized by having a given essence, but there is nothing about that essence that requires that there be any existing instances of it. A creature's participation in existence (one's share in being) never exhausts the essence. Rather, any finite being's essence limits that being's manner of existence. What one is (a dog, a human being, a rock, and so on) determines certain parameters for one's actions and operations. Any individual object's actual experience of doing anything and undergoing anything will fall within a certain range according to one's kind of being.

4 OVERVIEW

The philosophical treatment of questions about the existence and nature of God during the Middle Ages included various efforts to provide evidence and argument that would be rationally cogent and compelling. Some of the topics seemed accessible by faith as well as by reason. In making the effort to provide philosophical arguments, the thinkers of this period should not be thought of as attempting to supply grounds more solid than what faith provided. If anything, they tended to regard faith as a more certain source of knowledge than reason. But the high regard in which they held religious faith nonetheless meant, at least for most of them, no disregard for reason. To the contrary, they took the view that the powers of reason that human beings had been given by God should be put to good use. Hence, they should be used on the subject of the existence and nature of God above all.

In so doing, medieval thinkers devised various forms of argument in support of the truth of the claim that God existed and that the existence of God could be known on the basis of our knowledge of this world. Arguments of this sort were inevitably grounded on one of the principles that they regarded as self-evident and foundational, the principle of sufficient reason. Properly stated, this principle maintains that for everything that exists there is an adequate explanation, either in itself or in another. While there is a causal explanation in something else for all those objects that are within our direct experience, there must be one thing whose adequate explanation resides only in itself. This they held to be God.

But as individuals with religious faith, medieval philosophers also attempted to relate the view of God as known by this faith to the view of God that is possible when the human reason is engaged in philosophical considerations about divinity. Their recurrent interest in the divine nature and the attributes that may be predicated of God reflect their sustained interest in ascertaining how best to understand the claims found in the Scriptures. They tried to determine by philosophical means whether the things revealed by God could also be known by the human mind independently of that revelation.

NOTES

1   For an overview of study of the Bible during various periods within the Middle Ages, see Rogerson et al. (1988), vol. II: *The Study and Uses of the Bible.* The classic study on this topic by Beryl Smalley (1964) remains quite valuable. See also de Lubac (1959).

2   Judaism stressed divine transcendence in many ways, including the strict prohibition against idols, the sacredness of the very name of God, and the sternness of the prophets in such passages as Isaiah 40: 12–26. In the New Testament we find statements such as John 1: 18 ("no one has ever seen God") and 1 Cor. 13: 12 (that now we see only dimly as in a mirror, in contrast to heaven, where we shall see God face to face). In Islam, however, the theme of transcendence is predominant almost completely.

3   For a fine overview of ancient and medieval thinking about God and religion, see Reichberg (1998).

4   Even though there do not appear to have been any separate treatises in ancient philosophy on the existence or nature of God, these topics do regularly appear in the course of other projects, such as Plato's demonstration of the existence of providential deities in book X of the *Laws,* or Aristotle's accounts of the Prime Mover (that is, the first efficient cause) in *Physics* VIII.5. But scholars are divided about whether Aristotle ever intended to identify such metaphysical first principles with the concept of God. In *Metaphysics* XII.7–9, Aristotle envisions God as

thought thinking itself, in the form of a perfect sphere, to which the various intelligences are attracted and thus by final causality God is envisioned as the source of all motion and change in the universe. Plotinus' view of the One (or "first god") as the unchangeable and ineffable source from which everything else "emanates" (flows) can be found in *Enneads* V.2; for his view that the One is beyond being and beyond thought, see V.6.

5   See Gerson (1990), esp. ch. 3 on Aristotle and ch. 5 on Plotinus.

6   For Christians, the doctrine of divine providence includes the notion that God not only created the world, but designed it in such a way as to orient the various sorts of creatures toward what would fulfill them. Further, the Christian doctrine of the Incarnation implies, among other things, God's great love for humanity and a readiness to restore it after its fall in sin. These views also envision the possibility of friendship with God and the promise of perfect happiness (felicity).

7   In contrast to some ancient thinkers, who postulated a series of intermediate deities in order to account for divine governance of the world, medieval philosophers attacked the notion that any such intermediate agents were divine. Augustine, for instance, in the first ten books of *The City of God*, takes great pains to show that these intermediaries are really angels or demons, or just human beings whose great deeds won them a reputation for godliness. While appropriate honor may be due to great deeds, they are not gods, and any sort of worship (*latria*) would be idolatry (worship of idols).

8   See Burrell (1993).

9   One of the great tasks that Christian theologians always set for themselves as monotheists was to discuss the mystery of the Trinity, while staying alert to the paradoxes involved in asserting that the Godhead consists of three divine Persons. Although this topic is by any standard theological rather than philosophical, it invariably involves philosophical considerations, such as the very definition of "person." See Koterski (2004).

10 *Proslogion*, ch. 1, in Anselm (1998), pp. 84–5.

11 *Confessions* I.2, in Augustine (1991b), pp. 3–4.

12 For instance, *On Free Choice of the Will* II.6, in Augustine (1982b), pp. 48–9.

13 *Summa of Theology* I.8.1.c, in Aquinas (1945).

14 See the variety of texts from Eckhart's sermons and academic writings that are studied in McGinn (2001).

15 See, for instance, Pecham (1993).

16 This is not yet to mention the role played by God's free choice to bring into existence individual beings whose essences exist in the divine mind

as Ideas, that is, as diverse participations in the totality of perfections that exist in the simplicity of God's own being.

17 *Summa of Theology* I.2.3, in Aquinas (1945).

18 The term "ontological" is not a medieval label, but one that derives from modern philosophy. One can find it, for instance, in the attack on this type of reasoning that Immanuel Kant makes in the *Critique of Pure Reason*.

19 See *On Free Choice of the Will* II.6.14, in Augustine (1982b), where he speaks of God as one "to whom nothing can be granted superior." *Consolation* III.10, in Boethiius (2000), may also be a possible source of Anselm's phrasing. Boethius claims that God (the highest good) is "quod nihil melius excogitari queat" ("that than which nothing greater can be thought"). Descartes makes this approach his own in *Discourse on Method*, part 4, and in *Meditations* III.

20 The phrase "the fool who says there is no God" is a rhetorical trope found in various Psalms. The use of this term should not be mistaken as if it were saying that the psalmist is contemptuously dismissing the person who holds that there is no god. Rather, the psalmist has considered the matter and is rendering a considered judgment. Whatever one's reason for denying the existence of God, the truth of the matter (in the psalmist's judgment) is that we really are creatures who depend on God in more ways than we may know or be ready to admit.

21 *Summa of Theology* I.2.1 ad 2, in Aquinas (1945). For a sympathetic account of this argument within the context of Anselm's life and theological project, see Southern (1990), pp. 127–37.

22 For a survey of modern analysis of the ontological argument in its many forms, see van Inwagen (1998), pp. 54–8.

23 The "Five Ways" are found in *Summa of Theology* I.2.3.c, in Aquinas (1945). For a fine account of the structure of these arguments and of philosophical reactions to them, see Davies (1992), pp. 21–39.

24 For a thoroughgoing analysis of the nature of the argumentation in the "Five Ways" and a balanced evaluation of recent scholarly judgments about their validity, see Wippel (2000), pp. 442–500.

25 *The Guide for the Perplexed*, part II, ch. 1 in Maimonides (1963).

26 See Leaman (1998).

27 One also finds in various writings by Aquinas an argument from the need for a cause of existence that is itself uncaused. See his early treatise *On Being and Essence*, ch. 4. in Aquinas (1983). See also *On the Power of God*, ch. 7 in Aquinas (1952), and *Summa contra gentiles* I.22 and II.52, in Aquinas (1975).

28 For Aquinas' discussion of one-way real relations, see. e.g., *Summa of Theology* I.6.2 ad 1, in Aquinas (1945).

29 Bonaventure follows Augustine's lead in this as in much else. For the semiotic character of Bonaventure's entire metaphysics, see Cullen (2006). For a discussion of the biblical foundation for the scholastic doctrine of the analogous knowledge of God, see Dulles (1987), p. 31.

30 See, for instance, *The Trinity* V.1.2 and 2.3, in Augustine (1991a) for a discussion of this general approach, and VII.4.7–9 for comments on the problems one faces in trying to find appropriate human language when speaking about God.

31 *Itinerarium mentis in Deum*, in Bonaventure (1978).

32 *The City of God*, for instance, makes this argument again and again in books VI–X; Augustine (1984).

33 *Consolation of Philosophy*, book V, prose 6: "*interminabilis vitae tota simul et perfecta possessio*" in Boethius (2000).

34 For an interesting account of this position, attentive both to historical and contemporary issues, see Miller (1996).

35 This is the famous "Shema" – see Deuteronomy 6: 4. There is, of course, considerable discussion about whether the phrase should properly be translated as "the Lord our God is one Lord" or perhaps as "the Lord our God alone is Lord." It is a question about whether the text is making a claim about the utter unity of God. Perhaps it is just a claim about the fact that only the God of this people is truly God. By contrast, there are various supernatural beings whom other peoples worshiped as gods, but they are only some sort of fallen angels or demons, if indeed they exist at all. They may simply be the product of superstitious imagination. While modern thought tends to presume the latter, there is reason to think that for biblical writers the "gods" whom these pagans worshiped were only spirits who fulfilled the role of gods to their adherents. These demons returned various services to their devotees in return for adoration and sacrifice. See Psalm 96: 5, which reads: "For all the gods of the Gentiles are devils; but the Lord made the heavens." See also Deuteronomy 32: 16–17; Joshua 24: 15; Ps. 82: 1–8; Ps. 95: 3; Ps. 106: 34–41. Augustine seems to have understood these biblical references in this way, as, for instance, in *The City of God*, books 6 and 7.

36 The first of the five pillars of Islam, "La illaha il'allah." See Bearman (2002).

37 See, for instance, *Summa of Theology* I.11.3, in Aquinas (1945).

38 The regulative function of the attribute of simplicity may well be the reason why it often receives such prominence among the divine attributes, e.g., as the first implication derived after grasping God's nature as supremely perfect in *Monologion*, ch. 17, in Anselm (1998), p. 30,

or as the first attribute discussed in the treatise on the divine nature in *Summa of Theology* I.3, in Aquinas (1945).

39 Thomas Aquinas is often called the "Angelic Doctor" because of his special care in developing this subject; he made frequent recourse to the *Celestial Hierarchies* of Dionysius. Within his treatise on the angels in the *Summa of Theology* I.50–64, in Aquinas (1945), he argues that while angels can be directed by God to assume bodies, they do not naturally have a body or any material component. Hence, they are not individuated by matter (which is the principle of individuation within a species) in the way that physical creatures begin to have individual existence as beings distinct from others in their species by virtue of having different matter. The logical implication of this point is that each angel constitutes its own species (I.50.4), and yet even so each angel is a creature that receives existence according to a limiting essence. For a discussion of potentiality in regard to what an angel knows, see I.58.1.

40 As discussed below in chapter 7 on souls, potency and actuality are crucial metaphysical concepts for medieval understanding of the soul not only during bodily life, but also after death. The capacity for a soul to undergo the purifications of Purgatory, let alone to experience the joys of Heaven or the torments of Hell, is one of the basic premises of Dante's *Divine Comedy*, worked out by the poet with great reliance on scholastic philosophical psychology. For a recent treatment of this subject, see Cogan (1999).

3

THE DIVINE IDEAS

For medieval philosophers, the material universe is something that God created. But they disagree, and sometimes sharply, about the precise meaning of the theological claim that God created the world *ex nihilo* ("out of nothing"). As an article of their religious faith, they are all committed to the doctrine that God somehow created the world. Some maintain that we can provide a philosophically rigorous proof for the fact of creation, while others judge that we would never have known that fact without the benefit of revelation. When treating the related topic of divine providence,[1] they are all convinced that God knows creation in all its variety and details, but they disagree about how it is that God knows everything that there is to know about creatures. In fact, to think of the world precisely in terms of "creation" and "creatures" and not just in terms of "beings" or "kinds" or "natures" is one of the most distinctive aspects of medieval philosophy.[2]

To understand all reality other than God in terms of "creation" is to see it as dependent on God for its origin, for its continued existence, and for its good governance. This perspective differs in important respects from the views that take the physical universe always to have existed or to have come to its present state by evolution or to have emerged by chance. The religious commitments of medieval philosophers put the discussion of this whole topic into a different light. One of the recurrent components in their explanations is the notion of the divine ideas. By this notion, medieval philosophers tried to account both for the act by which God creates the world and for explaining how divine knowledge works. After considering the Platonic background for this concept, this chapter will consider certain patristic adaptations made in the basic model in order to render it compatible with biblical faith, and then some of the further adaptations made by scholastic thinkers.

1 THE BACKGROUND

What generates the philosophical problem to which the divine ideas are proposed as a suitable answer? The fundamental question here concerns the kinds of knowledge and activity involved in the divine creation of the world. How does God create the world? Does God know every last detail about each individual in the universe? Or is it the eternal archetypes of things that are alone fitting as objects of divine knowledge? On the one hand, there is the conviction that God's omniscience (a perfection that belongs to God as infinitely perfect) must necessarily include knowledge of the contingent events surrounding even the simplest and humblest creature. On the other hand, there is the long-standing philosophical presumption that the stable objects required for genuine knowledge are kinds rather than individuals. The degree of permanence that specific objects exhibit over time comes from the forms that stabilize mutable entities in the changing sensory world, and it is these forms that are thought to be the object of knowledge.

In addition to these metaphysical and epistemological considerations, medieval philosophers had to find a way to reconcile the claim that God providentially cares for each one of the vast variety of creatures with the equally basic position that God is unchanging, utterly one, and simple (that is, without the sort of component parts typical of creatures). As we noted in chapter 2 on the concept of God, much of the problem here concerns the difficulty of using human categories to think about God without inadvertently restricting God by the limitations that characterize all the finite beings of our direct experience. As an added complication, these thinkers believed God to be personal, and so needed to avoid making God into some abstract principle.

From the start, philosophical theologians of the Middle Ages readily embraced the general notion of the Platonic Ideas in order to explain how God creates and knows every creature. But over the course of time they found it necessary to introduce various qualifications and adaptations into this theory, most notably the incorporation of these Ideas into the very mind of God. In this way they tried to explain not only certain things about divine knowledge, but also about the intelligibility and intrinsic value of the created order.

The notion of the divine ideas is not merely some relic of the Platonic philosophy that somehow remained within the systems of patristic and medieval theorists without critical examination. Rather, it played a crucial role in the new versions of metaphysics that they developed in order to accommodate their belief that the universe was divinely created. Thinkers fundamentally sympathetic to Plato and Neoplatonism, such as Augustine, Boethius, and Dionysius, found the Platonic theory of Forms quite agreeable for this purpose. In the *Timaeus* of Plato they saw the figure of a quasi-divine craftsman whom Plato called the "demiurge" and took it as a useful model for understanding how God's creative activity might work once certain important alterations were made in this notion. Plato's demiurge, for instance, always needs to look up to the eternal Ideas as the models for his terrestrial craftsmanship. Medieval theorists, however, were unwilling to compromise God's sovereign freedom in any way by suggesting that God as the single cause of all things was somehow subject to any necessity outside himself. Hence, they envisioned the Ideas as within God's mind, rather than thinking of them as something that existed separately, to which the demiurge had to look for his models in fashioning a world.[3]

Even those medieval thinkers less inclined to Platonism retained this doctrine. Despite Aristotle's rejection of Plato's theory of Ideas, the thinkers who became Aristotle's disciples in the thirteenth century continued to adhere to some version of the divine ideas. They found it especially helpful in explaining how the vast multiplicity of creatures could originate by the free choice of a single cause of all things. Likewise, it assisted them in explaining how the teleological drives that are repeatedly manifested in much of nature could show so much intelligent design.

In this chapter we will first consider certain adaptations that patristic and early medieval thinkers make in the Platonic theory of the Ideas or Forms, especially by relocating them from outside to inside the divine mind. But merely to relocate the Ideas does not resolve all the problems. A second aspect of our study will be to consider the approach to God that the medieval period call the *via negativa* or negative theology – a sophisticated strategy for denying any limitations upon God. The Dionysian tradition retained an important role for these divine ideas, while championing negative theology and divine unity. What was seen as especially problematic here was the relation of God to the Ideas, for the notion of divine perfection was readily recognized to imply that there is no composition in God. Thinking out the implications of divine simplicity involved reflection on certain crucial differences between the human mind and the divine mind. The cognitive powers that belong to human beings need to be understood on the model of act and potency. But God is purely actual. So, whatever powers God may be said to have must be thought of as identical to his being and not as potencies that still need to be activated in the course of being focused on beings other than God himself. Further, it became clear that the divine ideas should not be thought of as some kind of products of God's mind that are somehow distinct from God. They are not themselves creatures, but aspects of God himself. They are the models for creatures, but they exist within God's own mind. Even though there are presumably many such divine ideas, there is only one God. Efforts to work out these relationships required considerable ingenuity. The final component of this chapter will focus on the notion of exemplary causality, a distinctive kind of causality exercised by the divine ideas in the creation and governance of the world.

2 PATRISTIC ADAPTATIONS OF THE PLATONIC DOCTRINE OF IDEAS

For a proper understanding of medieval philosophizing on the divine ideas and exemplary causality, there is a certain amount of theological background that is indispensable. Like his fellow Alexandrian Clement,[4] Origen found in the demiurge of Plato's *Timaeus* a remarkable parallel to certain passages in Scripture that employ the analogy of the artist or craftsman for describing God as the creator and designer of the universe.[5] Origen envisions the Wisdom of God as generating an intelligible world (*noetos kosmos*) that possesses from all eternity all the principles (*logoi*) of what will be created. Like an architect who constructs a house in accord with a mental plan, so divine wisdom brings about all the things that God intends to create. Here we find not only certain aspects that resemble details from Plato's account of the demiurge, who looks up to the Ideas for the models by which the world is created, but also certain biblical resonances, such as passages from the Wisdom Psalms and various part of biblical Wisdom literature.[6] These scriptural texts come relatively late in the history of the Bible and often reflect back theologically on the creation stories contained in the first chapters of Genesis. They tend to use the personified figure of Wisdom as a way to explain how God planned the world and providentially provided in advance for the restoration of its disorder.[7] For the later followers of Origen, such as Gregory of Nyssa, it is not only in the world of physical nature that we can see the design of God, but in our own human nature, for God has impressed a likeness of his own intelligence and goodness on us. God is like a sculptor who carves into a wax model the image of the figure he wants to fashion.[8]

One crucial difference between any of these texts and their Platonic source is in the location of the divine ideas. In his *De Opificio Mundi* ("On the Making of the World")[9] the Jewish biblical exegete and philosopher Philo of Alexandria explains God's creation of an intelligible world as a "model" (*paradeigma*) that God uses to "create" (*demiourgein*) the material world. Christian thinkers likewise tended to see the Ideas not as outside God, as if they were some sort of eternal essences to which the demiurge of Plato's *Timaeus* had to look in shaping and fashioning the already existing but unformed and sometimes recalcitrant matter into a world of things.[10] Rather, they are God's own ideas, eternally existing within the divine mind.[11] Plato's *Timaeus* tends to sketch the demiurge in broad outline rather than to draw a picture of this figure in any detail. The Platonic version of this figure is thus not the source of the ideas but rather a master craftsman who uses eternal ideas independent of himself to impose order on the disorder of matter. Nor is this Platonic figure an all-powerful deity. Rather, his work is a project of "reason persuading necessity" (*Timaeus* 48a1), that is, of having intelligence mold materials that are sometimes resistant into the intended design.[12]

For medieval philosophy, however, the divine ideas are invariably ideas that God has thought up as various ways in which he can manifest the diverse qualities and perfections that are aspects of his own divine essence.[13] Each of these ideas is some specific facet of God's own perfect being. Together they serve as diverse ways in which the all-good God shares his divine goodness with creatures. This understanding of divine cognition through divine ideas envisions the process as including something like the mental models that a human artist creatively thinks up in the planning stages of the work. The difference is that human artists cannot really think things up *ex nihilo*, but must invariably use materials that already exist in order to devise the models for any intended works of art and then fashion the actual artifacts. At best, human artists impose new forms on previously existing matter. By contrast, God uses himself as a model and makes the materials and the forms *ex nihilo*.[14]

Medieval thinkers regularly show themselves alert to the paradox involved in holding that something came from nothing. The alternative explanations available to them are basically three: (1) an eternal world coexistent with God, who functions to impose forms on pre-existing matter;[15] (2) a world that comes to be from the very being of God and that thus consists of some portions of God's own being; (3) a world that God creates out of nothing and that in this way receives an existence other than the being of God, even though it remains utterly dependent on God.

Given the biblical warrant found at John 1:3 for holding that the creation described in Genesis involved bringing things into being *ex nihilo*, Christian thinkers generally tend to resist what must have seemed a very attractive philosophical option, the theory of emanation. According to the Neoplatonists, the whole universe comes to be by the emanation or outpouring of the very being of the source (for Plotinus, the One). The basic problem here was that this position often led to pantheism. Those who upheld the doctrine of the direct creation by God of everything other than God opted instead for a view that is admittedly harder to explain but closer to what was received from revelation, the notion that God created everything "out of nothing." In order to make what sense they could of this biblical phrase, they were often ready to adopt and adapt the Platonic figure of the demiurge. In the *Timaeus* this master artisan is a craftsman intent on molding his pre-existing material on the basis of the perfect eternal models that he contemplates. The result is a world of beings that show varying degrees of imperfection in the copies. Thinkers of the patristic and early medieval period tended rather to envision God as a supremely creative artist who, in the timelessness of eternity, thinks up diverse ways in which his own perfections can be the models for creatures. This creator is thus responsible even for the existence of the ideas as limited ways of manifesting his own infinite qualities. He is not just a copyist who must use already existing models for fashioning his artifacts as well as his skills allow.

In the works of Augustine, we find the chief conduit for the doctrine of the divine ideas as it passed to later medieval thought. All the crucial aspects of the problem are in play for Augustine, but he leaves a number of the issues unresolved, such as the problem of how to reconcile divine simplicity with a plurality of these ideas. Borrowing a term from the Stoics, who spoke of the *rationes seminales* (the "intelligible seeds" of things), Augustine tends to call these divine ideas *rationes aeternae* ("eternal reasons"). He explains[16] that the Platonists recognized a sense of the need for a mediator between God and creation and virtually held the biblical doctrine of the Word (the *Logos*). If the Platonists lacked an understanding of the identity of this mediator as the Second Person of the Trinity who became incarnate as Jesus Christ, they at least saw the need for speaking about the ideal mind through which God created all things. Christians, he urges, understand this *Logos* to be the divine Son, eternally begotten of God the Father. Augustine stresses that there are *rationes aeternae* of all created things in the mind of God.

Alert to certain problems that inevitably appear whenever one starts to use intrinsically temporal human language about God, who is eternal and timeless, Augustine explores the creaturely status of time itself.[17] He often compares God to an artist who mentally conceives an idea of what is to be made before actually making it. This general approach becomes a standard feature of the philosophical understanding of God and the divine ideas by subsequent thinkers. Eternity is not just an endless succession of moments of existence but a genuine timelessness. For Augustine, even time is something that God created. In this light, it does not prove difficult for Augustine to portray any divine idea as an eternal and unchanging *ratio*[18] by which all individual things are created according to their types. It would, for him, be sacrilegious to imagine that God's mind were formed or determined by anything outside himself.[19]

Linked to the doctrine of the divine ideas, for Augustine, is a certain theory of knowledge that once again shows the need felt by these religious philosophers to make decisions about what they adopted, what they needed to adapt, and what they needed to reject from among the various views they received from their classical sources.[20] The Platonic explanation for learning in terms of the recollection of perfect Forms seen in a previous lifetime seemed to depend on a theory of pre-existent souls.[21] Hence, Augustine argues instead (for example, in the second book of *On Free Choice of the Will*[22]) in favor of the doctrine of illumination.[23] He conjoins this position with his view of how the mind learns eternal truths.[24] Using the analogy of visible illumination, in which the sun illumines objects by its own radiance, Augustine envisions God as bringing a person to learn eternal truths by shining an incorporeal light upon the soul.[25] There are clear echoes here of the Platonic theory of recollection, but it is detached from doctrines that he found unacceptable (e.g., reincarnation). For Augustine, it is the eternity of the unchanging truth in the divine ideas that makes it possible for human knowledge to possess the character of immutability that is the condition required for the security and permanence indispensable to stable knowledge. The senses might well provide occasions for considering these transsensory truths, but the senses cannot guarantee the needed permanence. Even if much of our thinking occurs as the result of the changing appearances presented through the senses, there is constantly a need to purify the "eye of the mind" so as to be able to see these ideas. Despite his recurrent treatments of this topic, Augustine offers little to resolve what would come to be one of the most problematic aspects of this doctrine in the course of the Middle Ages, namely, how to reconcile the apparently great and even infinite multiplicity of ideas with divine simplicity.[26]

One of the roads by which subsequent medieval philosophers took up this concept and gave it repeated critical examination proceeds through Boethius, while another moves through Dionysius and John Scotus Eriugena. The influence of Boethius throughout the entire Middle Ages arose especially from his formulation of the problem of universals (to be considered below in a separate chapter). From his *Consolation of Philosophy*, later generations of medieval philosophers received a distinctive approach to the problem of evil and the reconciliation of human freedom with the complete knowledge that God has of every creature. Crucial to that explanation is the thesis that God knows each creature's way of participating in the divine ideas by which he creates the whole world.[27]

The *Consolation* was composed during Boethius' imprisonment at Pavia when Theodoric, the Ostrogothic king of Italy and an Arian Christian, whom Boethius had faithfully served in various capacities, was jousting with Justin I, the Roman Emperor at Byzantium and a Catholic, not only in the arena of political power but also in that of theological controversy.[28] Scholars have raised questions about whether the Boethius of the *Consolation of Philosophy* may have departed from the religious convictions that are obvious in his theological treatises and adopted some form of Stoic resignation in the wake of his fall from office. But recent scholarship has tended to see a deep consistency of outlook between his theological works and the *Consolation*, and have suggested that it is the product of a thinker who had adapted Neoplatonic philosophy in ways suitable to preserve his religious commitments.[29] Even in those parts of the *Consolation* where it is the allegorical figure of Lady Philosophy who comforts the desolate Boethius after his loss of good fortune, the author retains the same modifications of Neoplatonic philosophy that he made in other writings, such as those pertaining to the divine ideas.

After situating himself (Book I, prose 4) in the Platonic tradition of seeking in the movement of the heavens the patterns (*exempla*) for the secrets of nature and the mysteries of human life, the author has Lady Philosophy explain that, despite the apparent vagaries of fortune, the world is ruled by the rational plan of God and not by chance.[30] Some of the crucial passages on this theme echo the Bible's Wisdom books.[31] There is presumably an allusion to Genesis's description of human beings as made in God's image in Lady Philosophy's reproach against Boethius' self-pity: "Other creatures are content with what is their own, but you, whose mind is made in the image of God, seek to adorn your superior nature with inferior objects, oblivious of the great wrong you do your Creator."[32] In the prayerful hymn of Lady Philosophy that stands at the very center of the whole book, Boethius not only envisions the divine ideas squarely within the mind of God. He also addresses the freedom of God in creating the world in this artistic fashion:

O Thou who dost by everlasting reason rule,
Creator of the planets and the sky, who time
From timelessness didst bring, unchanging Mover,
No cause drove Thee to mold unstable matter, but
The form benign of highest good within Thee set.
All things Thou bringest forth from Thy high archetype:
Thou, height of beauty, in Thy mind the beauteous world
Dost bear, and in that ideal likeness shaping it,
Dost order perfect parts a perfect whole to frame.[33]

In a comparable passage within his treatise *On the Trinity*, Boethius invokes the divine ideas as the rational plan by which God creates the world. Reflecting on the problem of how a multiplicity of ideas can be found within the utter simplicity of God, he explains that this multiplicity only arises from the limits of human intelligence in trying to grasp what the supreme kind of intelligence grasps in a unified and simple manner.[34] Later in the *Consolation*, Boethius clearly affirms divine simplicity when Lady Philosophy is explaining the difference between the apparently ever-changing wheel of fortune and the constancy of God's providential care for creation. "The simple and unchanging plan of events is Providence, and Fate is the ever-changing-web, the disposition in and through time of all the events which God has planned in His simplicity."[35] To show this point as reasonable, Boethius likens the creative work that flows from divine simplicity to human artistry:

> A craftsman anticipates in his mind the plan of the thing he is going to make, and then sets in motion the execution of the work and carries out in time the construction of what he has seen all at one moment present to his mind's eye. In the same way God in His Providence constructs a single fixed plan of all that is to happen, while it is by means of Fate that all that He has planned is realized in its many individual details in the course of time.[36]

What Augustine and Boethius especially contributed to the medieval understanding of the divine ideas was a sense that the basic Platonic notion of the Forms could be successfully adapted for Christian use. The change needed to do this is the relocation of the ideas within God's own mind, but without sacrificing divine simplicity or imperiling the notion of God's providential love for creation. Subsequent authors accepted and developed this aspect of Christian Platonism in greater detail, often in connection with biblical exegesis.[37]

3 DIONYSIUS AND ERIUGENA

A second stream of thought about the divine ideas is found in the works of Dionysius the Areopagite and John Scotus Eriugena. The figure whom modern scholarship often calls "Pseudo-Dionysius" is thought to have been a Syrian monk who wrote a number of highly creative treatises in the late fifth or early sixth century. His real name is unknown to us but he wrote under the pseudonym Dionysius, apparently to claim the mantle and thereby the authority of the Dionysius mentioned in the Acts of the Apostles (at 17: 34). That Dionysius had become a convert after St Paul's preaching before the statute of "the unknown God" in the Areopagus. Scholars have not been reticent about noting the connection between Paul's use of the reference to the unknown God on this statue and Dionysius' interest in "negative theology" to stress that there will always remain much unknown about God.

In general, negative theology refers to that brand of theological discourse that urges that we come to know God best by knowing what God is not. God is, for example, "incorporeal" (non-bodily but nevertheless real) and "uncreated" (not brought into being but always existing). Thinkers in this tradition tend strongly to doubt and sometimes even to deny that human language is adequate for speaking about the nature of God. This kind of theology is often called "apophatic," a term derived from the Greek word for "denial" or "negation." It stands in contrast to "kataphatic" theology, a term derived from the Greek word for "clear" or "explicit." Kataphatic theology involves making (direct or indirect) positive assertions about God's nature, for example, by affirming that God is "good" and "wise," or perhaps better, "all-good" and "all-wise." For this tradition, the goodness of God should never be limited to what "good" or "wise" means when these terms are said of any creature. The proponents of negative theology are generally ready to embrace prayerful silence in view of the essential mystery that they hold God to be. As a philosophical position, negative theology tends to be alert to the severe limits on what can be validly said about God directly by way of any sort of affirmation, or even indirectly by the sort of symbolic representations one often finds in the Bible. But the episte- mological humility at work here is not exhausted by the silence. It finds a way to express itself by means of what medieval logicians will call "super-eminent predication," the use of special terminology such as ("all-powerful" or "all-knowing") as a way to assert that God possesses in an unlimited way various properties and qualities that we experience in limited degrees. But to assert that God is "all-good" or "all-just" or "all-knowing" is not to claim that we human beings really understand what it is to be all-good or all-just or all-knowing. Rather, it is to assert that there is a validity in using these superlative predicates because in doing so we start from something that we do know in its limited forms. By these terms we are really just pointing toward what God possesses in an unlimited degree. Thus, by a care- fully controlled use of negation, we can work analogically toward the reality of the infinite by using language carefully to point toward the infinite perfection of God. We do this even though such infinite perfection always in principle exceeds anything that we could possi- bly grasp by the use of terms derived from the experience of finite realities.

The reserve that negative theology thus demands about both posi- tive and symbolic assertions is intended to keep one from falling into anthropomorphism or into any sort of expression that would be unfitting for the transcendence of God. But merely to say that God is not this or not that (for instance, not a rock or fortress,[38] despite the use of such metaphors as these in the Psalms) is not enough. We do not learn what we really want to know about something by listing things that something is not. For this reason, many of the medieval proponents of negative theology saw a need to balance the denial that there are limitations on God with affirmations of divine power and fullness. In this way they aimed to have their denials point to the fact that God is beyond anything that can be encompassed by human language.

Where there is an important disagreement among negative theolo- gians is over the question of whether this denial of limitation leaves us with any possibility for speaking about God at all. If we may still speak of God, how we may do so? For many thinkers in this tradition, and for Pseudo-Dionysius in particular, the care and diligence employed in the effort to say that there is no limit on the perfections of God still permit us to indicate the direction in which the infinite perfection of God resides. Thus we may use the language of super-eminence to call God "omnipotent" or "omniscient" even if our minds cannot (in principle) encompass all of what "omnipotent" or "omniscient" entails.

To say that God is "all-powerful" or "all-knowing" is not to suggest that we fully know what these terms include. It is simply to claim that we know from human experience in a limited way what power is or what knowledge is. We can then point toward unlimited perfection from this starting point. Phrases like "all-powerful" or "all-knowing" are thus intended to indicate the direction in which infinite power and infinite knowledge exceed the finite forms of power and knowledge with which we began the comparison. They can even bring into question whether human knowing is accurately understood when taken as a kind of "grasping." For by finite forms of these qualities we might well be able to encompass within the mind the reality that we are seeking to name. But in dealing with the infi-nite, all that we can do is to point toward God from a position that is more firm and clear to us. For some negative theologians, even to say this is too much. Hence, all that we may legitimately do is to be reverently silent. But for others, this possibility of knowledge by puri-fied negations and analogical terms means that we can make some genuine progress by a philosophical brand of theology. We are then not reduced to utter silence or to skepticism or to agnosticism. The purification of ordinary language can then help to accentuate the ineffability of God's intrinsic nature. The discipline involved in refus-ing to confine God to whatever we normally mean by the content of a given concept serves as a way to respect God as *semper major* ("always greater") than what we can say or grasp. The mystical tradi-tion within medieval thought stressed the use of analogical terms such as these "super-eminent" predicates.

It is especially through Dionysius that medieval theology came to think about negative theology. Four of his main works are still extant today: *On the Divine Names, Celestial Hierarchy, Ecclesial Hierar-chy*, and *Mystical Theology*.[39] Once these works were translated into Latin,[40] they introduced into medieval thought not only a number of fruitful distinctions among the ways that terms may be used of God (positively, negatively, and super-eminently); they also provided a new and powerful sense of the divine ideas as divine energies or exemplary causes.

In chapters 4 and 5 of the *Divine Names*, Dionysius asserts that various supersubstantial realities like Being itself, Goodness itself, Life itself, and Wisdom itself are not separate entities, not divinities independent of God, not angels, and not any sort of creature. Rather, they are proper names of God. They display God's exemplary causality, for they are paradigms or patterns for creation. By them, God is the origin and source of all that is. Thus, for Dionysius, the divine attributes that require such great reserve if we are to use them correctly have importance not only in giving us some limited but real grasp of God's essence and knowledge; they also play an important role in the metaphysical explanations offered for how created things have the natures that they do. The divine ideas are not to be thought of as static concepts. They are the dynamic causes by which God creates a world, gives it participation in his own divine perfection, and renders it eventually able to return to him as its source and goal:

> We give the name of "exemplar" to those principles which preexist as a unity in God and which produce the essences of things. Theology calls them predefining, divine and good acts of will which determine and create things and in accordance with which the Transcendent One predefined and brought into being everything that is.[41]

By means of this exemplary causality there is an immediate relation in the direct dependence of creatures on God at every level of creation. In this regard, Dionysius' picture is somewhat unlike the standard Neoplatonic system that is influential in so many other aspects of his thought. The pagan Neoplatonists tended to envision a vast hierarchy of beings mediating between the utterly pure source above all other beings and the progressively dense and impure material world. The multilayered levels of the intelligences functioned as intermediary causes and prevented the One from being sullied by contact with any level of materiality or multiplicity. It may well have been out of the conviction that the residual pagan elements of Neoplatonism needed to be conformed to divine revelation[42] that Dionysius stresses God's creative power and goodness as directly reaching throughout every level of being. Those beings that are closer to God in the hierarchy invariably show greater resemblances to their divine source, but they never detract from the direct influence of divine causality throughout the universe. Nor does the multiplicity of ways in which God's effects are manifest in creatures bring multiplicity within God. The plurality of divine ideas simply displays the variety that marks divine providence:

> I do not think of the Good as one thing, Being as another, Life and Wisdom as yet other, and I do not claim that there are numerous causes and different Godheads, all differently ranked, superior and inferior, and all producing different effects. No. But I hold that there is one God for all these good processions and that he is the possessor of the Divine Names of which I speak and that the first name tells of the universal Providence of the One God, while the other names reveal general or specific ways in which he acts providentially.[43]

As we will see in a chapter still to come, the metaphysical doctrine of the transcendentals penetrates Dionysius' vision of things, as it does so much of medieval thought. As the transcendent Good itself, God is the cause of everything that comes to be. God makes them good precisely by making them to be.[44] Goodness is thereby a feature of all being as being.

A latent problem in this way of conceiving the ideas as the exemplary causes of all beings in such a thoroughgoing fashion is whether and to what extent any of God's creatures (especially human beings, but the angelic intelligences as well) can have any freedom. For there to be the sort of freedom and self-determination that makes possible moral responsibility, it seems that there needs to be at least something that escapes divine determination.[45] Although this problem is not raised in Dionysius' text, the inner logic of the problem will bring it to the fore in later thinkers. The transmission of these Dionysian principles into the Latin-speaking world proved to be a rocky road. In the Greek-speaking East, Maximus the Confessor performed a valiant service for Dionysian thought by curbing certain trends in his thinking that verged on being theologically suspect.[46]

For the Latin Middle Ages, the most important route for the transmission of Dionysian ideas was through the translation of his works by John Scotus Eriugena. Dionysius' insights were thereby successfully passed on to later generations despite the recurrent suspicion that Eriugena's own work was pantheistic. His *Periphyseon* (known in Latin as *De Divisione Nature* and in English as "On the Division of Nature") employs much of what he learned from Dionysius, but now arranged in a fourfold division of the whole universe, which he calls "nature"[47]: (1) what is not created but creates (God), (2) what both creates and is created (the spiritual portion of creation), (3) what is created but does not create (the physical portion of creation), and (4) what neither creates nor is created (the matter out of which the physical universe is made). The claims of the final section of his text were frequently subject to criticism, for they can be taken to undermine the notion that God created everything *ex nihilo* ("out of nothing").

The second part features a prominent place for the divine ideas as a set of angelic intelligences. They are envisioned as a crucial component within a highly Neoplatonic view of the relationship between God and the sensory world. By portraying God as the cause of the angelic intelligences that in turn create the rest of "nature," Eriugena can still claim to make all of nature the expression of the divine will. In this way Eriugena offers one possible development of the Dionysian model, albeit one that never gained wide acceptance. In his text the divine ideas have thus become causes that are inferior to God and are in a certain way existentially distinct from the divine nature itself. And yet by virtue of his somewhat pantheistic way of expressing himself, Eriugena also seems to claim that these ideas are still divine and part of the being of God. So are the physical creatures that they in turn produce, and even the eternally uncreated matter out of which these physical creatures are formed. His system is a large-scale experiment for trying to think out what the complete dependence of everything on God might mean. For his critics, it risks collapsing everything into divine being by not having sufficient appreciation for the independence of creatures once they are brought into existence.

Despite the pantheism that rendered Eriugena's formulation unacceptable to most medieval thinkers, the recurrent attraction of this approach is evident from the ways in which Meister Eckhart and Nicholas of Cusa in the fourteenth century deliberately adopt many of these same themes.[48] Augustine and Boethius had relocated the ideas inside the mind of God, while Dionysius and his followers tended to identify the divine mind with the ideas. Where Augustine had stressed the ways in which all creatures bear the resemblance of God's perfections, Dionysius makes these divine perfections the paradigms or exemplary causes by which God's knowledge causes the world and gives creatures a share in God's own perfections. In commenting on *The Divine Names*, Aquinas cites Dionysius as his authority for the view that "from creatures we arrive at God in three ways, namely, by way of causality, by way of removal, and by way of eminence."

4 BONAVENTURE AND AQUINAS

Given their other tendencies and commitments, it is not surprising that Bonaventure and other Franciscans retain a basically Augustinian perspective on the divine ideas.[49] Anselm had taken up this topic in his *Monologium*, as did Peter Lombard, whose collection of quotations from Augustine became a famous textbook for the scholastic period.[50] But the notion came under severe challenge at the time of the recovery of Aristotelian natural philosophy (a topic that will be treated more extensively in chapter 6 on cosmos and nature below). The extent to which Aquinas remains convinced of the need for a doctrine of divine ideas, despite his otherwise wide-ranging embrace of Aristotle, shows how deeply this doctrine is fundamental for explaining how God creates everything that comes to be made.

Both Bonaventure and Aquinas continue to stress that we need to postulate divine ideas as the exemplary causes by which God creates the universe. But they both feel the need to interpret this doctrine in a way that does not compromise divine simplicity. Aquinas, for instance, argues that since everything that is within God is God, even the ideas are to be thought of as identical with God.[51] But after establishing that we must say that there are ideas in God, Aquinas spends the remainder of a lengthy treatise on the divine ideas showing how the plurality of ideas does not compromise divine unity and simplicity. For Aquinas, our need to speak of a plurality of ideas arises from the difference in the natures of things.[52] Since God is self-existent and uncreated, we have no reason to suppose that he needs these ideas to know himself. Within the divine unity that is God, God simply knows his own essence as the model and idea of all creatures.

But for a proper understanding of the artistry of divine creation, we need to postulate a plurality of ideas in God, conceived on the model of the productive knowing of a human artist.[53] Aquinas develops at some length the comparison of divine creative knowing with the sort of knowing involved in human artistry. He finds it preferable to do this rather than to liken it to the kind of human knowing that is involved in, say, the cognition that occurs by the abstraction of forms from data received by the senses. For Aquinas, God's knowledge is not dependent on receiving forms that already exist in objects but is creative of those forms. When he turns to questions of how things are what they are and how we can know them to be what they are, the divine ideas play a crucial role in his explanation. Truth, he urges, should be defined as "the conformity of thought and thing."[54] While human cognition of truth requires that the mind be conformed to the form of things, the truth inherent in things involves the conformity of the forms of things to the divine idea by which God has designed the natures of those things.[55]

The full account that Aquinas articulates of the divine ideas in works like On Truth and On the Power of God[56] systematically places this doctrine into conjunction with the doctrine of divine providence. Unlike those versions of the divine ideas that persist in the Platonic posture of having God (like the demiurge) contemplate the possibles according to their intrinsic necessities, Aquinas resists any notion of pure intelligible essences that are sufficient in themselves. Focused instead on God's providential care for individuals, Aquinas envisions divine ideas for the genera, the species, and even the accidents related to individuals, not as pure possibles but as existing individuals. In this way even matter is within God's knowledge. Matter never exists without having some form, but the idea of matter is part of the divine idea of some kinds of substance.[57]

Bonaventure holds much the same doctrine, but with a certain nuance. The ideas are envisioned as the expression of the divine truth by which God eternally utters himself in all possible participations. For Bonaventure, the exemplarism of the divine ideas ranks with creation and illumination as one of the greatest of metaphysical problems and as a specially fruitful path for philosophical concentration on God as the cause of all things.[58] Aristotle's thought on God had led in the direction of God as the unmoved mover and as self-thinking thought. In this view, God had neither cognizance nor care of the world. It was only by virtue of the attractiveness of God's own perfection that God served as the final cause of motion among finite objects that were envisioned to be as eternal as God himself. For Aristotle, there was simply no incentive to postulate a theory of creation or a theory of divine ideas. In fact, there were many good reasons to object to such notions because of the complications brought in by the associated Platonic doctrine of participation.

But confronted with the need to explain how the plurality of kinds of *creatures* could originate from a single God thought to be the cause of all things, Bonaventure embraces the Dionysian doctrine of the exemplary causality of the ideas. He saw it as an indispensable component of any acceptable metaphysics and one that made extremely good sense in itself. God, after all, is pure spirit. His substance is beyond our comprehension. The problem, however, comes from our side because of the intrinsic limitations of any human intellect. In himself God is wholly intelligible. But in knowing himself as fully as an omniscient being would, God must be thought to know himself in a single, encompassing, and timeless act rather than by the discursive sort of discovery-process that characterizes our activities in coming to know ourselves or to know any external object. In us, knowledge somehow involves obtaining a resemblance to what is known. We can rightly be said to become what we know, even though we do not cease to retain our own nature. But in God the act of knowing is identical with both the object known and with the knowing subject. For this reason God's knowledge of himself needs to be thought of as a kind of perfect resemblance. The completeness of this identification between the knower and the known surpasses any model that we might propose from human experience. But, happily, Christian theology suggests a way in which to honor the uniqueness of this resemblance and yet respect the doctrine that there is a Trinity of persons in the one God. For Bonaventure, this theologically known truth provides a crucial piece of information for the metaphysician. The eternal Word is the perfect image of Father, eternally begotten, God from God, one in substance with the Father and expressing in his person all God's knowledge,[59] not only in his infinite being as God but also as virtually containing all possibilities for manifesting his perfection. Bonaventure made Christ the center of all his thought, and for him nothing could be more true than that the Word of God is the home of the divine ideas, the archetypes of all the ideas that can ever play a role in knowledge and in being.

The successors to Bonaventure and Aquinas tend to place greater stress on the notion that these ideas express various possible essences and specify certain intrinsic necessities inherent in their very structures. Duns Scotus, for instance, takes them not as God's knowledge of his own essence or as the expression of this essence in all of its possible participations, but more as ideas that God has produced. Thus they are creatures that exist in God by virtue of being possibles.[60] With the main figures of later scholasticism and the increasing prominence of logic over metaphysics, this trend to make the possible (that which is non-contradictory) the rule of the real will have its effect on many areas of thought. In the domain of the transcendentals, for instance, truth and goodness will come to seem extrinsic rather than intrinsic denominations. In the area of the divine ideas, the focus on the logical necessities intrinsic to a concept entails a shift from concern about how to maintain philosophical respect for divine transcendence within a strong view of God's providential care for individuals, to a concern with the logical necessities inherent in a concept that even the mind of God needs to respect. We will see some of these trends in the following chapters on universals and transcendentals.

5 OVERVIEW

The question of the relation between God and the universe never ceased to intrigue medieval philosophers. For this reason, the notion of divine ideas remained of importance throughout the period. Borrowed from the philosophy of Plato, where the notion of Ideas as separate Forms in which the mutable objects of the contingent world were said to participate in the necessary and eternal existence of perfect essences, this concept became a staple of medieval metaphysics that remained crucial even for those thinkers who preferred Aristotle to Plato.

First, the notion of the divine ideas permitted medieval philosophers a way in which to account for divine creation of the world that distinguished God from the created world. By envisioning these divine ideas on the model of the ideas that artists dream up when mentally preparing to produce a work of art, these medieval theorists saw a way in which to credit the divine artist with the design of all created natures and yet to distance God from created natures. Each created nature bears a certain resemblance to its creator, for it is only on God that each nature is modeled. In this schema there is nothing else on which anything can be modeled. And yet none of the created natures is God and none of them has all the perfections of God. They have a certain regional independence. What exists harmoniously in the simplicity of the divine nature exists in actually distinct beings and their created natures.[61] As a metaphysical concept, the divine ideas provide a way for the theorist to affirm the freedom of the divine artist to think up countless finite ways in which to embody the qualities and perfections that exist infinitely within the divine nature.

Interestingly, medieval thinkers who use this concept clearly felt free to adapt it from its Platonic and Neoplatonic forms. From the start of the medieval period there was clearly a strong sense of the need to relocate the divine ideas from a separate sphere to within the divine mind, precisely in order to be faithful to the utter sovereignty of God. To have retained these ideas as somehow other than God, even as necessary essences, would have been to surrender something indispensable to the perfection of God. But for much of the period it seemed that only a modification and not a wholesale replacement of the epistemological assumptions of the Platonic version of the divine ideas was enough. For Augustine and his successors, a theory of divine illumination seemed to be a sufficient transformation of the doctrine of learning as recollection that was part and parcel of the Platonic doctrine of ideas. After the recovery of Aristotelian natural philosophy and the related Aristotelian doctrine of learning by abstraction, there is less emphasis on the doctrine of illumination. But the doctrine of the divine ideas remains a strong part of the metaphysical accounts of Aristotelians like Thomas Aquinas. For him, these divine archetypes stand as the exemplary causes by which to explain the divine creation of the world and as the ultimate anchor for all truth claims. As we will see at greater length in the chapter on transcendentals, Aquinas thinks that truth is best defined as the conformity of intellect and thing. While the truth of human speech requires the conformity of human minds to the structures of things, the truth of things (transcendental truth) is the conformity of things with the divine ideas of things, the archetypes in the divine mind by which God created the universe.

NOTES

1 Among ancient philosophers, the Stoics are particularly known for holding a doctrine of providence. But one can find references in earlier Greek thinkers as well, e.g., Plato's affirmation of providence in his *Laws* (887–8). The Stoics tended to envision providence abstractly rather than personally. See, for instance, *Discourses* 1.16, in Epictetus (1998) for a discussion of the divine supervision of the universe. Further, they tend to equate providence with fate or destiny. See, e.g., *Epistles* 107.11, in Seneca (1996).

2 Jan Aertsen brings out well the philosophical significance of the usage of the term "creatures" in comparison to philosophical terms such as "nature" as well as more generic terms such as "beings," "things," or "objects." See Aertsen (1988).

3 See Burrell (1993).

4 See *First Letter to the Corinthians* 20, in Clement of Alexandria (1960), and *Stromateis* V.14, in Clement of Alexandria (1991).

5 Especially Psalms 103 and 139; Job 28; Proverbs 8, esp. 8: 22–31; Sirach 24; and Wisdom 6–9.

6 *On First Principles* I.2.3, I.2.6, I.2.7, in Origen (1973).

7 Among the many passages one could also cite from the New Testament, consider Ephesians 2: 10, "For we are his workmanship, created in Christ Jesus for good works, which God prepared beforehand, that we should walk in them."

8 *On the Creation of Man* in Gregory of Nyssa (1972) and *On the Beatitudes* VI, in Gregory of Nyssa (2000).

9 *On the Creation of the Cosmos according to Moses* in Philo of Alexandria (2001).

10 See *Timaeus* 27c–47e, in Plato (1997), for his account of the demiurge's use of the Ideas as patterns for shaping the world.

11 See Boland (1996), pp. 53–8 for an account of Plotinus' contribution to the relocation of the Ideas into the Mind (*Nous*), the second stage of the emanation.

12 Not only Plato but also the subsequent Platonic tradition invariably thought of copies as ineluctably imperfect, to one degree or another, in

comparison to the original. This point would require considerable effort to overcome in the development of Christology and the controversy over icons. One of the critical points turned out to be determining how the second person of the Trinity could be a perfect image of the Father. See Schönborn (1994), esp. pp. 209–13.

13   By way of example, Augustine (1991a) reflects on God as knowing himself in *The Trinity*, books VIII–X.

14   *The City of God* XII.26, in Augustine (1984); and *Confessions* XI.5, in Augustine (1991b).

15   This position comes into renewed debate in the thirteenth century once the texts of Aristotle have again become available. While only certain radical Aristotelians of that day seem to have held that the world must have been co-eternal with God, figures like Aquinas took the view that one could not prove by philosophical reason alone the fact of a creation of the world in time. Contemporaries such as Bonaventure, by contrast, maintained that one could know the fact of a creation in time not only by faith but also by philosophical reason.

16   See *Eighty-Three Different Questions* q. 46, in Augustine (1982c), pp. 79–81, esp. at p. 81.

17   *Confessions* XI, in Augustine (1991b), contains Augustine's reflections on the problem of time. Augustine views time not in the Aristotelian manner of the measurement of bodies in motion but rather as a distention of stretching of spirit, and thus as something that God created. In certain ways his view is a development of the Platonic view of time as the "moving image of eternity."

18   The Latin term *ratio* is notoriously difficult to translate because of its breadth of possible applications. Its range of meaning includes "plan," "reason," and "pattern," as well as "idea" or "notion." As synonyms, Augustine also speaks of the divine ideas as the *formae rerum* ("the forms of things").

19   See *Eighty-Three Different Questions* q.46.2. in Augustine (1982c); see also *The Trinity* III.10.25, in Augustine (1991a) and *The City of God* XII.26–7, in Augustine (1984).

20   See Cochrane (2003), esp. pp. 399–516.

21   For Augustine's reasoning in coming to the view that he needed to be agnostic on this question, see chapter 7 on the soul below.

22   *On Free Choice of the Will* III.30.55–31.62, in Augustine (1982b); see also *On True Religion* 3.4 and 10.19, in Augustine (1979).

23   See Nash (1969) and Matthews (2001).

24   See *The Teacher* 14.45–6, in Augustine (1979); and *On Free Choice of the Will* III.5.13, in Augustine (1982b).

25   See *De Magistro* 12.40, in Augustine (1979).

26 See *The City of God* VIII.6 and VIII.10, in Augustine (1984).

27 There are many good translations of the *Consolation of Philosophy*, including Boethius (2000). In the *Consolation* Boethius alternates between passages in prose and in poetry, and so the scholarly convention for citation of passages from the *Consolation* is to indicate the number of the book, and then to indicate the number of the poem or prose segment. For Boethius' shorter works, see Boethius (1978).

28 For a detailed account of what is known and what is suspected in this fascinating story, see Chadwick (1981), esp. pp. 46–68 and 247–53.

29 See Nash-Marshall (2000), esp. pp. 18–30, where the scholarly controversy is reviewed; see also Relihan (2007).

30 See *Consolation* Bk. I, prose 6; poems 5 and 6; Bk III, poem 6; Bk IV, poem 6, in Boethius (2000).

31 Among the many examples that can be supplied, *Consolation* Bk III, prose 12 ("It is the supreme good, then, that mightily and sweetly orders all things") echoes Wisdom 8: 1 ("[Wisdom] reaches mightily from one end of the earth to the other, and she orders all things well"), in Boethius (2000).

32 *Consolation* Bk. II, prose 5, in Boethius (2000).

33 *Consolation* Bk. III, poem 9, lines 1–9, in Boethius (2000).

34 *On the Trinity*, ch. 2, in Boethius (1978). In addition to making the argument in the *Consolation* that merely knowing anything does not cause it to occur (Bk. V, prose 3), Boethius uses the same strategy that we find here as part of his resolution of the problem of reconciling divine omniscience and human freedom by comparison with the way in which human cognition surpasses any form of animal cognition, we may projectively imagine how divine cognition surpasses human cognition. See *Consolation*, Bk V, prose 4, 5, and 6, in Boethius (2000).

35 *Consolation* Bk. IV, prose 6. See also Bk. V, prose 2, in Boethius (2000).

36 *Consolation* Bk. IV, prose 6, in Boethius (2000).

37 For the history of this development through the twelfth century, see Dronke (1988) and Chenu (1968), esp. pp. 60–79.

38 For instance, at Psalm 18: 2 (RSV): "The LORD is my rock, and my fortress, and my deliverer, my God, my rock, in whom I take refuge, my shield, and the horn of my salvation, my stronghold."

39 Often called the *Corpus Areopagiticum* in scholarly studies, these treatises are available in a recent English translation in Dionysius (1987). *The Divine Names* offers a philosophical analysis of the divine attributes, while *The Mystical Theology* sketches the method of affirmative and negative theology. *The Celestial Hierarchy* discusses the nine choirs of angels (arranged in three triads). *The Ecclesiastical Hierarchy*

concerns such ecclesiastical topics as the sacramentals, clerical ranks, and various liturgical rites. Jaroslav Pelikan discusses the range of scholarly conjectures about the author of this material in Dionysius (1987), pp. 11–24, while Jean Leclerq recounts the influence of Dionysius on the medieval Latin West, pp. 25–32.

40 The first Latin translation of the *Corpus Areopagiticum* seems to have been done early in the ninth century by Hilduin of Saint-Denis. Hilduin also composed a hagiographical biography that identifies Pseudo-Dionysius with Dionysius the first bishop of Paris. See *Passio sanctissimi Dionysii* in Hilduin (1994). But the near unintelligibility of this translation prompted John Scotus Eriugena to complete a new translation in 862. Among his later translators are Robert Grosseteste and Marsilio Ficino.

41 *The Divine Names* V.8 at 824c, in Dionysius (1987), p. 102.

42 For a fine analysis of how deeply indebted Dionysius is to such pagan Neoplatonists as Proclus, see Boland (1996), pp. 115–42. See also Perl (2007).

43 *The Divine Names* V.2 at 816c–d, in Dionysius (1987), p. 97.

44 See *The Divine Names* V.4 at 817c–d in Dionysius (1987), p. 98.

45 The term that Dionysius uses for "predetermination" here is *prooris-moi*, the same term used by St Paul and various Greek patristic writers for "predestination." On this general problem faced by Judaism, Christianity, and Islam in regard to how best to understand the freedom of creatures, see Burrell (1993).

46 In particular, Dionysius' writings were thought by some to show signs of Monophysitism. According to this view, there is only a single nature in Christ, and not a dual nature (divine and human). The Council of Chalcedon in AD 451 determined that orthodoxy requires one who wishes to profess the Christian faith to hold that the Divine Person of the Word (the Son of God) assumed a human nature at the time of the Incarnation.

47 The Dublin Institute for Advanced Studies has been progressively producing a complete scholarly English translation of the *Periphyseon*. For a translation of the first three books, see Eriugena (1987) and for the fourth book, Eriugena (1995). A fine overview of Eriugena can be obtained from Carabine (2000).

48 For a fine account of this theme in Eckhart, see McGinn (2001), esp. ch. 5: "The Metaphysics of Flow." On Cusa's approach, see Hopkins (1986).

49 See *Quodlibet* 9, q.15, in Henry of Ghent (2005); and *Glossa in quatuor libros sententiarum Petri Lombardi* I, d.36, nn. 4–8, in Alexander of Hales (1951), pp. 357–60.

50 See *Monologium* 10 in Anselm (1998); and *Sentences* I, dd. 35–7 in Lombard (1971).
51 *Truth* 3.1, in Aquinas (1993a), pp. 139–41.
52 *Truth* 3.2, in Aquinas (1993a), p. 147.
53 *Truth* 1.2 and 3.3, in Aquinas (1993a), pp. 11, 152–4.
54 *Truth* 1.1, in Aquinas (1993a), p. 6.
55 *Truth* 1.4, in Aquinas (1993a), pp. 17–18. For an excellent study of this topic, see Pieper (1989).
56 Aquinas (1993a) and (1952).
57 See *Truth* 3.5, in Aquinas (1993a) and the parallel passage at *Summa of Theology* I.15.3 ad 3, in Aquinas (1945).
58 *Collationes in Hexaemeron* I.8, in Bonaventure (1970), p. 330.
59 *Collationes in Hexaemeron* III.4, in Bonaventure (1970), p. 343.
60 See *Opus Oxoniense* I, 35, in Scotus (1950).
61 See *Consolation of Philosophy* Bk. V, prose 6, in Boethius (2000).

4

THE PROBLEM
OF UNIVERSALS

If there is a single problem that engaged medieval philosophy more than any other, it is the problem of universals. Throughout the period the nature of universals was the object of recurrent investigation, not only because of its perennial importance to philosophy but also because of its significance for certain theological issues. The problem concerns the relation of the one and the many, and it has metaphysical, epistemological, and logical dimensions. Despite the rigorous discussion that it received by many a medieval philosopher, there always remained considerable disagreement about how the problem should be resolved, and even about just what the precise questions to ask were.

In general, the problem of universals involves explaining how different objects can be members of the same kind (a problem in metaphysics), how it is possible for us to know individual objects as instances of a kind (a problem in epistemology), and how general terms should properly be used (a problem in logic). The way in which one answers the questions at one level has direct implications for one's options at the other levels. Despite the added complexity, the recognition of the interdependence among these basic questions helps one to see the connections of these philosophical disciplines to one another. For medieval thinkers, these philosophical distinctions would have implications for various theological issues such as the Trinity (according to Christian belief there are three persons in one God) and the Incarnation (in Christ there is a union of two natures – human and divine). These theological issues involve questions about the relations of individuals to their kinds, the reality-status of natures, species, and essences, and the propriety of using general terms collectively.

1   THE RANGE OF THE QUESTION

It may be helpful to begin with the topic of universal terms and concepts before considering whether there are any universal things that exist separately from individual objects. It is a question about what sort of foundation there is to justify the use of the universal terms and concepts that are characteristic of human language and thought. Consider the difference between a proper name and any common noun. The words "Dionysius the Areopagite," for instance, designates the name of a specific individual in the Acts of the Apostles. It may, of course, happen that other individuals in the course of time have had or have taken the same name (such as the author of the sixth-century treatise *On the Divine Names*), but the mere fact that more than one individual bears the same proper name does not necessarily make such a name a universal term, for these words are usually intended to designate a particular person. If there are plural individuals by the same name and if the context does not make it clear which individual is being referred to, the use of that name without further specification could lead to ambiguity. The many things that we can truthfully say about either the first-century individual named "Dionysius the Areopagite" or the sixth-century author who used this pseudonym will invariably involve the use of words that are genuinely universal terms, such as "human," "male," or "Athenian." Used in appropriate combinations, they can allow us to identify a specific individual with increasing specificity, even though the terms themselves are general in character.

Strictly speaking, a word is a "universal" term when it is said about various things that we recognize as somehow alike, that is, beings that are of the same kind in some respect (however many or few of them there may be). The precise range of a universal term's possible references can be more broad or more narrow, so long as we mean the word generally for the whole set of things that we take to be of this kind. In this regard, universal terms such as the rather broad universal term "dog" or the somewhat more narrow but nonetheless universal term "cocker spaniel" apply to all the members of the classes that they name. Then, by adding appropriate specifying words to these universal terms, we can talk about an individual as a specific member of the set (*"this* is *my* cocker spaniel, Buttons") or about some typical instance without specifying any particular individual ("these are the traits typical of *a* cocker spaniel") or even about the type in general of which any given individual would be an instance, a token, a representative ("cocker spaniels tend to make fine pets").

The generality that is intended by a universal can be found not only in nouns (such as those used in the above examples), but in other parts of speech (for instance, the verb "to bark" or the adjective "brown"). But whatever the part of speech in question, the word is a universal term insofar as it conveys a meaning that is generally *applicable* to all instances of what it designates. To say that a common noun is a universal term is not to claim that there is universal agreement *in fact* about the matter under discussion. It is not to say that everyone who uses the term shares exactly the same understanding, either as regards the precise meaning of the term or about the specific range of things to which the term refers. Different speakers of the same language (sometimes even within the same conversation) can use the same universal term but with different meanings. To the extent that they do so, the discussion may be quite taxing until the speakers agree to use a given term with the same meaning. But even before they have come to any agreement about what they are going to mean by a given term in their discussion, each of the conversants is using a given term universally insofar as the person speaking is intending to use that term of all the instances to which it seems to apply. The claim involved in calling a term a universal is simply that the term bears a meaning that is applicable to the entire range of items that the one using the term wants to designate.

Ordinary communication requires that those speaking with one another use a given term in at least roughly the same way, and the logical rigor needed for valid argumentation depends on using a given term in exactly the same way. But this is not to presume that words should always be used in just one way. Recognizing that human language use is flexible, medieval philosophers distinguished among the univocal, the equivocal, and the analogous uses of a term. A given term is used *equivocally* when the meanings that it bears are unrelated (for instance, the "bark" of a tree and the "bark" of a dog). It is used *univocally* when it always bears precisely the same meaning in a given context (for instance, the term "bark" when used in a context where only the sounds that dogs make is under discussion and in no other sense). Finally, a term is used *analogously* when it bears meanings that are different but related (as when we say that a dog is "healthy" and that a certain diet or exercise regimen is "healthy"). Having distinctions like these available makes it possible to understand universality in a sophisticated way as a formal feature of general terms, whenever and however they are used. By adding further words to a given universal term, it is always possible to craft suitable distinctions about the ways in which terms are being used so as to indicate the relevant aspects of sameness and difference. Even so, each of the newly qualified terms will again be serving as universals, precisely because these terms will be providing ways to group similar things together.

A given term can thus be used universally, regardless of whether a particular person is using that term with a well-formulated definition. Whether any term is sufficiently well crafted for making sharp distinctions, or so broad as to risk ambiguity, it is nevertheless "universal" so long as it permits us to group together whatever seems similar, for it provides a way to think about things according to kinds. The related question about whether there really is any such thing as a "kind" points to the metaphysical aspect of the problem of universals.

Does the human ability to recognize recurrent features in diverse objects and to say (by using universal terms) that they are "of the same kind" imply that there is something universal that exists separately from the particular instances? If this dog is a cocker spaniel, and that dog is another cocker spaniel, isn't there something real about "cocker spaniel" to which both these dogs and both these sentences are conforming? The distinctness of one object from another, even in those cases where the features of one are exactly replicated in the other, could lead us to answer that question negatively: only the particular objects exist, and the only thing that is universal are the words that have applicability to any and all members of the class. Alternatively, because of the ready way in which words name things, their properties, their activities, and their relationships, it would be easy to assume that there must be a one-to-one correspondence between words and things. If we can use universal terms correctly, there is an inclination to suppose that there really are universal things that correspond to universal terms. Aristotle's criticism of the Platonic doctrine of the Forms centers on this very point by urging that there is no reason to assume that what we rightly distinguish in speech and thought must exist separately in reality.[1] Just because we can talk about the distinction, say, between the quantitative aspects of a door (e.g., that it has a rectangular shape, six feet by three feet, and an inch wide) and the materials of which it is made (wood, for instance, or steel), the validity of this distinction in no way entails that the quantitative and the qualitative dimensions of the door exist separately from one another. Do "universals" exist in their own right, or does "universal" only properly refer to a mental way of considering what is the same about different things?

The metaphysical aspect of the problem of universals thus emerges in the course of reflecting on what would need to be the case in extramental reality to justify our mental unification of many distinct instances of, say, red things under a common concept *red* and thus for our use of a common word like "red" (whatever the appropriate term in a specific language). Unless there really is something common to the individuals that make up a given kind, something that we do not create, control, or alter by our speech or by our thought, it would appear to be unjustified to use the same general term with regard to distinct individuals. Yet, even if there is some common reality, we never seem to experience the existence of a kind directly, but only the existence of distinct individuals. The philosophical issues here include questions about the precise metaphysical status of the features that we recognize to be common among individuals and about the proper ways to express such commonness.

Medieval philosophers recurrently asked themselves a number of important questions in this regard, including: What, if anything, do general terms name? Do they name things, or is it merely that they are names that we use for particular things that we see as the same? If only particulars exist (whether these particulars are independent beings such as *this person* or *this dog* or *this rock*, or the various specific *actions* and *qualities* and *quantities* and *relationships* that belong to particular items), what is it that justifies our naming them all by the same term? If one answers that question by speaking about the common form that various individuals share, what is the precise status of this form? If we want to say that each of the members of a given kind has the same form, how do we deal with the problem that each item presumably is a different instance of this allegedly common form? Does the common form that they somehow share have any independent reality of its own distinct from the instances in which it recurs? On the other hand, if the forms that structure individual objects are internal to each object, then in what way may we say that there is a form "common" to these various individuals? What exactly is the basis that justifies the use of a common term? Thus there are questions here about the relationships among things as they exist independently of our thinking as well as about the ideas and concepts by which we think about things, and also about the words and terms by which we express what we mean.

Simple as the answers to these questions may seem at first, the difficulties latent in each of the answers that have actually been proposed quickly became evident in the history of medieval philosophy. Knowing absolutely anything seems to involve mental recognition of both sameness and difference. The mark of sameness-in-kind is that every member of that kind possesses the same trait or property, even if the members of this kind possess it in different degrees. So, unless there is something genuinely common to many individuals, there is no reason to think that there really is anything like a "kind" present at all. At best, our groupings (what we would call "kinds" in this scenario) would be merely the result of a pragmatic or even an arbitrary imposition of order on what is really different. But what is arbitrarily asserted by one person may be arbitrarily denied by another. Hence, to be philosophically compelling, all such claims to have a genuine "kind" need to be rooted in some objective reality that is independent of the person making the claim; there needs to be a foundation in reality for the claim of likeness or resemblance.

In our sensory experience of the world we never encounter "general things" but only particulars. Although we need to posit the real existence of kinds in many areas of life,[2] we never meet kinds or types directly in themselves. We encounter only individual objects, each with its own form or structure, and, on the basis of our recognition of patterns and similarities, we assert that there are kinds or types. When we find enough similarity in the various things that we observe, and sometimes an exact replication, we are entitled to claim that these various items are members of the same kind. In fact, knowing anything at all seems invariably to involve some recognition of the kind to which it belongs, that is, an appreciation for some unity within the multiplicity of experience. When the question of knowledge is considered metaphysically, the burden of explanation is that we need to say just what the status of this common aspect is. If gaining knowledge about anything involves coming to appreciate how the things that are being known are in themselves, then it is not enough to say that the commonness is only a product of our minds. If knowledge were something entirely created by the mind, then claims to know anything would not really involve a receptivity to things as they are, but only the construction and imposition of some arrangement on things. By contrast, acquiring knowledge of anything involves seeing the sameness amid difference and appreciating the differences within things that are in many other ways similar. The process of gaining knowledge cannot succeed without making certain distinctions that record genuine differences and dismissing distinctions that one finds to be without a real difference. If one agrees that constructivist approaches to knowledge are self-defeating, one will be more inclined to grant that similarities are something real that the knower is receiving through the knowledge process.

One simply cannot think or speak about kinds or types without using general or universal terms. Nor can there really be kinds or types unless there is something common, something genuinely the same, among different individuals. The foundation of this conviction is the experience that there is something that is repeatedly found in different entities. This experience of sameness is what justifies at least in principle the use of a single term for all these instances. Even if no one ever happened to notice a certain kind of thing (an undiscovered species of animal, for instance), the sameness of the diverse objects that make up this species would still be available for discovery and articulation.

What is this generality that is such an essential feature of the kinds of objects? What is involved in the recognition of generality that is so crucial to any sort of human knowledge? And what is the generality that marks the terms by which we classify kinds and types? These questions help to identify the range of discussion about the problem of universals in the medieval period. Historically considered, there is considerable justification for dividing medieval thinkers into two general camps on this question, the realists and the nominalists, however many subgroups might be further specifiable within each camp.

2   REALISTS AND NOMINALISTS

As we have seen in chapter 3, most medieval philosophers exhibit some readiness to affirm that there are ideas in the divine mind that are the basis (the exemplary cause) for the distinctive kinds of things that human minds are able to discern and to express by means of universal terms. What medieval thinkers disagreed about is how best to explain these relationships. The typical positions taken on the question of the status of universals are what ground the labels "realist" and "nominalist" that are often used in the history of philosophy to distinguish two general approaches on this topic, namely, the view that universals really exist independently of human minds and the view that universals are merely names (*nomina*) supplied by human minds. In the course of the Middle Ages a considerable technical vocabulary emerged for the discussion of this topic.

The Greek term that the Latin language renders by *universalia* ("universals") is *ta kath'olou* ("through the whole," as in the phrase "what is the same *through the whole* range of individuals of the same kind"). Admittedly, philosophical argumentation can rely on etymological explanations only so far, but sometimes there is an insight to be gained by the use of this means, and that is true in this case. The Latin term *universalia* suggests "being turned toward one thing" and thus a unification of the many, especially in the sense that a single term (and perhaps the concept for which the term stands) is appropriate for turning our thoughts toward the kind to which the individuals belong or the property that various objects have in common.

Among ancient philosophers, Plato's position on the separate existence of the Ideas or Forms stands at one extreme on the realism/nominalism spectrum, while Aristotle's position needs to be located somewhere on the nominalist side of the scale, but closer to realism than to unmitigated nominalism. Aristotle does not stand at the extreme point of declaring that universals are merely names that we arbitrarily impose on things. Rather, in his view it is a term that is universal, but the reason why a term can be applied universally to the diverse items in a group is that there is some foundation in reality for classifying various particulars under a common concept. One can see at work here the importance both of making distinctions and of unifying multiplicities in order to make cognitive progress and achieve genuine knowledge. Aristotle offers the theory of learning by abstraction to explain how the mind acquires its concept of things – abstraction here names the process of noticing what is common to some multiplicity.[3] By contrast, Plato's position in the *Republic* and other dialogues focuses on learning by recollection and implies that there really is an archetype by which we can recognize the features that are repeatedly found in individual things.[4]

In medieval discussions of this topic, the question about the status of universals was advanced by the use of some important distinctions. First, the general designation *universalia post rem* ("universals after the thing") is used for those concepts that are formed by human minds after reflection on what is common among various individual items of experience (e.g., the terms for biological groupings such as species, genus, family, order, phylum, and kingdom). Second, the term that is used to name the common aspects repeatedly found within distinct individual things (whether or not these aspects ever become the focus of human conceptual thought) is *universalia in re* ("universals in the thing"). Third, the exemplars for these aspects and structures and kinds as they exist in the mind of God the Creator are called *universalia ante rem* ("universals prior to the thing").[5] All three of these types of universals (general concepts, common features within things, and exemplars in the mind of God) can be named by universal terms (*nomina universalia*) that apply to all the instances of a given class in any given human language.

Within these general parameters, what makes some medieval philosophers "realist" and others "nominalist" is the difference in their stances on the question of the existence of universals. A readiness to affirm the extra-mental reality of at least some universals marks one as a "realist" of some sort. But there are considerable differences of opinion about just what sort of universals may rightfully be said to exist. Hesitancy about such classifications, especially because of a given thinker's focus on the individuality of every real being and a concomitantly greater readiness on the part of that thinker to associate generality with our way of holding before the mind the commonness of diverse real beings, involves one in some sort of "nominalism." But there are diverse forms of nominalism, including the pure form that holds that universals are merely names and nothing more, and the various conceptualist versions of nominalism that tend to regard only concepts as universals in the strict sense and yet to affirm that, in order to explain the observed unities in the world of our experience, there must be some basis in reality for this commonness that is the result of the divine ideas.

Nominalists tend to find the claims of realists at some level incoherent or even metaphysically impossible. Even if the form or structure that is the organizational principle of one thing is found in exactly the same position and arrangement in another thing, each thing (strictly speaking) has its own form and cannot provide formation or structure for another thing without ceasing to organize the first thing.[6]

Realists prefer to focus on the need to posit the existence of universals as indispensable for the stability of our claims to know the structure of an essence, for that is what we know whenever we truly come to know anything. But thereby they assume the burden of trying to explain how these separately existing universals can perform their causal role in forming the particulars of their kind. Accordingly, those who are realists on the question of universals can offer a vigorous challenge to nominalists about knowledge: what is this commonness or sameness that we know whenever we know anything to be of the same kind? Nominalists operate from their greatest strength when stressing the reality of individual objects and in this they do not have the problems that face the realist claim that universals must somehow really exist. But they still have to explain how we can really know what we claim to know about the kinds or types of things if there does not exist some real foundation for the groupings that we use when we employ any general terms as the names of common properties or kinds.

To try to resolve the problem by saying that general terms merely have pragmatic advantages or are just the result of habituation within a linguistic community does not answer the epistemological question of how we really know what we do know. It would reduce knowledge to the power of asserting and imposing an order on things. It would be to give up on the claim that has long been regarded as central to genuine knowledge, that is, that knowledge is a matter of mentally grasping things as they are, without creating, controlling, or altering what one is grasping. Admittedly, the question of what constitutes authentic knowledge is complex. As one often sees Socrates demonstrate in the dialogues of Plato, genuine knowledge has to be more than mere opinion or a lucky guess.[7] One must, of course, make allowance for the many different types of knowledge (including personal experience, history, mathematics, music, science, religion, art, and so on). In a metaphysical sense, knowledge is a change in the being of a knower when the knower has mentally received the form of whatever is known. But, to speak in a very general way, there is also good reason to think that knowledge is justified true belief.[8] Knowledge is a form of belief in the sense that one does truly affirm it; if one did not really hold or assert a claim, one would not be properly said to know it. Further, what one holds must be true, for no one would say that when one holds a position that is false it is knowledge. Third, one must have adequate justification for holding the true belief; otherwise, it is presumably a mere opinion, a good guess, or a case of luck that one has gotten the matter right. The synthesis of these factors in a person's experience involve the unification of experience in a number of ways, including the recognition of what is common to diverse experiences, the use of common terms to express this recognition, and the grasp of the reasons that warrant holding the belief with firmness and conviction. Stated more succinctly, unity is the principle of all knowledge. Knowledge involves unifying the multiplicity of experience under common concepts. But the justification for an assertion of unification is that there are real unities and commonalities in things. If one cannot show these to be the case, one needs to withdraw the claim to have knowledge on a given question and acknowledge that one has only an opinion.

The very factor that makes nominalism attractive – its parsimonious refusal to multiply entities unnecessarily[9] – is the very aspect of the theory that makes it difficult for nominalists to account for how genuine knowledge comes about. With realism, the situation is just the reverse. If one holds that universals have some real status, one will be able to call on them in giving an account of our knowledge, but one will need to explain how such entities can genuinely exist and operate in the way they must do for this account of knowledge ever to be possible.

3   THE SOURCE TEXTS: PLATO, ARISTOTLE, PORPHYRY, BOETHIUS

The text that gives rise to the medieval controversy over universals is a Neoplatonic commentary on Aristotle's *Categories*, the *Isagoge* ("Introduction") by Porphyry.[10] But the problem at issue is already pervasive in the works of Plato. One can see in Platonic philosophy at least one version of the realist position (depending, of course, on one's interpretation of some notoriously difficult passages in the dialogues). Whatever the particular concerns that are predominant in any one of Plato's dialogues (justice, for instance, in the *Republic* or courage in the *Laches*), the conversation of the dialogues returns again and again to questions about the *eide* and *ideai* (Forms and Ideas) in which the objects of our normal experience are said to participate, however perfectly or imperfectly.[11] Whatever the answer to questions about the interpretation of specific texts, one may confidently say that any philosophy that posits a separate realm of perfect Forms as the basis for the commonness among individuals of the same type (e.g., by way of participation) and as the ultimate source of our knowledge of this commonness (e.g., by way of recollection) would be a strong instance of realism on the question about the status of universals.

It is not only Aristotle but Plato himself, in some of the late dialogues such as the *Theaetetus*, the *Parmenides*, and the *Sophist*, who raises profound problems about how participation and recollection are supposed to work. The *Theaetetus*, for instance, is an elaborate exercise to show that knowledge cannot be adequately explained apart from reference to the forms of things and to some process like recollection. The *Sophist* includes a re-examination of the question of the sorts of things of which one should and should not expect there to be forms, as well as the question about the relative compatibility of the forms with one another in composites.[12]

Aristotle often speaks of *ta kath'olou* ("universals") when discussing terms that are predicable of plural instances. While there certainly are texts in Aristotle's works that speak of eternal essences in a fashion reminiscent of his teacher Plato, Aristotle seems generally to have thought of universals as common terms.[13] He tends to treat them as predicates that apply generally to a whole class or kind. They are ways to name the form or structuring principle that is common or repeated in all the members of a kind and that justifies the claim that these distinct entities actually belong to the same class or species. This approach puts emphasis on the individuality of all real objects. Thus, in some ways Aristotle's position on universals may be rightly described as a form of nominalism. But his efforts in the *Posterior Analytics* at establishing the criteria for scientific knowledge and his evident convictions in many other writings about the many areas of life for which we can rightly claim to know all sorts of things reveal his commitment to the view that there are foundations in reality for these claims to knowledge. The reason why Aristotle's texts on the question of the existence of universals are so difficult to interpret is precisely the fact that there is something real about the essence that many individual beings share. There is, admittedly, much scholarly discussion about how to reconcile certain passages in Aristotle's *Categories* with certain passages in the *Metaphysics*. This is true especially on the question about whether the primary instance of the category "substance" (*ousia*, being, essence) refers to the individual or to the kind.[14] In the *Categories*, Aristotle tends to see the primary sense of "substance" as referring to individual beings, and to regard genera and species as "substance" only in the secondary sense (the kinds of being). But the *Metaphysics* offers passages in which essences are called substances in the primary sense, and individuals are held to be the instantiations within time of these eternal essences.[15] It is understandable that he would criticize Plato for assuming that what can be thought about distinctly must also exist separately. But in doing so it is hard to avoid merely relocating the problem of how generality works at some other level without really resolving it (e.g., in the distinction between primary and secondary substances, that is, individuals of a kind and kinds). What is clear from the writings of Aristotle is that he sees a basis in reality for predicating the same universal term of the different members of a given class. Further, he holds that we come to know the form that is the warrant for this sort of predication by abstracting the form from the various instances in which it recurs.

Porphyry's *Isagoge* ("Introduction") is an overview of Aristotle's *Categories*. In the history of medieval thought this text frequently served as the starting point for philosophizing on this subject. Despite the claim about being an introduction to the categories that seems to be made in the title, this text does not dwell at any length on the ten categories of being and of language that are Aristotle's main concern in that work. Rather, its focus is on five concepts of a higher or more general level of abstraction, namely, genus, species, difference, property, and accident. In the tradition of reflection on this topic, these five meta-categories came to be called the five "predicables."[16] While Porphyry himself maintains an intriguing agnosticism about the status of universals, his work raises certain basic questions about universals. These questions came to be the immediate source of questions for generations of medieval philosophers in ways that proved extremely fruitful:

> I shall beg off saying anything about (a) whether genera and species are real or are situated in bare thoughts alone, (b) whether, as real, they are bodies or incorporeals, and (c) whether they are separated or in sensibles and have their reality in connection with them. Such business is profound, and requires another, greater investigation. Instead I shall now try to show you how the ancients . . . interpreted genus and species and the other matters before us.[17]

Translated into Latin early on during the medieval period, first by Marius Victorinus and then by Boethius, the *Isagoge* became a regular member of the group of texts by which logic was taught and an engaging stimulus for thinkers of very different temperaments and outlook.

The first of Boethius' two commentaries on the *Isagoge*[18] sets the question of the categories of being and of language within the large-scale view of philosophy as the project of seeking wisdom by disciplined study and an ascetical form of life.[19] His second commentary includes an extensive treatment of the topic of universals, including his own attempt to answer the question that Porphyry had raised without resolving. Although Boethius' position is often described as "moderate realism" in the secondary literature, it might be more accurate to say that he is an epistemological realist. He identifies quite clearly the conditions that would need to be satisfied for a universal thing to exist and then denies that any real being of our experience could satisfy those requirements. What wins him the title of "moderate realist" is his strong sense of the metaphysical difficulties that arise in trying to answer the need for universal terms and general notions to have some foundation in reality. He is ever mindful that when we make the abstractions that we do in coming to know anything, there has to be a real basis for our claim to have knowledge.

Boethius' argumentation is revealing. For any universal to exist, it would need to be common to various individuals in its entirety simultaneously (not just successively). The problem is that the various things whose being this universal is supposed to constitute are distinct in their being from one another, and this presents a contradiction. While one and the same thing could enter into the constitution of different beings at different times, it cannot be present as a whole at the same time in each of them in such a way as to make them distinct beings.[20] For Boethius, the resolution of the question of universals turns on a proper understanding of intellectual abstraction. It is a matter of distinguishing between the ways in which an object's form is found in individual sensible objects and the way in which that form is understood by the mind. By the process of abstraction, we are able to separate intellectually what is not separate in reality. Hence, for Boethius, universality or generality refers to the mode by which the mind separately grasps a form that does not actually exist separately from the matter for which it is a structural principle.[21] Considered then as an intellectual way of representing what is within a material object as a structural principle, a universal is not a thing in itself but a mental representation with a foundation in things. In this way Boethius avoids the contradiction that Aristotelians brought against the Platonic position for apparently requiring universals to be present wholly and simultaneously in the distinct being of different individual things. Meanwhile, the relocation of the Platonic Ideas to within the divine mind allows philosophers a way to honor the Platonic insights about what is needed for guaranteeing the essential features of individual beings that belong to the same kind.

In the twelfth and thirteenth centuries, the recovery of Aristotle's writings and the stimulus provided by the Islamic commentaries generally reinforced the basic approach taken by Boethius. Of particular importance here is the practice of the Persian thinker Avicenna in distinguishing between considerations of a nature taken simply and absolutely in itself and of the same nature as it exists in a particular object. He argues that a common noun like "horse" that expresses a certain nature as it exists in one particular object or another is predicable of many individuals. For this reason, Avicenna holds that a general term may be used in the singular or in the plural. But when the word is used to express a nature considered in itself (such as "horseness"), the term is neither singular nor plural, but simply universal.[22] Philosophically, then, the question becomes whether a nature or an essence is being considered in regard to its instantiations or being considered absolutely, in distinction from anything that participates in it.

Variations on this distinction between the simple and absolute consideration of a common nature and the consideration of the same nature as it is found in individual beings and as it determines our concepts (that is, the thoughts of a mind that has learned about the essence of some being by an appropriate abstraction) can be found in many thirteenth-century philosophers. Aquinas, for instance, takes up this general Avicennian approach as he articulates his views of essence and existence.[23] What proved very appealing about this approach is the presence of the same epistemological focus as that used by Boethius, now supplemented by a more complete understanding of the Aristotelian doctrine of abstraction. When an essence or nature is considered apart from all questions about its existence in any particular instantiation, one can focus on that nature or essence in its structural clarity. But when one is considering the same nature as it exists in particular objects or in the mind, one can also attend to the recognizable sameness amid the differences that are part of its individuated existence. That is, one can focus on the same nature considered precisely in relation to the various material conditions of its existence in physical objects.

In the writings of the twelfth-century thinker Peter Abelard, we find a quite distinctive approach to the problem of universals. This approach received renewed attention in the fourteenth century. One can discern here the long-lasting influence of Porphyry's unresolved questions by noting that one of Abelard's most significant treatments of the problem occurs in a section of *Logica Ingredientibus* ("Logic for Beginners") entitled "Glosses on Porphyry."[24] There is much scholarly controversy about the correct interpretation of Abelard's admittedly difficult text. But what is widely recognized is that Abelard is using Aristotle's definition of universal as found in *On Interpretation*, namely, that a universal is what can be predicated of several things.

The questions on which Abelard focuses are semantic in character,[25] especially when he asks how universal terms accomplish their function of representing in a general way what occurs repeatedly in diverse objects. In his search for a "common cause" that can justify "the imposition of universal terms," he settles on what he refers to as the "status" of those things to which the universal term is to be applied.[26] In his examples, he makes clear that by the term *status* he does not mean to suggest that a universal is some existing thing. Rather, it is a way to designate that which true propositions about the objects in question signify. A universal is thus not some abstract entity like the Platonic idea of Dog that justifies the use of a general term "dog" for Buttons and Rover. Rather, what is signified by "being a dog" provides the needed justification. It is the status of being correctly asserted to fall under a given concept that is the common cause of allowing a universal term to represent generally what occurs in each particular case. That we can truthfully assert "being a dog" (or any similar expression of a status) of Buttons or Rover may well depend on our making an abstraction. But this approach places the justification for universal terms on a different act of intellect, the judgments that we make, rather than on what Aristotle called the first act of the intellect, the apprehension of forms by abstraction. The subtle shift here to a semantic explanation of universals (rather than a metaphysical explanation in terms of distinct forms) seems to be an attempt to accentuate what it is that the mind contributes, namely, the recognition that something has a certain status independently of any mental activity.[27]

4   LATE SCHOLASTICISM

By the fourteenth century, as a result of decade after decade of meditating upon the recovered texts of Aristotle, there was a widespread conviction about the impossibility of maintaining anything like the

Platonic theory of Forms. To do so would mean holding that nature of things had a separate existence from things themselves. Yet, by anyone's reckoning, fourteenth-century versions of the problem of universals became incredibly complex. Part of this trend might be explained simply in terms of the type of scholasticism prevalent during this age.[28] The increasingly technical precision possible when a philosophical question is subjected to steady generations of academic scrutiny made it possible for schemas of enormous complexity to be developed. But there was also a shift in what seemed to be problematic and in need of philosophical explication. The conviction that the nature of things are internal metaphysical constituents of the being of things was quite strong. What seemed to need explaining was difference rather than sameness. As a result, what we find emphasized in these later discussions about the problem of universals is the topic of individuation. The various theories of individuation that are produced are attempts to provide an account of the numerical distinctness of individuals in terms of something other than the nature that makes individuals members of a given species.[29]

William of Champeaux, known best perhaps for being the teacher with whom Abelard so violently disagreed, argued for accidental properties as that which individuates. But this position won little acceptance. Aquinas took the view that matter under determinate dimensions was the principle of individuation for physical substances, as he argues in detail in *De Ente et Essentia* (*On Being and Essence*).[30] One consequence of this view is that immaterial substances such as angels could only be numerically distinct from one another on the basis of their form. Unless one were ready to hold for the notion that there is such a thing as spiritual matter, as some of the Franciscans were willing to do, each immaterial substance (each angel, for instance) would need to be regarded as different in species from every other. Aquinas accepts this conclusion. But, dissatisfied with this implication, other thinkers generated their own distinctive solutions to the problem of individuation, including the theory of intentional distinction produced by Henry of Ghent[31] and the notion of *haecceitas* ("thisness") within the theory of formal distinction offered by John Duns Scotus.[32]

Henry argued that the individuality of actual beings requires no other factor (such as "matter" or "existence") to be added to the intelligible essence; it is enough, he thought, to show that an individual is internally undivided and not identical with any other individual. Scotus argues against those philosophers who wanted the principle of individuation to be something negative – the view that something is individual insofar as it is *not* anything else and insofar as it is *not* internally subdivided, such as a heap or pile. The difference between individuals of the same species cannot be their common nature; that would be the factor that distinguishes them from beings of a different species. Instead, he urges that the principle of individuation should be regarded as something positive and part of what the individual is, and yet not something that itself needs to be individuated. He calls this factor *haecceitas* ("individual difference" or "uniqueness"), which he understands as a principle that contracts the common nature to the singularity of each individual.[33] The advantage of this position seems to be the way in which it handles the problem of universals. Scotus stresses the individual essence in each object as what we know when we know that object. But the residual difficulty for which this position received much criticism is a perceived ambiguity about the relationship between the individual essence unique to each individual and the common nature that this individual essence is supposed to be contracting into singularity.

William of Ockham studied at Oxford, where Scotus had been extremely influential. He took Scotus' approach to the problem of universals very seriously but ultimately rejected not just the stronger forms of realism but any form of realism, in favor of an uncompromising nominalism.[34] For Ockham, universals are *not* outside the mind at all; they are concepts *in* the mind (and thus universal only in the Aristotelian sense of being "predicated of many").[35] There is nothing at all that is universal in the Boethian sense of being metaphysically "common" to many individuals of a given species. What kind of thing is a universal concept? Is it an intentional object, distinct from the thinking of it, or is it simply the act of thinking and thus a quality inhering in the soul? Ockham prefers the latter. Against the Scotist proposal that the common nature is genuinely identical with (but formally distinct from) the *haecceitas* or individual difference that is supposed to contract the nature to singularity, Ockham has a twofold objection. If the specific nature and the *haecceitas* are really identical, they cannot be formally distinct; but if they are formally distinct, they cannot be identical. Ockham also rejects the Avicennian and Thomistic view that the same thing can be singular or universal, depending on the different ways in which we are considering it, for in his judgment what a thing is in itself cannot depend on how anyone is thinking about it.

For Ockham, universality can only be the property of a sign, that is, a property of some act of thought or of the linguistic expression of that act. The problem of universals is thus not an epistemological problem of accounting for the ways in which the intellect abstracts a common nature that is inherent in individual objects that have been perceived by the senses. Nor is it a metaphysical problem of understanding how common natures are individuated in order to have existence as single entities. Rather, the problem of universals is the logical problem of explaining how general terms are used within propositions so as to refer to the individuals they signify. The solution to this problem, he thinks, is a matter of the careful use of the technical devices of logic for quantifying and specifying the reference of the terms used in propositions.[36] Among other late scholastics in this tradition, John Buridan is especially noteworthy for developing the nominalist position in metaphysics and logic through a focus on the representational apparatus that is common to all human beings and what undergirds their various conventional languages.[37]

5   OVERVIEW

Philosophical progress is often made by means of careful distinctions. On the question of universals, philosophy progressed during the medieval period by developing distinctions that have proven to be relevant for the identification of various aspects of the problem. Thinkers who put their focus on the problem of universals in regard to logic and semantics crafted certain distinctions that helped to clarify the question about whether something that one is thinking about in distinction from other aspects of the same being also needs to exist separately in reality. Thinkers who stressed the need for there to be a basis in reality for assertions about the commonness that belongs to instances of the same kind provided important distinctions about the proper use of universals in epistemology and in metaphysics. And within the realm of metaphysics, the universals that one needs to use in discussions about the sameness and the difference among beings of the same kind permits metaphysical progress in the understanding of essence and existence.

For the further understanding of the problem of universals, we need to bear in mind the question of the divine ideas that we have already considered (since medieval thinkers regarded the divine ideas as the ultimate source of the commonness of essences that recur in individual beings) and the question of the transcendentals (the part of metaphysics that deals with the properties of being as being that cross distinctions among categories), to which this book now turns.

NOTES

1 Aristotle (1984) makes this argument at various places in his works, e.g., *Metaphysics* I.9 and XIII.4–5.

2 While professional philosophy tends to deal with these questions in treatises on logic, some of the most interesting discussions of this topic in the Middle Ages come from the domain of biology and medicine. Mortimer J. Adler (1940) traces the philosophical problems that emerged for the notion of biological species in his *Problems for Thomists: The Problem of Species*. See also the works of Galen, the philosophical physician whose works were studied and translated throughout the Middle Ages: e.g., Galen (1963), *On the Passions and Errors of the Soul*.

3 See *De Anima* III.5-7, in Aristotle (1984).

4 See *Republic*, esp. V.477b and VII.529b; *Meno*, esp. 75d–e; and *Theaetetus*, esp. 197a–199a, in Plato (1997).

5 See chapter 3 on "Divine Ideas." For a detailed account of this whole topic, see Klima (2004).

6 There is also the important question about the unicity or plurality of substantial forms within a single substance. The question here concerns whether there can be more than one substantial form within a genuine substance. Aquinas and his followers argued that the unity of a true substance comes from a single substantial form that is the organizational principle of a composite being that makes it really one being, even if composed from different kinds of material; by contrast, mixtures are aggregates of distinct substances that are not genuinely united but only juxtaposed in the same general area. Bonaventure and many of his

fellow Franciscans argued for the plurality of substantial forms within a composite being under the hegemony of some dominant form; by taking this position they argued that they could better explain the residual substructures of a composite substance without imperiling its unity as a whole.

7   This is the theme of many of the Socratic dialogues, including, for instance, the encounters between Socrates and various Sophists in *Gorgias* and *Protagoras* in Plato (1997).

8   This is a view that is discussed in *Theaetetus* at 201a–d, in Plato (1997).

9   Some form of the principle of parsimony has been used by thinkers since antiquity, but the principle has been associated in a special way with William of Ockham because of his frequent use of it as a methodological principle for economy in theoretical explanations. Hence, it is often known as Ockham's Razor. Although the rule is widely recognized to be an aspect of his thought, the specific formulations of this that are usually cited are nowhere found in his texts, such as *plurality is not to be assumed without necessity* and *what can be done with fewer assumptions is done in vain with more.*

10   A number of these important source-texts are gathered in Spade (1994). For the text of Porphyry's *Isagoge*, see Spade (1994), pp. 1–19.

11   See *Republic* VI.508a–511d; *Laches* 199c–200b, in Plato (1997).

12   See *Sophist* 243d–e, 248e–253c in Plato (1997).

13   See *On Interpretation* 7.17a38–b1: "I call universal that which is by its nature predicated of a number of things, and particular that which is not; man, for instance, is a universal, Callias a particular," in Aristotle (1984).

14   See, e.g., Gill (1989).

15   See *Categories*, esp. 5.1 and 5.11; *Metaphysics* VII.4.1029b11–1030b13, in Aristotle (1984).

16   These five predicables have a semantic function. They allow the classification of all other predicates.

17   Porphyry, *Isagoge*, in Spade (1994), p. 1.

18   A fine summary of the textual history of Boethius' role in the story can be found in Chadwick (1981), pp. 131–52. See also Marenbon (2003a).

19   Pierre Hadot (2002) has been especially prominent in reminding the scholarly community that ancient philosophy was almost invariably an ascetical discipline and way of life. For the importance of philosophy as a way of life in medieval philosophy, see de Libera (1993).

20   Boethius, "Second Commentary on Porphyry's *Isagoge*," in Spade (1994), pp. 20–5.

21 See Spade (1994), pp. 25: "And so these things exist in singulars, but are thought of as universals. Species is to be regarded as nothing else than the thought gathered from the substantial likeness of individuals that are unlike in number. Genus, on the other hand, is the thought, gathered from the likeness of species. This likeness becomes sensible when it exists in singulars, and becomes intelligible when it is in universals. In the same way, when it is sensible it stays in singulars, but when it is understood it becomes universal. They subsist therefore in the realm of sensibles, but are understood apart from bodies."

22 See Morewedge (1973), pp. 32–6.

23 For example, in *On Being and Essence* in Aquinas (1983). See also the commentary on this text by Bobik (1965).

24 In Spade (1994), pp. 26–56, esp. pp. 37ff. on Abelard's position.

25 For further development of the significance of this observation, see Klima (2004) at #6 and Deely (2001).

26 See Spade (1994), p. 42. For Abelard's discussion of the difference between abstraction and judgment as different acts of the intellect, see Spade (1994), p. 50.

27 In Abelard's technical language one can detect this effort at advancing the question by a semantic strategy: "Yet the multitude of the things themselves is the cause of the universality of the name. For as we remarked above, there is no universal that does not contain many things. But the universality a thing confers on a word the thing does not have in itself. For surely the word does not have signification by virtue of the thing. And a name is judged to be appellative in accordance with the multitude of things, even though we do not say things signify or are appellative." Spade (1994), p. 56.

28 As Richard W. Southern has shown, the scholastic humanism that had been so stimulating and culturally enriching in its early and mature period eventually turned arid. See Southern (1995, 2001). For a discussion of a comparable situation in Islam, see Goodman (2003), esp. ch. 3 on the humanistic aspects of Islamic philosophy.

29 For a detailed account of the problem of individuation, see Gracia (1994).

30 More specifically, *On Being and Essence*, ch. 4, in Aquinas (1983) distinguishes between various senses of matter, including prime matter as the principle of pure potency at the root of all substantial change, and determinate matter (matter under dimensive quantity) that he took to be the principle of individuation.

31 See Marrone (1985).

32 See Ingham and Dreyer (2004), pp. 108–16; see also Noone (2003).

33 See Spade (1994), pp. 57–113 for six questions on individuation from Scotus' *Ordinatio* II, d.3, part 1.

34 For a more detailed study of this subject, see Panaccio (1999) and Spade (1999a).

35 William of Ockham (1998), *Summa Logicae*, esp. #15: "That the Universal is Not a Thing outside the Mind," pp. 79–82. Additional texts from Ockham's *Ordinatio* on this subject can be found in Spade (1994), pp. 114–231.

36 William of Ockham (1980).

37 For a general orientation to Buridan, see Zupko (2003), esp. ch. 1, "Language." See also Buridan (2001).

5

THE TRANSCENDENTALS

It is not until late in the scholastic period of the Middle Ages that one begins to find treatises formally given the title "Metaphysics," and yet there can be no doubt that reflection on the great problems of metaphysics was a central preoccupation throughout medieval philosophy. For some thinkers, the proper subject-matter of metaphysics as a discipline was centered on the being of God as the creator and source of all finite beings. This approach fits well with one possible interpretation of the term,[1] for the Greek etymology of "metaphysics" allows it to be taken to refer to what is "beyond" (*meta*) "the physical" (*ta physika*). Other thinkers prefer to concentrate on the ontological classification of the various types of being (infinite and finite, spiritual and physical). Still others see this discipline as organized around study of the principles of being, and they focus on such grounding axioms as the principles of identity, non-contradiction, causality, and sufficient reason.

But yet another fruitful way to appreciate medieval thought in the area of metaphysics is by considering the concept of the transcendentals. At least one scholastic, John Duns Scotus, claims that metaphysics is the science of the transcendentals,[2] and a later figure, Francisco Suárez, systematically develops the implications of Scotus' suggestion about the centrality of the transcendentals for the science of metaphysics in his massive *Disputationes Metaphysicae*.[3] Jan Aertsen even claims that it is attentiveness to the transcendental properties of being as being that distinguishes medieval philosophy from other periods in the history of philosophy.[4] The claim of medieval metaphysicians is that these properties are inherent in the being of all things and thus only intentionally distinct from a given thing's being. By contrast, the approach of many contemporary metaphysicians is generally to regard properties as actually constitutive of things.[5] Like the developments that occurred on such topics as analogy and univocity, essence and existence, or nature and creature, the progress made in reflection on the properties of being as being came as medieval thinkers considered certain theological problems of their own tradition in juxtaposition with the perennial problems of metaphysics as they found them being raised in texts from ancient Greek and Roman philosophy. They read these texts in light of their religious faith. The recurrent attention that they gave to the problems of substantial unity, intelligibility, and value received a range of answers that we can better appreciate by considering the philosophical roots of the concept of the transcendentals and some representative medieval approaches to this topic.

1   MEDIEVAL REALISM

Because of the vast differences between medieval and modern approaches to metaphysics, it may prove helpful at the start to distinguish in a general way the "realism" typical of medieval thought (with its focus on the objectivity of our knowledge of being) from the "idealist" turn of modern philosophy (where there tends to be special focus on the knowing and desiring subject). In contemporary philosophy, the term "transcendental" is often associated especially with Kant and German Idealism. It is out of his concern with discerning the a priori conditions for the very possibility of our recognition of objects that Kant thinks of his own project as "transcendental philosophy." For him, the world of objects is in an important way constituted by the human mind, and he uses "transcendental" to refer to those aspects of the thinking subject that transcend experience and are the grounds for having anything as an object of thought.[6] He warns against supposing that the metaphysical notions that are generated by reason correspond to anything in the world of being. He urges us to take them not as the "properties of things" but only as "certain logical requirements and conditions inherent in any perceptions of things." They might be helpful for organizing our experience, but we must always treat them critically and never suppose that they refer to reality as it is in itself.[7]

By contrast with the "idealism" typical of modern philosophy, much of medieval philosophy is "realist" in character by virtue of its claim that we are able to understand things as they are in themselves and to know being as being. In this respect metaphysical realism as practiced by medieval philosophers differs from those philosophical positions that deny the possibility of knowing the being of any object except in relation to a subject who is thinking of that object. Contemporary phenomenological approaches to philosophy, for instance, generally tend to speak of beings in terms of "objects for us" and the "field" in which they appear to us; considered from this approach, the claims made by realist philosophies seem almost too strong in principle, if only because they are usually articulated without reference to the thinking subject. For this approach, we can never know objects in themselves, but always and only as objects for some knowing subject.

Whatever their differences among themselves, medieval philosophers tend to be "realist" and to anchor their metaphysics in the transcendental properties of being as being. It is not that they are not alert to the relevance of questions about the knowing subject, but they handle those questions differently. For instance, when delimiting the range of sensory-qualities available to each of the specific sense-organs, Thomas Aquinas offers a caution that he repeats in so many other contexts that it virtually becomes formulaic for him: "Whatever is received is received in the manner of the receiver."[8] Colors he takes to comprise the proper object of sight. The healthy eye is able to receive a certain range of colored perceptions. Sounds constitute the proper object of hearing. A healthy ear is by its nature capable of receiving a certain range of tones. The qualities that a person receives through sense-perception are thought to inhere in beings independently of any knowing subject, but each material sense-organ, so long as it is not diseased or disabled, has access to a delimited range of such qualities that constitute its proper object.

While focusing on objects in themselves, the philosopher must always remain mindful that there are factors in the subject that could distort the experience (illness, weariness, decrepitude, and so on) just as there are factors in the situation that could distort the experience (dissonance, distance, climate, and so on). But if the situation is normal and the sense-organs are healthy, the person experiencing these sensations can in principle come to know the object's sensory-qualities in themselves. The subjective condition for this to occur is that the qualities must be within the scope of what a given sense-power can receive.[9] The perceiving subject is a necessary condition, one might say, for the sensation-experience to take place. The involvement of a suitably receptive subject should not be presumed to have altered or distorted the reception of the qualities of the object being sensed.

For Aquinas, the human mind thus has the capacity to know objects as they are in themselves. The mind, for him, is an immaterial power and thus has no limit in principle on what type of forms it can receive. It is in principle able to receive and understand the forms that are present in any type of being whatsoever. What it actually receives from any given being can (with sufficient attention and investigation, depending on the specific case) genuinely disclose what that being is in itself precisely because of the transcendental truth or objective intelligibility of the being. To articulate this sort of view about the possibilities and the limitations of human cognitive powers is an essential part of the effort by Aquinas and many philosophical realists in the medieval period to give appropriate respect to receptivity on the part of the knower as necessarily prior to any creative or constitutive activity in knowing (such as our mental efforts to construct classification systems or to elaborate theories). These thinkers regularly conceive the goal of knowing in terms of grasping the object as it is in itself, without creating, controlling, or altering what we are trying to grasp. The metaphysical presupposition of transcendental truth that makes such a view of the knowing process possible is one aspect of the theory of the transcendentals.

Medieval metaphysicians thus tend to take the transcendentals not as the sort of predicates that are only the result of the way in which we conceive or explain what we are talking about,[10] but as true and real attributes of beings. They are not understood as our own mental constructions for handling what surpasses the bounds of possible experience, but as the most general of properties of being as being. These properties (especially "unity," "truth," and "goodness"[11]) are thought to be coextensive with "being" in their reference (that is, every being as being is one, true, and good), but distinct in meaning (that is, each one signifies a different aspect of being as being).[12] Any being whatsoever is *one* (*unum*) insofar as it is undivided and thus exhibits transcendental *unity*, whether it is divisible or indivisible.

Likewise, any being as being possesses transcendental *truth* (*verum*) by virtue of its *intelligibility*, whether it ever actually comes to be known by anyone or not. And by having certain *qualities or perfections* that can be communicated to others and that can thus be *desirable* to others, every being whatsoever reveals transcendental *goodness* (*bonum*), regardless of whether it is actually the object of any desire or not.

Two of the crucial aspects of the doctrine of the transcendentals thus seem to be inconsistent with one another: (1) no transcendental adds anything to being, but only makes explicit something inherent in the term "being," and yet (2) transcendentals like *bonum* and *verum* do imply certain "extrinsic relations" (*bonum* with the will, *verum* with the mind). The first aspect implies that the transcendentals are intrinsic features of every being as being and thus are in things independently of any relation they have to anything else. The second seems to be in conflict with the first by implying that these transcendentals are not *inherent* in things but dependent on some extrinsic relations.

The apparent conflict can be resolved by noting that these claims are made from different perspectives. To claim that transcendentals are *inherent* in things is to claim (1) that the existence of every being must correspond to its essence in order for that being to be. This doctrine also claims (2) that the existence of every being is desirable (in the sense of having certain perfections that make it a possible object of desire). On the other hand, the claim that transcendentals also imply extrinsic relations is, in the case of *verum*, to recognize (3) that it is possible for the existence of every created being not to correspond to its essence. (One can, for example, speak of a person *not* being what he should, of his not realizing his potential, of not corresponding to his essence.) This is the obverse of the point that in the uncreated being of God, essence is always exactly identical to existence. The existence of every created being is *verum*, precisely because the being is created and thus corresponds (to a greater or lesser degree) to the divine idea.

The medieval understanding of the transcendental properties of being is deeply connected to the ways in which these thinkers understood the being of God. As we have seen elsewhere in this book, philosophical considerations of God in the medieval period put great emphasis on divine transcendence, that is, on the way in which the being of God is utterly beyond the created world.[13] God is not regarded as simply another being within the universe, but as the creator of all beings, the source of all perfections, and the cause that sustains everything in being. This is to recognize that human minds can never adequately comprehend *what* God is even when they come to know *that* God exists. But whatever the essence of God is, it transcends the categories of human experience. To speak in this way is, one might say, to use the term "transcendence" in a *vertical* way. In the hierarchy of being, God's infinite being is above all finite beings, not just as the noblest member of the set but as really outside the set. God's essence is something we may be able to point toward, but we must never claim to comprehend or encompass it.

Although our present concern with the transcendental properties of being is related to divine transcendence, especially in regard to God's creativity and omniscience, the idea here is to focus not on *vertical* transcendence but on a kind of *horizontal* transcendence. Most of the properties that we come to be aware of in the beings of our experience are quite specific to the particular type of being under consideration and therefore belong to the discussion of the "categories" as relevant for coming to know what a given type of being is. By contrast, a focus on the transcendentals is important for coming to understand every being as a being. This is to say that, in principle, all beings are able to be understood by us because there is some form present in a given being that is structuring that being and that is already actually understood by God. Likewise, it is to say that all beings are fundamentally good – not in the sense that all are equally desirable by everyone, but simply that every being as such has some perfections that make it a possible object of desire. Transcendental goodness refers to a quality intrinsic to that being as created by an infinitely good God and capable of being attractive.[14] These properties[15] of being as being are "transcendental" in the horizontal sense of the term as "cross-categorical" – they range across all the categories rather than being category-specific. For some medieval philosophers, the linkage between divine transcendence and the transcendental properties of being is held so strongly that they only allow the transcendentals to be predicated of God alone (being itself).[16] Others envision the transcendentals as extending not to all beings but only to God and to some creatures whose participation in being especially resembles the being of God.[17] But others find that this approach would imperil the thoroughly horizontal sort of transcendence that they see a need to defend in metaphysics for the sake of realism in epistemology (that is, the position that we are able to know objects in themselves). While occasionally adverting to these differences of opinion, the remainder of this chapter will focus on the main medieval tradition that takes the transcendentals as properties of being as being and thus found in each and every real being.

2 THE PHILOSOPHICAL ROOTS OF THE CONCEPT "TRANSCENDENTAL"

Medieval reflections on the transcendentals draw on both philosophical and religious sources. Ancient philosophers were clearly committed to the basic intelligibility of all reality, and they tended to formulate the first principles of metaphysics in ways that privilege one or another of the transcendentals (without, however, using this term). Plato's *Republic*, for instance, treats the Idea of the Good as the source of all being and knowledge.[18] Aristotle explicitly notes the correlation of being and unity.[19] In identifying the One as the font from which everything that is emanates, Plotinus develops themes from both Plato and Aristotle into a doctrine of transcendental unity that becomes the basis of his entire philosophy. Out of respect for the pervasive influence of Neoplatonism throughout the Middle Ages, we may consider his views at slightly greater length here.

Like the Idea of the Good, the One of Plotinus contains within itself all the perfections that are separately manifest in the outflow of diverse beings from the One. But any being, however distant from its source in the One, exists only insofar as it is one, and disunity entails the dissolution of being.[20] Insofar as unity is lost, being is lost. Mindful of Parmenides ("from nothing, nothing comes"), Plotinus seems never to have thought of anything coming into being from nothing or of anything's destruction into nothingness by utter annihilation. Rather, he envisioned the generation of anything as coming about by the introduction of some limiting form that makes it this one or that one. The destruction of any being, for him, means the break-up of what was unified into things that are not intrinsically connected or integrated, even if they may still happen to be spatially next to one another. For Plotinus, all reality emanates from the utterly ineffable One. Every reality at any level is one, however tight or loose that unity may be.[21] Plotinus' attentiveness to transcendental unity thus echoes the far-reaching respect of Plato for goodness in such central texts as *Republic*,[22] where he names the Idea of the Good as the source of all being and all knowing and regards all other beings as participating in this form of all forms, however otherwise delimited by participation in the other forms.

Somewhat more generally, the Greek quest for a scientific (and not just a mythological) explanation of the universe operated under the assumption that all reality is in principle intelligible. When this presumption about universal intelligibility is reflected upon thematically, it constitutes the kernel of the doctrine of transcendental truth. One of the integral assumptions at work here is that any genuine instance of knowledge worthy of the name is stable over time. But for knowledge to be stable, what one knows must be at least relatively fixed and unchanging. In most cases one can only have intellectual access to these stable essences by means of highly changeable and often changing sensory impressions. The investigation of sensorily known qualities by appropriate methods can disclose the object's intelligible form. It is the thing's form that is the real object of intellectual investigation, for coming to understand anything involves reducing the many to the one – that is, finding what is really common among the many instances that present themselves as somehow similar. Understood in this way, the quest for knowledge of the abiding natures of things can be envisioned as a process of discernment that often proceeds by tracing back perceptible effects to the structures of the beings that produced them.[23] What makes the success of such cognitive efforts possible in principle is the presumption that there is something in things that can be discovered by suitable means of inquiry. It is this assumption that is at the root of the concept of transcendental truth.

No one thinker within ancient philosophy gives a systematic and interconnected account of the transcendentals as such. But in the medieval period there is considerable and sustained attention to the various questions that give rise to a philosophy of the transcendentals. Among the factors responsible for the medieval development is the significant difference in metaphysical outlook that comes with seeing the universe as something purposely created rather than simply a given. The difference here corresponds in some ways to the shift from the idea of God as the highest being within the universe to a being that is the source of everything that exists and yet radically different from the cosmos. The universe as a whole and every being within it are seen as dependent on God for both origin and continued existence. The recognition of this sort of dependence provides the grounds for some thinkers to mount arguments for the existence of God. In addition, this way of understanding the relation between God and the universe as something that God has created also invites new reflection on the nature of being and its properties. There is, for instance, a new urgency to the question about whether every being as being can be thought of as good when one confronts the reality of evil, suffering, and pain from the assumption that an infinitely good God has created everything that exists. We will consider this question in greater detail in section 5 below.

3 TRANSCENDENTAL UNITY, TRUTH, AND GOODNESS

Let us now take up in turn each of the main properties of being that were identified as transcendentals: unity, truth, and goodness.

For anything to lose its unity would be to be destroyed as a being. This need not mean that it is entirely annihilated, but that it ceases to be what it was. The destruction of a unified being usually means that it is broken up into various beings, each of which has a unity of its own. But whether a given being is thought to be divisible (in the way that any physical object can be broken up into other things) or indivisible (e.g., God or a human soul), any being as being is "one" (*unum*) in the sense of being actually undivided. To say this is to say more than the term "being" says, but only by way of a negation ("being *not* actually divided now").

The importance of this claim can be seen, for example, in the extensive debates about substantial unity discussed below in chapter 7 on soul. Some medieval thinkers stress the plurality of forms in their efforts to account for the persistence of qualitative features across substantial change. One see this, for instance, in the doctrine of the virtual presence of elements in a compound, according to which various qualitative features associated with particular elements or chemical compounds persist even after the destruction of, say, the animal whose matter they constituted. Other thinkers emphasized the need for asserting that there can be only one substantial form in each substance if that substance is to be a genuine unity. They argue for its indispensable role in organizing and unifying any composite being at any one moment and over the course of time. Without it, what appears to be a substance would in fact only be some sort of group or collection that is accidentally unified, perhaps by proximity or cooperation to some degree or other, but not deeply unified in the distinctive way that a substance is unified. In both cases, the philosophers who are party to these debates ground their thinking in the importance of affirming that unity (at some level) is a fundamental property of being. The loss of unity is tantamount to the cessation of a given being's existence and its dissolution into something else.

The term used to express this transcendental property, *unum*, does its work by using a latent negation, that is, by asserting that any being as being is "actually undivided." In this way, the term *unum* is making explicit something that was latent in the term *ens* (being). The term brings out the point that every being as being is one, whether the being is actually undivided because it is simply *indivisible*, such as God or the human soul, or merely that it is *presently undivided* but in principle divisible, such as a human body, a plant, or a rock. Some beings are divisible into homogeneous parts that would still be of the same type when separated into smaller lumps (such as a clod of earth). Others have heterogeneous parts and would lose the substantial form that makes them to be what they presently are if they were to be divided (such as a horse or a tree, depending on which parts are cut off and how). In short, many different types of unity are possible in this way of looking at reality. What the transcendental *unum* signifies is that every being as being has unity of some sort as an intrinsic feature of its being.

Closely related to transcendental *unum* is what some medieval metaphysics name as a distinct transcendental – we might call it *individuality*, but different philosophers use distinctive names and explanations for this aspect of being. Aquinas, for instance, speaks of *aliquid* (literally, "something") as a transcendental term for explaining the fact that everything that exists is an individual distinct even from other individuals in the same species. Duns Scotus uses this notion as philosophical bedrock for his metaphysics by focusing on the *haecceitas* ("thisness") of every being as being. Some of his critics think that he emphasizes the point to such an extent as to risk the intelligibility of being. A being's intelligibility comes from the possession of a common form by the many beings of any given type or kind. But, considered in another respect, Scotus is simply working out the consequences of the Aristotelian insight that the basic unit of being is individual substance, whatever difficulties for epistemology that insight may introduce.

Further, everything that is real may also be called "true" – not in the sense that it is actually known by any human mind, but in the sense that the structure of its own being is what gives it a certain intelligibility. This is the truth of things, and a thing itself must "conform" to its *structure* in order to be. This is the source of the correspondence character of "truth." This use of "true" is not the standard sense of the word, for propositions and statements are usually the sorts of things that we call true; namely, we call those propositions true when what we say or think conforms to reality, either by affirming what is, or by denying what is not.[24] What warrants us in speaking about the truth of things and not just the truth of propositions is a metaphysical reflection on truth as the correspondence of thought and thing, conjoined with an acceptance of the creaturely status of all reality other than God. The basic insight in regard to transcendental truth is this: prior to any mental grasp of a thing by a human mind, there is already a relation by which the thing conforms to the corresponding idea in the divine mind (a point discussed at greater length in the chapter on divine ideas).

In the ordinary use of the word "truth" in regard to statements, we are normally thinking of the correspondence between what the statement expresses and the way things are. The technical term that is often used for the notion of correspondence is *adequatio*, the "making equal" or conformity of thought to thing.[25] *Adequatio* suggests a direction to this conformity, for in order to generate truthful propositions, the human mind is what needs to change in order to receive mentally the already existent structures of whatever is to be known. From what it receives, it is able to abstract an adequate understanding that will accurately represent realities that the mind did not create, control, or alter.

But, of course, the direction of the conformity that is involved in the truth of human statements (thought conforming to thing) does not exhaust the possibilities, for it is also possible for things to conform to thought. In the sphere of human experience, we find this to be the case in practical and productive uses of the mind, such as when a painter or a sculptor creates a work of art that realizes its mental model, or when statesmen devise a political form for achieving what they want to accomplish by an order of governance. By analogy with human artistry, the divine artistry of the creator (as we have seen in chapter 3 on divine ideas) does not just think (*cogitare*) about what already exists, but thinks things up (*excogitare*). It would be an error to suppose that divine knowing is limited to operating by the sort of processes that are typical of human knowing – by receiving and abstracting from what is received – as if divine knowing were dependent on objects for information in the way that we are.[26] In human knowing, the mind receives and abstracts the form that makes a given object what it is. The substantial form is what makes it the kind of substance it is. The various accidental forms make it have the various properties and traits that it has. For any being to be a reliable source for true propositions, it must have structures of this sort. But those structures are already known by the divine mind, whose knowing (as we have seen in the chapters on God and on Divine Ideas) is what gives every being its existence and preserves it in being. Taken in this way, there is a truth that any finite thing has by virtue of the conformity of thought and thing – not the conformity of human thought to thing, but of thing to divine thought. Within the notion of transcendental truth is the idea that every being is sustained in existence by the omniscient God's act of knowing.[27] It is because there is such a form that the being can in turn be known by a human intellect. As a true instance of its kind, each thing is intelligible to human minds suitably disposed to study and appreciate them for what they are. In this way medieval thinkers can account for error as well as truth in our knowledge-claims. Human minds can make hasty and ill-founded judgments about the things under discussion. But human minds that operate with suitable receptivity to the contours of being can find in the truth of things a ground for strong knowledge-claims about the nature of things, without ever thinking that they had exhausted the nature of anything.[28]

Finally, every being by the very fact that it exists is "good" (*bonum*) in that it has, by virtue of its being, various perfections that can be communicated to another. As with the other transcendental terms, the term "good" adds something to being, not by adding something other than being (for there is nothing other than being available to add). Rather, it adds to being by way of making explicit something that the term "being" does not directly suggest, namely, by predicating an extrinsic relation (the suitability of the being for desire by a will) that follows from the intrinsic property of any being as having certain qualities and perfections that can be communicated to others.

Transcendental goodness is not the same as moral goodness, but it is its ground. Similarly, transcendental truth is not the same as propositional truth, but is its ground. To assert that every being as being is transcendentally good is not an assertion of moral rectitude or ethical approval. Moral goodness does have a basis in metaphysical goodness, but only when further distinctions are made. In particular, moral goodness refers to free and voluntary choices made in accordance with the right order of loves.[29] The rightness of this order of one's loves depends on respect for the hierarchy of goods, such that one loves the highest good the most, that one loves goods of the same level equally, and that one loves inferior goods proportionately.

The refinement of this basic schema is the work of ethics proper and so outside the scope of this chapter. But for the moment it will be enough to say that medieval theories of ethics almost invariably[30] include an intellectual component. Putting the right order into one's loves requires that one know what the divinely ordered hierarchy among the goods are from which one must choose. At the basis of the claim for an objective basis to the order among goods is the doctrine of transcendental *bonum*, that is, the principle that there is in every being a goodness according to its kind, for every being as being is good in the sense of having qualities and perfections that can be communicated to others and thus good for them according to their kind.

In the case of moral goodness, the question thus turns on what is appropriate for human desire and choice. Moral goodness refers to what we as human beings ought to desire, love, and choose as genuinely perfective of our own being and those for whom and with whom we choose. Human actions (and their correlative human desires and loves) are good when ordered toward choices that are genuinely perfective of human nature. When human actions or their correlative loves and desires frustrate human nature and the ends for which God made it, there is something morally wicked. But, as medieval philosophers like to remind us, the morally evil ends to which we may put something do not render the object evil, but only our own action.[31] The object remains metaphysically a good, precisely because transcendental *bonum* refers not to our choices but to the being itself as apt for being perfective of another (however much we may abuse it).

To take some simple examples, if we should steal an apple, or an idea, or abuse the liberty of another human being, neither the apple nor the idea nor the other person becomes evil. Each of them remains precisely what it was, with whatever sort of qualities, properties, and perfections it may have and to whatever degree it has them. Our theft of something to which we are not entitled, or our abuse of some good, renders our action, our desire, or our choice morally repugnant, not the object with which we are dealing. On the other hand, things that are transcendentally good can also be good for us. Nourishing food, for instance, is a genuine good for us precisely because the good that is communicated to us when we consume depends on the goodness it already had in its own being.

This goodness is a perfection that can be communicated to another but that would be good even if it were never communicated to anything else. From another perspective, the idea that every being as being is good can seem counterintuitive in the face of plagues and pests, viruses and mosquitoes. But once again it is crucial to remember that the claim being made for transcendental *bonum* is not that everything is "desirable" from the human perspective, let alone that everything "ought to be desired." Rather, the claim is only that any being as being has certain qualities and perfections and thus is able to be desired. How or under what specific conditions any particular object may actually be desired always remains to be determined, particularly in the case of something that we humans find destructive or obnoxious.

As a metaphysical claim, the doctrine of transcendental *bonum* is not about our human convenience or pleasure, but about the way reality is. Whether something in particular is actually found attractive and actually desired by any of the other beings in its vicinity depends on various aspects of the situation and the nature of the beings involved (e.g., whether a given being is hungry, thirsty, lonely, and so on, and whether the other being appears to have the sort of qualities and perfections that would in any way be satisfying).

The proposition that "all being is good" is as fundamental to medieval philosophy as the proposition that "all being is true," but it is easy to misunderstand. It is not a naively optimistic assertion about this being the best of all possible worlds. Nor is it intended as some broad moral approbation, say, along the lines of Rousseau's comment about the essential goodness of every human being prior to the destructive influence of civilization. Rather, it is to be understood in much the same way as the statement about transcendental truth, that is, as asserting that goodness is a term convertible with being. The reason for this assertion is that anything can, in principle, communicate whatever qualities and perfections that it possesses to another, and hence can be desirable for another. It is on the same basic reasoning that truth is said to be convertible with being, for anything that is can, in principle, be known by another, and hence it is intelligible for others. What the term "true" (*verum*) said in this way of any being adds to the term "being" comes about by an extrinsic denomination – that is, by way of predicating a relation to an intellect other than the being in question, specifically, the relation of being actually known by a divine intellect. In the case of *bonum* an extrinsic denomination is also involved, the relation of suitability for desire by another (whether actually desired or not).

Transcendental *bonum* is a property of being as being that owes as much to religious as to philosophical insight for its articulation. Where Plotinus had concentrated on the One as the originative source for the emanation of all reality, his own source (Plato) had located the Idea of the Good as the Form of all Forms, the source of all being and knowing.[32] In fact, much of this reverence for the Good permeates Plotinus and the entire Neoplatonic movement in both its pagan and Christian forms. One of the points of greatest attraction for its adherents is its commitment to the notion *bonum est diffusivum sui*, the idea that the good is self-diffusive. Like a fountain, the good is envisioned as pouring forth in abundance, for example, in the cooperation that tends to be elicited by friendliness or in the expansion of knowledge, which never decreases by being shared. Extrapolated as a metaphysical principle, the identification of goodness with being has a long history as a basic insight of metaphysics.

What made the idea of the good especially appealing for medieval philosophers was its prominence in the biblical account of creation. According to Genesis, God created the world in six days and then rested on the seventh. Whatever the modern controversies over how literally or symbolically to understand the reference to "days," medieval exegetes had no hesitation in interpreting[33] this biblical terminology to refer to periods of time that far exceeded a 24-hour period, not least of all because the sun needed for measuring out days and nights was not created until the fourth day.[34] What intrigues them far more about the text of Genesis was the refrain at the end of each day: "And God saw that it was good." This declaration gave them reason to affirm that God had made everything that exists and that everything that exists was good. God at least could see this goodness, they felt, however obscure the picture could sometimes be from a human perspective. Reconciling these views with the undeniable presence of wickedness and suffering prompted much fruitful reflection, to which we will turn in section 5 below. But medieval philosophers had reason to understand goodness as a property of being as being from both philosophical and revealed sources.

4 THE CONVERTIBILITY OF THE TRANSCENDENTALS

Because the predication of the transcendental terms "one," "true," and "good" involves properties that are coterminous in reference by terms that differ in meaning, medieval philosophers often assert that these terms are "convertible with being."[35] Now, for a metaphysician to speak about the being of anything invariably raises questions about essence and existence, that is, questions about *what* something is and about *whether* it is. As we have noted in chapter 4 on universals, reflection about being in the sense of existence entailed questions about whether the terms were being used univocally, equivocally, or analogously, for it was important to determine whether one meant exactly the same thing when one spoke about the existence of, say, God, angels, human beings, animals, or stones. An important part of these considerations involved making a proper distinction between being in the sense of *existence* and being in the sense of *essence*, for the ways in which things exist differ, and the definitions of the essences of things are intended to reflect those differences. But, if we abstract from the way in which anything exists and concentrate instead solely on its presence, that is, simply on the fact *that* it exists, there is need for simple univocity in our terminology. The notion of the analogy of being is intended to capture these relationships of sameness and difference by noting both the preservation of a certain identity in the various uses of the word "being" as well as to have a controlled sense of the differences in essence and the relationships among these different types of beings.

The theory of the transcendentals extends these considerations by allowing deeper reflections on the various properties that belong to the common concept of being. To say that the transcendental terms are convertible with the term "being" is to assert that, in addition to any properties that are specific to the essence of a given genus or species (such as being flat or round, being alive or being an inorganic compound, and so on), there are certain properties intrinsic to any and every being to which a metaphysician needs to attend. Not only does the metaphysician study the simple fact of presence, but also the attributes of unity, intelligibility, and quality that are concomitant with presence, regardless of the specific type of unity or any of the particular details about the being that can be known or desired when the being is considered as an individual or as an instance of a kind. For anything to lose its unity would amount to cease being what it was. For anything ever to be known, it must already have intelligibility. And for anything to be desired (regardless of whether the desire is morally appropriate), it must have some sort of quality or perfection that can appear attractive as a perfection that could be communicated.

Among the things most fascinating for medieval thinkers about terms like "good" and "true" is an important difference between transcendental and categorical terms. While most of the properties of a given entity belong only to that specific being (the individual features of the cocker spaniel "Buttons," for instance) or to the type of being that it is (the features that are typical of cocker spaniels), transcendental properties are those that cut across (that is, transcend) the various categories of being and may be said of every being precisely insofar as it is a being. In pondering this logical distinction, medieval metaphysics also tended to see a correlative difference with regard to being.

In medieval commentaries on Aristotle's *Categories*, one can see this complex interrelationship of logic and metaphysics. The book schematizes a classification of the forms of things under ten headings, namely: substantial forms and the nine accidental forms *quality, quantity, relation, place, time, position, state, action,* and *affection.*[36] The modern tendency to refer to these items by abstract nouns should not make us forgetful that Aristotle, perhaps to avoid any question-begging, actually stated them a bit more awkwardly but thereby open-endedly as questions: *what is it? what kind? how much? related to what? where? when? how ordered? having doing what? undergoing what?*[37] Here, and throughout his writings, Aristotle seems regularly to have made the assumption that all beings can in principle truly come to be known without alternation or distortion by the activity of a suitable disposed knower.

His medieval interpreters asked whether these were categories of words, of mental concepts, or of things that exist independently of our minds. In their responses, they generally follow Boethius, who is in turn following Porphyry, in treating Aristotle's *Categories* as primarily concerned with words but also thereby with the ideas and the things that these words name. All subsequent philosophizing about categories tends to reflect concern with this fundamental question of the relation between words and things, as well as with questions about the relation between the actual forms of things and the mental forms by which we claim to know things, let alone the terms by which we express the forms of being and of knowledge. Substance and the various accidents are then the names for the various forms of being, that is, structural features of beings that could be grouped under various categories. In the *Isagoge,* the "Introduction" to the logical writings of Aristotle that inspired much medieval speculation about logic and metaphysics (such as the problem of universals), the Neoplatonist Porphyry arranged these categories in a way that elicited from later hands a diagram called "Porphyry's tree,"[38] which came to be included in many medieval manuscripts of the *Isagoge,* a table by which one could descend through a series of dichotomous divisions, for instance, from *substance,* through *body, animated body, animal,* to *rational animal* as the lowest level of species, within which one would find only individual instances. At each stage the table records the types of properties possible for that level of classification. In his approach to logic, the terms that name the properties of specific kinds of objects are categorical predicates (sometimes called "first-order" terms in later philosophy), while the terms that in turn name groups of logical terms such as "genus," "species," and "difference" are called the "predicables" ("second-order" terms).

By contrast with the categorial predicates and the predicables, the "transcendentals" are a group of terms that name certain properties that are convertible with being because they are found in every being that exists. These terms bring out one or another feature of every being as a being, and thus they are coextensive in reference with the term "being" but different in meaning or sense. For Aristotle, the categories of being (substance and the nine types of accidents) permitted a classification of the various forms of finite being found in our experience. Methodologically, medieval philosophers, especially in the scholastic period, followed the path of *resolutio* ("analysis") in their research on the natures of things, particularly by the classification of an object under study within such categories as substance, quality, quantity, and relation. But in the course of their reflections on metaphysics, they found that the same method of *resolutio* brought them to a number of irreducible notions: being and certain properties of any being regardless of category, especially unity, truth, and goodness.

The general concept of the transcendentals is then quite clear: for anything that one can properly call a "being," one is also justified in designating that object as one, true, and good. To appreciate the significance of this far-reaching claim, it will help to examine their convertibility with being and to consider what each of these means in turn. The actual Latin term *transcendentale* and its cognates seem to be of rather late medieval vintage,[39] but throughout the scholastic period (even among thinkers otherwise very different in outlook) there is a strong conviction that there are certain such properties whose terms are convertible with "being." The focus on "convertibility" apparently comes from the "terminist" logicians who took special interest in the theory of predication found in Aristotle's *Topics*, where he discusses the case of certain subjects and predicates that are related in such a way as to be interchangeable within a proposition.[40] The terminist logicians noticed that certain terms can apply to everything of which one may also use the term "being,"[41] but that the meaning that each one conveys is distinct. In fact, the way in which these terms add something to the meaning of being is achieved, paradoxically, either by a negation (e.g., *unum* in the sense of being undivided) or by the careful use of an extrinsic denomination (that is, by a name that indicates the relation of one being to some other being, e.g., *verum* in the sense of being able to be understood by an intellect or *bonum* in the sense of being able to be desired by a will). Since there is nothing other than or outside of being that could be added to being, there is nothing positive that the attributes named by these properties can bring; rather, what these terms in effect supply is an explicit mention of something that the term "being" does not directly of itself suggest, that is, by the naming of a property that is an intrinsic attribute of every being insofar as it is a being. This sounds, at first, unproblematic, but latent in the use of extrinsic denominations is a problem that will occupy generations of metaphysicians, namely, whether the reference to intellect and will in the definitions of *verum* and *bonum* does not actually imply a need for the subordination of metaphysics to logic and for the idealist or subjectivist turn that is one of the marks that differentiates modern philosophy from medieval.

The discussion of the transcendentals by scholastic metaphysicians became more formalized in the commentaries on certain claims regarding *bonum* ("good") made in Boethius' treatise *De hebdomadibus* ("On the Sevens"). This text, also known from its opening line as *Quomodo substantiae* ("How substances are good . . ."), had become a kind of metaphysics textbook in the twelfth century.[42] It is a Neoplatonic meditation on the relation between being and goodness that arises from trying to answer a question whether every being is good insofar as it is. It first received commentary from the likes of Gilbert of Poitiers and Clarembald of Arras, and later by Aquinas.[43] Following the method of analytic resolution (the breakdown of a concept into its ultimate constituents), such thinkers as Philip the Chancellor, the Franciscan Alexander of Hales, and the Dominican Albert the Great undertook a search for the "most common features" (*communissima*) of being that, like being itself, cannot be resolved into anything else.

Although Boethius' text is thoroughly philosophical in character, it also had a certain biblical resonance that is important to the evolution of the medieval doctrine of the transcendentals by virtue of the allusion in the title (*On the Sevens*) to the goodness that God finds on each day of creation, as we noted above in the third section of this present chapter on transcendental *bonum*. The metaphysical claim that every being as being is good in the sense that each being has some qualities communicable to others seemed to be a correlate for the biblical vision that all things are good because made by God who is all-good. Philip the Chancellor's *Summa de bono* arranges his treatment of the transcendentals around the notion of goodness.[44] Although clearly dependent on Philip's work, Alexander of Hales prefers to take unity as his preferred model for trying to understand and define the irreducible properties that are convertible with being. What apparently drives this change is concern that a genuinely transcendental property should not be thought to add anything to being, but references to goodness seem to do that insofar as goodness seems to be defined by reference to a will that finds the being attractive. *Unum*, by contrast, adds only the negation of "being undivided." In his own account of being as being in Book XI of the *Metaphysics*, Aristotle had named only unity as convertible with being when he observed that "it makes no difference whether that which is be referred to being or to unity. For even if they are not the same but different, they are convertible; for that which is one in also somehow being, and that which is being is one."[45]

In order to preserve the notion that a genuine transcendental should name a property of being as something that is found in every being and that can be named without reference to any other being, some thinkers are willing to name only the property of unity as a transcendental, whereas others prove willing to list *verum* and *bonum* as transcendentals, despite the fact that they seem to introduce extrinsic denominations as properties of being. In writings like the *De Veritate*,[46] Aquinas defends this view by emphasizing that the extrinsic denominations (that is, the references to intellect and will in the definitions of transcendental *verum* and *bonum*) follow upon an intrinsic denomination, namely, the form of the being that is the source of intelligibility and the various qualities and perfections of the being that could be communicated to others that are ultimately the reason for calling it *bonum*. Later figures like Suárez try to handle the problem by couching the definition of transcendental truth in terms of a "suitability" (*habitudo*) for being known and the definition of transcendental goodness in terms of a similar suitability for being desired, but other figures in the generation after Suárez, such as Christoph Scheibler, worry that definitions of this sort actually risk eviscerating being by naming it not on the basis of intrinsic properties but on the basis of extrinsic features. In fact, Scheibler even invents a "new" transcendental that he calls *perfectio* in order to capture what earlier thinkers meant by *bonum*. He fears that Suárez has opened *bonum* to being thought of purely as an extrinsic denomination.[47]

The philosophical issue at stake here in what might seem an arcane dispute is actually a medieval version of the ancient problem that was sounded long before in Plato's *Euthyphro*. Are things good because they are loved (a situation that would make goodness depend on something outside the being itself) or loved because good? The latter situation presupposes that being has an intrinsic goodness that then evokes an appropriate response from a suitably disposed will. In venturing to define the transcendental *bonum* in terms of will, late scholastic philosophers around the time of Suárez thus seem to be moving toward the subjective turn that will eventually be made in classical modern philosophy.[48]

5   TRANSCENDENTAL *BONUM* AND
THE PROBLEM OF EVIL

We may conclude this account of the medieval understanding of the transcendentals by noting its importance for the perennial problem of evil and suffering. For biblical religion, it is clear that all that exists is created by the one God. Chapter 1 of Genesis reports that on each day of creation God looked at what was made and saw that it was good. In various Psalms and certain portions of the Bible's sapiential books[49] there are passages that are dedicated both to giving praise for the design with which divine intelligence crafted everything that has come into existence and to praying for better understanding of God's works, so as better to appreciate their creator. But the philosophical problem of explaining how there can be evil in a world entirely created by a good God requires special explanation.

Historically, this question provoked a rethinking of the Platonic assumption (an assumption that Christian Neoplatonists found very congenial) that all beings are good because they flow from the Idea of the Good. That the problem of evil had troubled ancient Platonists is evident from their occasional remarks about the nature of matter.[50] But ancient philosophers seem to pay more attention to the problem of how to preserve God unsullied by matter and undisturbed by evil than to providing a justification for the fact of evil or the frequency of suffering by the innocent in a world wholly made by a good God. For the Christian metaphysician, it is scandalous to think of the Creator of everything (including matter) as responsible for evil. Hence, this problem required a reconsideration of the entire scheme. The development of a theory of the transcendental properties of being played a role. The importance of these religious commitments for philosophers can be seen in texts from the earliest part of the Middle Ages, such as the reflections of Augustine on the nature and origin of evil[51] and the prominence that Dionysius the Areopagite assigned to goodness among all the divine names.[52]

The doctrine of transcendental *bonum* permits the development of a general explanation of evil, both as wickedness and suffering, that is of great sophistication. Evil in any of its forms is quite real, but it is real as a privation of a good that ought to be present rather than as a positive form of being in its own right. Blindness in a human being, for instance, is the real lack of the ability to see in a type of being whose nature includes the power of sight. A toothache, to take another example, is a real feeling of sharp distress and suffering that arises from the lack of integrity in the enamel that ought to cover a tooth and protect the nerve within. Or, to take a moral case, the theft of some money is the real lack of the due order of loves that ought to include respect for property. In each of these cases, the proper description of the specific evil is invariably rooted in a being that has various qualities and perfections as a being of a certain kind. Evil is not a being in its own right, but some sort of lack in regard to being and its goodness. It has reality as a privation that can only be suitably described by reference to being and the transcendental property of goodness.

This notion should not be confused with the position taken in various eastern philosophies, that evil is ultimately illusory and that enlightenment consists in recognizing even pain and suffering to be as illusory as the self that they seem to affect. Rather, evil is quite real, especially in the pain and suffering that people experience, but the pain and suffering (physical, moral, spiritual, etc.) are forms of discomfort in the real substances that are sentient animals (including human beings) when some goodness that would normally be expected for healthy living is diminished or even totally lacking. The real pain of a toothache comes from something like the absence of tooth enamel and the consequent exposure of a nerve to hot or cold, against which it would be shielded in a healthy tooth. The pothole in the road that could disjoin the axle of a wheel that strikes the rim of the hole is similarly an absence of the being that would constitute a smooth path. And at the moral level, the evil intention in the heart of a thief or an adulterer that leads to some wicked act of taking what is not one's own is quite real. That is, it is a really efficacious motive that results in a real action with real consequences. Yet these ethical cases also manifest the privative character of evil: the absence of the right order of loves that morally ought to invoke respect for what belongs to another and then, as a result of the action taken, an absence of the order of justice, for individuals come to be deprived of what is rightfully theirs.

This way of looking at things, in which everything that exists is good, in some degree, according to its kind and to the degree that it is structured and acting according to its kind, thus allows the philosopher to offer a metaphysical account of evil (physical and moral) that in no way denies the reality of evil, especially in cases of pain and suffering, without needing to treat evil as if it had positive reality in its own right like any other substance. As medieval philosophers considered this question, the objections to such a practice was both religious and philosophical.

Borrowing heavily from the Neoplatonists, Augustine gives the first systematic articulation of the privative character of evil.[53] One can see the alternatives to the position that evil is privative in character in the Manichean view that Augustine explored for many years before his acceptance of the Neoplatonic insight and his own development of the point.[54] Augustine reports that he was long unable to comprehend how evil could be real unless it were something, but he found that he could not reconcile his sense of the need to imagine it as if it were a being in its own right with the claim that God made everything that exists and that God saw everything that was made as good. The Manichean position seemed much more plausible, that there were contrary forces at work in the universe, and that the goodness of the principle of light made all that was spiritual and good, while the wickedness of the principle of darkness generated all that was material and wicked. The Manicheans taught that the mixture of good and evil in the world of our experience could be explained by the cosmic conflict of these forces, and that even our personal striving for goodness could be taken as the natural and expected inclination of our spirits as fragments chipped off the good spirit in the course of the fray and now embedded in the chunks of bodily matter that continuously resist such altruism with their base and earthly inclinations.

The seventh book of the *Confessions* records the culmination of Augustine's long intellectual and personal struggle with this position. He credits God's grace with ultimately providing him with the strength to overcome the temptations to sin and to heal the hardened habits of disordered love that confused his thinking and motivated his bad conduct. But prior to that moment of spiritual conversion, he experienced an intellectual conversion through the preaching of Ambrose and the reading of certain Neoplatonists. A crucial part of the removal of these intellectual roadblocks was what we have been calling transcendental *bonum*. Combined with the insight that God's own nature is spiritual rather than material, and thus to be known with the mind as transcending the limited and always insufficient forms that are the vehicles of imagination, this doctrine of the goodness of all being as being and the real but privative character of evil was a philosophical breakthrough that in turn liberated Augustine for his somewhat later religious conversion.

For the subsequent history of medieval philosophy, this doctrine was regularly a source of fruitful reflection. Boethius, for instance, makes it central both in his theological treatises and in his famous *Consolation of Philosophy*. Spiritual writers in the Augustinian tradition take it as a firm footing for their own ruminations on God, creation, and human rectitude. Even those like John Scotus Eriugena, who are more inclined to follow out the implications of Neoplatonic principles, even at the risk of theological heterodoxy, see no reason to question this insight, and by the scholastic period this doctrine is firmly fixed as a foundation-stone for their system-building syntheses. Only with the subordination of metaphysics to logic in the period of nominalism does adherence to this doctrine come unraveled, as do the doctrines of transcendental *unum* and *verum*.

Boethius makes pivotal use of the doctrine of transcendental *bonum* in his *Consolation of Philosophy*. As in Augustine's *De libero arbitrio*, Boethius envisions the problem of evil as needing to account for the reality of evil in a world made by God alone and to preserve human freedom and responsibility in the face of God's omniscience and omnipotence. Hence, the frequent task of writers in the area of theodicy has been to accommodate claims for real human freedom simultaneously with claims about God as all-powerful, all-knowing, and all-good. Boethius' solution to the complex problem of evil expands on the stratagem of Augustine: that God's eternity places him outside the order of time, and thus able to know what his creatures are freely choosing to do without his causing them to make the choices they make any more than, in our own more limited situations, our knowledge of what other people are doing does not cause them to do what they do. This position is not without its problems, of course, as the vigorous debates on this topic ever since give witness. But that it provides a plausible position on the problem of divine knowledge and human freedom of choice is in part due to the doctrine of transcendental *bonum* and the privative character of evil that Boethius readily adopts from Augustine.

NOTES

1   Although Aristotle's own works tend to refer to the book that we know as his *Metaphysics* as a treatise on "First Philosophy," the term "metaphysics" has subsequently become the name of this whole discipline.

2   See *Questions on the Metaphysics of Aristotle*, Prologue, in Scotus (1997), p. 1. In fact, the whole of the prologue is an attempt to make the case for seeing the proper subject-matter of metaphysics as the transcendentals. For a recent discussion of this point, see Frank and Wolter (1995), pp. 30–1.

3   Portions of the two printed volumes that make up the *Disputationes Metaphysicae* of Suárez (1998) have been translated; unfortunately, the disputations most concerned with the transcendentals in general (##1–3) have not yet appeared in English. But for a fine account of this

material, see Gracia (1992). Unity is treated in disputations ##4–6, truth in disputation #8, and goodness in disputation #10.

4   See Aertsen (1996), pp. 19–23, 434–8; and Aertsen (1999). See also volume 11 of the journal *Topoi* (1992), which was given over to a variety of fine articles on the transcendentals in medieval philosophy.

5   For instance, Plantinga (1996). Note the difficulties that arise for any theorist who insists that "evil" is a primitive property rather than a privation of some due good.

6   See Kant (2003), B113–14, where he explicitly alludes to the scholastic doctrine of the transcendentals while distancing himself from it. For a discussion of this point, see also Pieper (1989), pp. 19–20.

7   For a thoroughgoing study of Kant's views on this topic, see Allison (2004). For a more general picture of the transcendentals in the tradition of German idealism, see Solomon (2003) and Ameriks (2000).

8   *Quidquid recipitur recipitur secundum modum recipientis.*

9   Unless one is the victim of some form of synthesia, in which one can apparently hear colors or see sounds, but this would be a condition on the part of the knower.

10 That is, there are second-order terms such as "genus" and "species" that are predicated not of things but of other terms, in order to classify and organize the first-order terms that directly refer to reality.

11 There is considerable discussion among medieval philosophers about how many transcendentals there are. In *De Veritate*, q. 1, for instance, Aquinas (1993a) lists six transcendentals: *res* (literally "thing" but here in the sense of having a specific nature) and *aliquid* (literally "something" but here in the sense of being an individual within a species) in addition to *ens* ("being"), *unum* ("one" in the sense of being undivided), *verum* ("true" in the sense of being able to be known), and *bonum* ("good" in the sense of being able to be desired for the communication of some quality of perfection). Other thinkers attempt to make the case for such candidates as *pulchrum* ("beauty") and for pairs of transcendentals such as "finite/infinite" and "necessary/contingent." See Pieper (1989), esp. pp. 32–4.

12 For Kantians, *transcendental categories* are those which are the necessary conditions of experience and cognition, but for medievals *transcendentals properties* are the necessary "conditions" of the beings of things. There is nothing than cannot be "good," "true," "a *res*," etc. It is for this reason that thinkers like Boethius and Aquinas insist that all that is is *unum*. See *Consolatio* III.11–12 in Boethius (2000).

13 Régis (1949), pp. 39–40, n.47, has suggested that Francisco Suárez appears to have been the first to have distinguished between

transcendental and transcendent in his *Disputationes metaphysicae*, disp. 3, sect. 2 in Suárez (1998), vol. XXV, pp. 107–9.

14   The assertion of transcendental *bonum* does not involve the claim that a given being is necessarily good-for-us, either for our species or for any one of us as individuals, but only that the being has the qualities and perfections endemic to its kind. A virus, for instance, might be quite bad-for-us, and any predator is bad-for its victim.

15   Among the technical terms used for "properties" in medieval discussions of the transcendentals is not only *proprietates* but also *passiones*, e.g., in Suárez's third disputation, which is entitled "De passionibus entis in communi et principibus eius" ("On the properties of being in general and its principles").

16   Typical of this view is Meister Eckhart. See Eckhart (1974) and Dobie (2003).

17   For a discussion of Scotus' views on this topic, see Dumont (1992).

18   *Republic*, Bks. VI–VII, 504b–518d in Plato (1997), e.g., 508e–509b: "This reality, then, that gives their truth to the objects of knowledge and the power of knowing to the knower, you must say is the idea of good, and you must conceive it as being the cause of knowledge, and of truth insofar as known. . . . The objects of knowledge not only receive from the presence of the good their being known, but their very existence and essence is derived to them from it, though the good itself is not essence but still transcends essence in dignity and surpassing power."

19   *Metaphysics* XI, 3, 1061a15–17 in Aristotle (1984).

20   See *Enneads*, IV.3 and VI.4–5 in Plotinus (1966–88).

21   *Enneads*, esp. VI.4–5 in Plotinus (1966–88), with its alertness to the argument for the unity of being in *Metaphysics*, esp. X.2–3 in Aristotle (1984).

22   See *Republic* VI–VII, but especially 508e–509a in Plato (1997).

23   See Frankfort (1977).

24   Anselm of Canterbury offers a classic statement of this view in his "On Truth," ch. 11, in Anselm (1998), pp. 151–74 at pp. 165–6.

25   *Veritas est adequatio rei et intellectus.*

26   Boethius initiates a long tradition of comparing divine knowing to human artistry in his *Consolation of Philosophy*. See Bk. V, prose 4, in Boethius (2000).

27   In working out the consequences of this position, Aquinas, for example, holds that God must be recognized to be the cause even for the existence of morally evil actions. God is not responsible for them as evil (that is the result of a wrong choice by some human will) but for their existence as the actions of beings whom he sustains in existence and whose evil

he allows in order to preserve the freedom of choice of rational agents, whose actions must be allowed to have their consequences. See *Truth* 3.4, in Aquinas (1993a).

28　Aquinas' comments that we cannot ever exhaustively know the nature of even a fly, but that this does not mean that we cannot genuinely know things. To know something means to have mentally received the form of the object. One could, for instance, have grasped the substantial form of a thing but not have grasped all of its accidental features.

29　The idea of the *ordo amorum* ("order of loves") is articulated by Augustine and remains fundamental for ethics throughout the medieval period. See, for instance, Augustine (1995a).

30　One of the reasons why Abelard's ethical views provoked such an intense reaction was his departure from this standard. See Abelard (1971), ch. 11.

31　For instance, *The City of God* I.18, in Augustine (1984).

32　See *Republic* VI, in Plato (1997).

33　For an account of the sophistication of medieval biblical interpretation, see de Lubac (1959), vol. I (1998). See also Smalley (1964).

34　See *The City of God* XI.7, in Augustine (1984).

35　See, for instance, *Truth* 1.10: "ens et verum convertuntur," in Aquinas (1993a).

36　*Categories* 4.1b25–7, in Aristotle (1984).

37　*Categories* 4.1b25–7, in Aristotle (1984).

38　See *Isagoge* in Porphyry (1887), p. 4, ll. 21–5. For discussion, see Kneale and Kneale (1962), esp. ch. 4, "Roman and Medieval Logic," pp. 177–297.

39　See Pieper (1989), p. 15, n.6, for the attribution of this point to Albert the Great.

40　*Topics* I, 8, 103b7–17, in Aristotle (1984). For an account of some of these logicians, see Thom (2003) and Broadie (1993).

41　By the time of Suárez, there is considerable formal discussion of *entia rationis* ("beings of reason") as distinct from *ens reale* ("real being"), and concomitantly discussion about whether purely mental being (fictious beings such as hippogryphs), as well as beings expressed through the use of negations (such as "the immaterial") and in terms of privations (such as "blindness") are also characterized by these transcendental properties. See the translation of disputation 54 in Suárez (1995).

42　*De hebdomadibus*, also known as *Quomodo Substantiae* in Boethius (1978). For the importance of this book in the later Middle Ages, see Chenu (1968), ch. 2: "The Platonism of the Twelfth Century." For an overview of this period, see Dronke (1988).

43 See the commentaries of Clarembald of Arras (2002). For a more general discussion of this pint, see MacDonald (1992).
44 Philip the Chancellor (1985).
45 *Metaphysics* XI. 3.1061a15–17, in Aristotle (1984).
46 *Truth*, q. 1 and q. 21, in Aquinas (1993a).
47 Scheibler (1617).
48 Likewise, in the readiness to emphasize "suitability" to be known by an intellect instead of focusing on the aspect of a being's having a form that stands in a relationship of *adequatio* with the divine intellect, there is some evidence of a trend toward having logic decide questions of metaphysics (rather than seeing logic primarily as an "instrument" for doing philosophy). The essentialism that is characteristic of rationalism in early modern philosophy manifests a further step in this direction, in its taking the principle of contradiction as the rule for what is real, but the development of that point is beyond the scope of this book.
49 There are many ways to classify the Psalms. Among those often listed as "Wisdom Psalms" are Psalms 1, 36, 37, 49, 73, 112, 127, 128, and 133. Among the "Wisdom books" are Proverbs, Job, Qoheleth, Sirach, Song of Songs, and Daniel.
50 See *Enneads* I.8, in Plotinus (1966).
51 See *Confessions*, esp. Bk. VII, in Augustine (1991b).
52 See *The Divine Names*, ch. 4, in Dionysius (1987), and the commentary on this passage in *Periphyseon* 510a–b, in Eriugena (1995).
53 See *Confessions* Bk. VII in Augustine (1991b).
54 Augustine acknowledges his debt to Plotinus on the matter of the privative character of evil, but the text of Plotinus, perhaps owing to the gnostic predilections of his editor Porphyry, remains ambivalent. While some passages in Plotinus are such that could have inspired Augustine's understanding of evil as privative, there are also such passages in which Plotinus equates evil with matter, according to the patterns of gnosticism and dualism.

6

COSMOS AND NATURE

The standard medieval view of the universe is considerably different from the one to which we are now accustomed, not only in its geocentric orientation but also in its religious and moral significance. Even when medieval philosophers are addressing problems that seem independent of questions about the structure of the universe, such as how human choices can be free in the face of divine omniscience or what the ground for morality is, there is always a distinctive view of nature and cosmos that is operative in the background.

The dividing line between the changeless patterns of movement typical of the heavens and the ever-changing dynamics of this world is, for them, the orbit of the moon. Yet, despite the constant flux that is characteristic of the sublunary world, there is in every type of creature an enduring "nature" that is the source of the patterns of growth and activity typical of things according to their kind. In this way, the concept of nature helps to explain stability amid all the change. By contrast, the celestial world that begins with the orbit of the moon is a region of luminous beings carried on translucent spheres and the unchanging patterns of their motion. The intricate interactions of these spheres are entirely fixed and only give the appearance of irregularity until one comes to understand the laws of the cosmos.

Generally, the philosophers of this period are mindful that what they receive from antiquity about the cosmos is a model for calculating how the heavens appear from the earth and not a direct representation of the cosmos's physical structures. But, as C. S. Lewis notes in *The Discarded Image*,[1] this distinction is often blurred in popular culture and is sometimes forgotten or neglected even in learned discourse. The basic model comes to be as firmly fixed in the popular mind as today's heliocentric picture. An appreciation of the careful distinctions made in regard to nature and the cosmos is crucial for understanding medieval thought.

This chapter will consider the basic concepts of nature and cosmos in tandem, beginning with the Ptolemaic understanding of the world. As with other topics treated in this book, it will help us to distinguish between what is received from ancient philosophical sources and what comes from religious traditions. This distinction will in turn assist us to appreciate the ways in which medieval philosophers transform what they receive. That God created the entire universe is taken as a given. But understanding what the structure of the cosmos is and how our world fits into the larger picture is an enterprise in which medieval thinkers readily assimilate the theories of earlier philosophers. That God had created every kind of being that ever existed is clear to them. But it is equally clear that once the kinds of things were created, beings of each kind tend to act and be acted upon according to their natures without the need for special divine intervention most of the time. The notion of "nature," as used by medieval philosophers, refers not to the great outdoors or to the entire set of things that exist independently of human artifice. In their technical usage, it refers to the inner constitution of things, the interior source within beings for their stable patterns of growth, development, and activity that are typical of each kind of being. This notion of nature has roots in ancient philosophy as the principle that grounds the stability and order of beings in universe. But by its juxtaposition with the religious notion of divine creation, it receives a fundamental transformation in the medieval period. Instead of being envisioned as simply an eternal fact about the world like the archetypal Ideas of Plato or the eternal essences of Aristotle, "nature" comes to be taken as revelatory of divine providence at work within each type of being in the cosmos. It is the structuring element that God built into all the beings of this world in such a way as to bring each type of creature toward its perfection as well as to manifest diverse aspects of the divine designer.

Further, when this concept is applied specifically to human growth and activity, the combination of Aristotelian teleology with the religious notion of God's plan for his creatures gives "nature" a new and decisive role in ethical theory. Various medieval philosophers speak of the natural law to designate the moral law that God has written into human nature. The natural moral law can be discovered by careful rational reflection on human nature. In this way nature offers a route to philosophical insight about the sort of habits that ought to be developed as virtues (or avoided as vices) and into the kinds of choice that one should make (or avoid) in the course of a human life. By observance of the natural law, one might realize the potentialities of which human beings are capable and which their divine creator desires for them. In this way the idea of nature is crucial for medieval philosophers as a way to move from moral theories that accentuated the notion of divine command toward the development of theories of ethics with a natural basis for moral norms and moral virtues.

1   THE PTOLEMAIC UNIVERSE

Today we understand the Earth to be a planet that annually orbits around the star that we call the Sun while rotating once daily on its own axis. Our solar system is located on one arm of the Milky Way Galaxy, which is itself but one among many galaxies in a vast universe whose contours are still being mapped.[2] The medieval view is geocentric. The moon, the sun, and the various planets are envisioned as being carried along on transparent crystalline spheres. These spheres rotate in such a way as to make the celestial bodies that they carry appear to travel on uniformly circular paths around the fixed and immobile earth. In the far background there is a sphere of fixed stars that is embedded in the *primum mobile* (the "first" or outermost "movable" sphere).

This view is often called the Ptolemaic universe. It is named for Claudius Ptolemy, the author of a Greek work that Latin readers come to know through an Arabic intermediary as the *Almagest*.[3] His account is the source for most of the astronomical theories that are repeated throughout the Middle Ages, even in the period before this text is itself translated into Latin. There is a steady record of observational activity by individuals who recorded their observations and suggested revisions to his account. The revisions tend, for the most part, to make an already complex model even more complex, the better to explain phenomena such as the apparent retrograde motions of some of the planets.[4] By using such devices as an interconnected set of spheres that rotate at different speeds and in different directions, these models are increasingly able to account for the motions perceived in the sky. But the use of physical mechanisms of this sort makes it all the more possible to confuse a model designed to calculate how celestial motions will appear from the surface of the Earth with a physical model for representing how celestial bodies actually are in themselves.

Prior to the development of the telescope and the new model for the cosmos that telescopic data would encourage, the basic Ptolemaic model seems to have been almost universally accepted without serious question. It appears to harmonize rather easily with the Bible, even though the Ptolemaic model is not itself derived from the Scriptures but produced by thinkers in ancient Greece working under assumptions of their own. Unusual phenomena like comets or the aurora borealis tend to be treated as divine portents and not to elicit a new model for the cosmos in the way that the extraordinary event of a supernova in November 1572 later did. The new evidence acquired through the use of telescopes, such as the discovery of moons around Jupiter, finally led to the sort of questioning that brings about the discarding of a geocentric model in favor of the heliocentric model developed by Nicolaus Copernicus[5] and supported by the new mathematical physics of Galileo Galilei.[6]

Although the controversy that erupted over some of the writings of Galileo in support of Copernicus has many undeniably ecclesiastical dimensions, it would be a mistake to treat it purely as a quarrel between religion and science and thus to forget the role played by Aristotelian cosmology and philosophy of nature. There are really three parties to the debate: proponents of the new science, interpreters of biblical revelation, and natural philosophers trained on largely Aristotelian ideas about the earth and the heavens. Even the title of one of Galileo's works (*Dialogue concerning the Two Chief World Systems*) suggests his awareness that it is a clash of models that is in question here. As recent scholarship on the case has shown,[7] Galileo himself sees the issue not as a simple conflict between science and religion but as a complex issue on which one needs to distinguish carefully between certain interpretations of the Bible, a number of a priori philosophical commitments about the nature of the cosmos, and the results obtainable by the hypothetical method of modern science. Interestingly, at Galileo's trial in 1616, Cardinal Robert Bellarmine, the Inquisitor, does not forbid Galileo from conducting further research but he does forbid him from continuing to offer his own private interpretations of the Bible, for this is outside his expertise. Bellarmine also reminds him to remain philosophically alert to the hypothetical status of the new heliocentric model while pursuing his search for appropriate confirmatory evidence.[8] Without going into further detail about the Galileo affair, we can appreciate how this well-known case brings out the point that cosmological theories invariably involve certain philosophical problems that are intrinsic to the use of models and that the theorists of that time and of the Middle Ages were mindful of this.[9] A century before Copernicus, for example, Jean Buridan expresses the view that the motions discussed by astronomers using the Ptolemaic system are enough to "save the appearances" of the heavens, whether they were truly physical motions or not. Comments such as this reveal an awareness of the fact that it is a calculative model that is being used to explain the appearances of things that are difficult to examine directly.

The Ptolemaic system[10] gives special attention to the motions of the stars that appear to "wander." In fact, the term "planet" is derived from the Greek word for "wanderer." This system tries to account for the complex patterns of the motion of the planets as seen against the background of those "fixed stars" that do not seem to move in relation to one another but only seasonally as a whole field. From the surface of the earth the fixed stars of the "firmament" appear to move in unison. It is as if they were embedded in a huge sphere somewhere far above the earth that moves along a large arc around a pole (in the northern hemisphere, the North Star). The main assumption here is that the earth is immobile and at the center of a series of transparent spheres that turn around the invisible pole. Each sphere carries along one of the "planets" (namely, the Moon, Mercury, Venus, the Sun, Mars, Jupiter, and Saturn). Their perceived orbits, however, need to be calculated as a function of the combined motions of the various interconnected spheres. The apparent motion of any given body forwards or backwards is the result of the sum of the interconnected motions of various other spheres and the planets that these spheres carry. But in recounting the process for making the calculations used to explain the appearance of the heavens, it is easy to slip into treating the calculative model as if it were a physical model.

2   TRANSMISSION OF THE MODEL

Written in about AD 150, Ptolemy's *Mathematical Compilation* comes to be known to medieval readers of Arabic as *al-Majisti* and later to the Latin world as the *Almagest*. In addition to this work, there are four texts that chiefly conveyed to the scholastic period of medieval philosophy the body of received knowledge about the natural world: a partial translation of Plato's *Timaeus* by Chalcidius,[11] Martianus Capella's *The Marriage of Philology and Mercury*,[12] Macrobius' *Commentary on the "Dream of Scipio"*,[13] and Boethius' *Consolation of Philosophy*.[14]

The ultimate philosophical source for Ptolemy's model is the *Timaeus*. In this late dialogue Plato envisions the earth as a motionless sphere at the center of a vastly larger sphere that is populated by the fixed stars that rotate around the earth. Nested in between them, he pictures a series of concentric spheres, on each of which there is fixed one of the wandering stars. While each of these transparent spheres has a uniform rotational movement, the combination of their movements produce the motions of the planets as they appear from the viewpoint of someone on the surface of the earth. The details of the explanation, however, Plato leaves unresolved. Successive generations of astronomers take up the challenge of reconciling this basic model with the detailed observations of Greek and Babylonian astronomers. In his treatment of the subject in *On the Heavens*,[15] Aristotle comments that observations generally verify the basic model. Subsequent astronomers work on increasingly intricate refinements so as to fit even the recalcitrant data into the basic format of the main model.

Once equipped with a Latin translation of the *Almagest*, medieval scholars, with their interest in intellectual systematization,[16] continue to refine the Ptolemaic model. Eventually, the accumulation of unresolved anomalies gives rise to Copernicus' frustration over the inadequacies of the model and his ingenious development of a new model in the sixteenth century. Reviewing their work historically discloses how strongly a priori their commitment is to the notion that nothing but a motion at constant velocity in a perfect circle is "worthy" of heavenly bodies.

However curious we may find this notion, we should not suppose that it is arbitrary or groundless. Aristotle distinguishes between the sphere of "nature" (*physis*) and the sphere of the "heavens."[17] The sublunary world is mutable and quite distinct from the superlunary world, whose utterly regular cycles of movements suggest that it is immune from decay and change. The dynamics of the changeable world he considers to be the proper object of a disciple that concentrates on *physis* – the Greek term that is rendered into Latin as *natura* and that passes into English by such words as "physics." Despite the etymological connections of the Greek term *physis* with growth and life, the cognate term in English (physics) suggests to us something inanimate and lifeless. We are accustomed to think of physics in terms of the laws of motion ever since Galileo and Newton mathematicized the discipline.

For Aristotle, *physis* has a biological resonance, and he employs an organic model as the basis of his entire theory of the natural world. The root verb *phyein* means "to grow." What specially marks the sublunary realm that we inhabit is an incessant series of life-changes such as conception, birth, growth, maturation, reproduction, death, and destruction.[18] To account more generally for the variety of changes observable in terrestrial things (including the inorganic), he articulates in the *Physics* the notion of being as a unified entity ("substance") with various qualitative, quantitative, and relational features ("the accidents") and then accounts for changes in a being's substantial and accidental forms by a theory of the four types of causality, with "material cause" and "formal cause" referring to the constitutive elements and structures of anything, "efficient cause" to the agents that induce changes, and "final cause" to the goals, purposes, and outcomes that are the result of the operation of structures and agents. Living things can take in new material and excrete what is no longer useful, and yet remain the same beings over the course of a certain period of time. By analogy with the biological perseverance of a given entity despite even the total (but gradual) replacement of its matter, Aristotle thinks that he can also give a suitable explanation for the changes experienced by inorganic entities as well as by artifacts. As a philosophical response to the paradoxes of being and becoming that Parmenides had posed long before,[19] he thus offers his generalized account of being and becoming as a physical theory about substantial and accidental change, rooted in an organic model. He thereby systematizes and improves the many efforts at natural philosophy that been attempted by various pre-Socratic philosophers.[20] In a sense, he is relocating entirely within the terrestrial realm the distinction that Plato makes between the ever-changing physical world of material objects and the unchanging intelligible world of the Forms.[21] He does this by using a biological model for handling both inorganic and organic objects and by setting the boundary between the mutable and the immutable at orbit of the moon. Above the sphere of the moon, he takes there to exist beings whose composition and motion are of a different order.

The sublunary realm Aristotle thought to be composed of the four elements (earth, air, fire, and water) in various proportions and arrangements. It was the "nature" (*physis*) of each kind of being in the terrestrial realm that provided the stability typical of each species, for the individuals of a given species are made up of some regular combination of these four elements. The individuals within a given kind are the subject of development and activity that are specific to each kind according to recurrent patterns. Since each of the elements had certain distinctive qualities (fire is hot and dry, air is hot and moist, water is cold and moist, and earth is cold and dry), he believed that his natural philosophy could explain not only the interactions of objects according to their kinds but also the sensations that sensate beings like ourselves experience when we encounter beings of various types. Our very bodies are made of the same elements as the rest of the world and can register the ways in which they are affected by other beings with these fundamental qualities. In this way the theory of physics that he articulates for the terrestrial world has a quantitative dimension, but it is not primarily quantitative in the way that contemporary physics tends to be. Rather, it has a profoundly qualitative character in its fundamental components.

By contrast, Aristotle thought that celestial bodies were fixed and unchanging in their patterns of perfectly circular movement. Hence, he presumed that they must be comprised of something other than the four elements that constitute changeable substances. This fifth element (in Latin, *quinta essentia*) was regarded as something real but unchanging. Despite the anomalies involved here, the distinction between sublunary and superlunary proved long enduring. The doctrine that the heavens must be made of a different sort of stuff in order to be everlastingly immutable proved extremely difficult for medieval theorists to shake. One can, however, detect efforts to do so as early as the works of the sixth-century Byzantine philosopher John Philoponus.[22] Later on, scholastic theologians are much inclined to include among their arguments for the proof of God's existence the universal applicability of the principle of causality. But one of the implications of seeing the principle of causality as universally applicable and capable of pointing to the need for there to be an uncaused cause is inevitably the obliteration of any distinction between sublunary and superlunary realms in terms of the type of material of which things are composed. Increasingly, medieval theorists recognize that the realm of natural or physical causality cannot cease at the orbit of the moon. By virtue of progress in this regard, the realm of the supernatural comes to be recognized as referring only to spiritual (that is, immaterial or non-physical realities) and not to the celestial bodies of the heavens.

The steady adherence to this basic picture means that a vast number of technical correctives are needed in order to make the calculations match the observed data. In their ongoing efforts to perfect the model, the theorists tend to divide their material into two parts by composing separate treatises "On the Sphere" and "On the Planets." About 1220, John of Sacrobosco, for instance, issues a treatise "On the Sphere"[23] that becomes the standard account of the structural feature of the geocentric model of the cosmos. One notices here both empirical and a priori arguments for holding that the shape of the earth and the encompassing heaven are spherical. A raft of technical terms (e.g., equant, solstice, horizon, and zenith) are developed to calculate the apparent motions of celestial bodies as well as the seasonal changes noticed in the rotation of the sun and in the field of fixed stars. With each generation the problems that emerge for matching calculated predictions to the observational data seem to grow more cumbersome. There are occasional figures such as the Islamic scholar Thābit ibn Qurra[24] who tries to replace various Ptolemaic devices wholesale with strategies of his own for calculating the periodic variations in the gradual drift of the equinox and solstice points to the east along the zodiac. But in line with the basic mechanisms of the model for handling the sun and the fixed stars as clustered in concentric spheres, these theorists persevere in the project of "saving the phenomena" by proposing and refining the calculative mechanisms. They introduce, for example, the epicycle (the small circle on which a planet is imagined as being carried while moving along the circumference of its sphere) and the equant (an imagined point at which the celestial motion of the various bodies would actually appear as uniform in velocity).

The treatises "On the Planets" tend to concentrate on calculating planetary motions as they appear from the surface of the earth as a composite of distinct motions whose resultant sum can be determined on the basis of certain mathematical tables.[25] The range and accuracy of these tables steadily surpass what Ptolemy had provided. Islamic materials are introduced into the Latin West such as through the translations made by Adelard of Bath[26] in the twelfth century. The philosophical justifications are aided by the Greek materials that Robert Grosseteste and others arrange to have translated.[27] For easier understanding of how to use these tables and the model that undergirded them, elaborate computational instruments are developed. The astrolabe, for instance, employs a concentric series of wheels to serve as physical models of the orbits of the plants, the ecliptic, the equant, and the epicycle.

3   NATURE AND FREEDOM

The increasing use of mechanical models has the effect of confirming the cohesiveness of the whole system. But the technical developments in the machinery also raises theoretical questions about the apparent incomparability of Ptolemaic eccentrics, equants, and epicycles with Aristotle's view of concentric spheres with uniform motion around a common center of focus.[28] Further, the use of these devices always risks the possibility of mistaking a computational model for a physical model. Interestingly, the development of such practical instruments served medieval astrologers nicely. They needed to be independent of weather in dealing with the position of the planets for the casting of horoscopes. But it is important to distinguish astrology from astronomy. Popular fascination with the magical and superstitious approaches to the heavens can easily obscure the real progress that was being made in the development of natural philosophy during the Middle Ages.

Throughout the medieval period, one finds in properly philosophical texts a sustained interest in understanding the cosmos astronomically combined with a principled opposition to astrology.[29] This latter goal is connected with efforts to provide a sound philosophical defense of free choice of the will,[30] and it is important to appreciate this question as a crucial aspect of the medieval philosophy of nature. It is precisely by the progressive disenchantment of the cosmos that there was further progress in philosophical understanding of human nature as well as in the area of cosmology. By the efforts to understand the entire physical universe in terms of natural causes rather than in terms of occult magical forces, philosophy secured some of the theoretical foundations for defending the view that human beings can make free choices and are not ineluctably under the control of fate.[31]

The problem is, of course, highly complex. The very effort to break away from the fatalism associated with astrology by explaining the cosmos in terms of natural ("secondary") causes directly engenders other philosophical problems. How there can be human freedom in a world that is under universal causal determination? How there can be genuine human freedom if God is truly omniscient? This dual problematic regularly proved to be a stimulus for medieval philosophizing on the subject. In some formulations, the prospect of theological determinism arises from certain positions that can be taken on questions in natural philosophy about time and temporality. But from early in the medieval period there is also a recognition that regarding God as within time is a misleading way of asking these questions. Doing so risks implying that God has a mode of knowing that is like our own – in particular, that God is able to know our freely chosen actions only by watching how they turn out. Such a formulation of the problem, as Boethius shows,[32] invariably leads to a situation in which one would have to deny that God truly knows our free choices "in advance." If God had certainty about our choices in advance, then these "choices" could never be otherwise than they way they do turn out, and hence would not really be "free" choices that could have been otherwise had we so chosen. But if our choices are truly free and truly do not even exist until we make them, then there is nothing for God to know "in advance," prior to the moment of our choices, even if this outcome seems to compromise divine omniscience. Much in the spirit of Augustine, Boethius urges that the formulation of the question as a matter of divine *foreknowledge* actually generates a false problem. God is not within time, but above or outside of time. God's eternity should not be envisioned as the endless duration of an infinite succession of moments, but as a timeless moment in which all is present at once in the mind of the maker. God's perfect knowledge of such free creatures as ourselves is thus more like the knowledge of an artist than the knowledge of a spectator.[33]

Recognizing that a strong theory of secondary causes in the terrestrial realm threatens to subject human freedom to total causal determinism, medieval philosophers articulate a philosophy of human nature that includes a defense of the spirituality of the soul, as we will see in the upcoming chapter on the concept of soul. They articulate a notion of the soul as having a rational nature that is real but includes various spiritual powers like intellect and will, and thus one that is neither entirely subject to physical causality nor entirely exempt from physical causality. What makes it possible for medieval philosophers, especially those in the Aristotelian tradition, to assert both is the claim that the rational soul of a human being is united to a body as the substantial form of the individual, but that it is also capable of existing on its own after death. Its powers of intellect and will do depend on various bodily powers such as the senses, but they are not reducible to those material aspects of embodied being on which they depend during life in this world. The mind, in modern terminology, depends on the brain but is not reducible to the brain. The will is manifest in the drives and desires of the flesh and the emotions but is not reducible to them. The will is a rational appetite and can increase or decrease in freedom insofar as the person develops in self-mastery.[34]

By virtue of this approach to the problem in terms of matter-form composition (a theory called "hylemorphism" from the Greek words, respectively, for matter and form), medieval thinkers believed themselves able to defend the freedom of human choice. They could thus simultaneously hold that a human being is subject to any number of physical influences (even by the stars) without having to deny the reality of free choice. By having souls that include such immaterial powers as the intellect and the will, human beings can make genuinely free choices. These faculties are the immaterial powers natural for the souls of rational beings, and they can allow us to resist the physical forces operating on us and inclining us toward one option or another. When human nature is seen in this way, the background picture of a cosmos in which various planets, stars, and constellations continually exercise various degrees of causal influence on earthly life thus does not imply that human freedom is constrained by fate. This view of things stands in contrast to more fatalistic visions of the human person in which freedom is largely limited to whether one will cooperate with one's ineluctable destiny. Those views appear more credible to the degree that the Ptolemaic model of the cosmos is taken not as a calculative model but as a physical model that links the celestial and terrestrial regions in an all-encompassing network of causal chains.

There are considerable philosophical and religious reasons for opposing any such fatalism. Presumably one wants to maintain the sovereign freedom of God and the moral responsibility that comes with human freedom. By alertness to the kind of model at work in representations of the cosmos, one will be in a stronger position to defend human freedom from astral determinism and to handle related questions, such as the relation of human free choice to divine providence. As we have noted above, medieval thinkers tend to be heavily reliant upon the *Timaeus* of Plato for their understanding of the structures of the created world. Yet, many of them judge one of the central aspects of Plato's teaching to be completely unacceptable in this regard: the notion of a world-soul that animates and regulates the universe. In one way, the notion of a world-soul is attractive to them. It seems to provide the entire cosmos, and particularly its most noble constituent, humanity, with an especially close relation to the Creator. The idea of a world-soul provides a kind of spiritual affinity. But much as they tried to adapt the notion so as to make it religiously acceptable, it proved recalcitrant to an orthodox interpretation and had to be abandoned.[35] The following chapter will consider the range of views about soul that were developed instead by medieval philosophers, but first we will consider the implications of the concept of nature for moral philosophy.

4   NATURE AS A SOURCE FOR ETHICS

The recovery of the Aristotelian concept of nature that was made possible by the translation of Aristotle's texts during the twelfth and thirteenth centuries (first from Arabic and later from Greek) is indispensable for the development of medieval views on the natural moral law. It provides a new and helpful way to think about the moral sphere in terms that are at once intrinsic to human existence in this world and linked to its divine source. By virtue of their religious commitments, medieval thinkers understand God the Creator as the author of all natures, including human nature. Human beings, they reason, bear a special relation to the Creator, for they exhibit not only the relationship that any effect bears to its cause, but also the special similarities that come from being "made in God's image and likeness." The Aristotelian way of understanding nature as the teleological (end-directed) dynamism within any given kind of thing had allowed Aristotle himself to articulate an ethics of virtue without direct reference to God or to law.[36] But the recovery of this view of nature within the deeply religious context of the Middle Ages enables scholastic thinkers to produce a rich, vibrant theory of natural law ethics. Seeing God as the author of every nature permits them to identify the intelligence that directs even those kinds of being without intelligence to their own set of ends. God's providential wisdom has established an end worthy of personal beings made in the divine image and likeness. By various innate tendencies, God provides certain natural inclinations by which human beings are motivated to realize this end. Yet they remain free to make their own choices and are morally responsible for what they choose. This remarkable synthesis of nature and freedom in a unified moral theory struck many medieval philosophers as deeply consistent with what they know by revelation, and yet as philosophically powerful and cogent in its own right.

Thomas Aquinas is the most well-known proponent of this approach, but in fact there is a wide range of natural law thinkers from the middle of the twelfth century to the end of the thirteenth. Their argumentation is predominantly philosophical, even though various theological commitments derived from the Scriptures and from religious tradition (such as the doctrines of original sin and the redemption of humanity by Christ) play a crucial role in shaping their understanding of natural law.

The typical medieval conception of natural law ethics can be distinguished from its ancient models (especially the rather fatalistic view of natural necessity championed by the Stoics) by the role assigned to divine providence. It also differs from most modern versions of natural law. Beginning with sixteenth-century political thinkers like Hobbes and Locke, modern natural law proponents place much more stress on rationality and on human autonomy. They often do so out of a desire to have a rational, universal, and objective basis for moral claims.[37]

The general idea of natural law ethics in the medieval period is that reason can discover in human nature a law implanted by God, the author of that nature. The confidence that scholastic thinkers feel about this prospect is made possible by the creative philosophical work on nature stimulated by the retrieval of Aristotelian natural philosophy. The general Aristotelian notion of a thing's "nature" as its internal principle of structure and development is applicable to humanity as much as to any other species. But the sense of "nature" envisioned by almost all scholastic philosophers is typically correlated with the notion of "creature."[38]

Because they have a created nature like any other species does, human beings can be considered from the perspective of their natural patterns of growth and development without abandoning the notion that they stand under the government and guidance of divine providence. Yet the crucial passages in Genesis and in the letters of St Paul that mark out various important differences between human nature and any other created nature vastly complicate the picture. The difference is not that human beings lack a nature, but that human beings alone naturally bear the image and likeness of God in their possession of freedom and rationality. The Christian tradition, especially in the Augustinian interpretation that dominates most medieval exegesis, sees human nature as deeply wounded by original sin and thus not entirely trustworthy for giving us moral insight. Although redeemed by Christ, all human beings still suffer the effects of this original sin.

The main effects of original sin are thought to be threefold: darkened intellects, weakened wills, and certain disordered inclinations. It is precisely these disabilities that make thinkers prior to the Aristotelian revival suspect that the concept of nature is an unlikely source for much reliable moral knowledge. Even those scholastic thinkers who become most enthusiastic about nature as a source of moral knowledge retain a strong conviction about the need for grace if one is to gain eternal salvation. This makes for interesting questions about the precise relation of morality to one's salvation. On the other hand, a strongly pessimistic view of the extent of the damage induced by original sin renders natural law theories of any sort suspect to some thinkers and leads them to prefer divine command theories of morality instead.[39]

Precisely because of the cognitive, volitional, and affective afflictions brought on by original sin, proponents of natural law ethics invariably need to ascertain just which features of human nature are normative and which are not. They also have to face the task of how human reasoning relates to divine revelation in moral matters. There are questions about the relation of nature to custom, legislation, social practices, and political arrangements. Medieval ethics could, of course, have evolved along other lines, by giving prominence to such notions as society considered as an organic body or to the idea of the three orders of society, but the notion of nature predominates in later medieval discussions of ethics after the recovery of the Aristotelian sense of this cosmos.

A brief mention of certain common objections to natural law ethics today may help in elucidating the medieval view. First, for some, the very idea of a fixed common nature is unacceptable. There is often a strong sense, for instance, that human plasticity is sufficient for us to refashion ourselves almost indefinitely and that natural boundaries are all, in principle, able to be crossed, given enough time and energy. A second objection arises from absence of belief in God, and this is often coupled today with belief in evolution. Nature then seems more a matter of the extent to which a given species has developed thus far rather than something morally normative. At best we may be able to ascertain what is most effective for survival or flourishing, whether for individuals or for the group. But to assign any more weight than what is biologically pragmatic would seem unwarranted. Third, proponents of the hermeneutic of suspicion have voiced the notion that the theological aspects of natural law theory are but the signs of the imposition of the views of the powerful on the powerless under the guise of nature as if it were something objectively normative. Finally, there have been significant objections of a technical philosophical nature. Usually these have been associated with the charge of the "naturalistic fallacy," the objection formulated by G. E. Moore on the basis of David Hume's reflections on the difference between fact and value and the allegation that it is logically impossible to derive an ought from an is, that is, the impossibility of deriving moral conclusions about obligation from descriptions of how human nature simply is.

These typical objections to natural law ethics mainly arise in some of the areas where medieval thought differs most from modern thought.

1 Medieval concerns with the problem of universals, as we saw in chapter 4, make for great attentiveness to what distinguishes differences in kind from differences in degree. There is much to learn from medieval treatments about the predicables genus and species and universal that is crucial for evaluating the claims of natural law ethics.[40]

2 A philosophical commitment to atheism would presumably preclude religious versions of natural law ethics. But one could equally well ask if the cogency of natural law ethics might not require one to reopen the question of God's existence. Scholastic philosophers never regard the idea of human nature as inflexibly static or overly narrow. They see its dynamism to reside not in the evolutionary generation of one species from another but in the teleological drive to growth and maturation of an individual within a given species. What is permitted, forbidden, or obligatory varies in relation to the individual's stage of development as well as the specific situation. But this relativity to such objective factors as the pattern of maturation natural to a species or the obligations that one may bear by reason of one's situation (being a parent or a spouse, for instance) is not a matter of arbitrariness but only of specificity.

3 If anything, it is the divine command versions of morality rather than theories of natural law ethics that raise a worry about the imposition of the views of a theological authority. The ultimate

sanction here seems to be that "God commands such and such." The authority in question has enormous influence in stating and interpreting what it is that God commands. By contrast, natural law ethics is the sort of moral theory that proposes intelligibility as a fundamental aspect of any moral criterion, and thus by its very nature it invites reason and discussion rather than authoritative pronouncement.

4 Regarding the charge of the naturalistic fallacy, there has been much recent fruitful discussion about whether there really is a logical fallacy here.[41] In general, it is important to remember that medieval versions of natural law ethics do not understand the natural law approach as a matter of reading off a static or complete set of dos and don'ts. Rather, natural law involves a kind of moral reasoning that was philosophically insightful even while respecting religious beliefs about a providential creator, a sinful humanity, and divinely initiated process of human redemption.

5 THE TRANSFORMATION OF ANCIENT SOURCES IN THE MEDIEVAL DEVELOPMENT OF NATURAL LAW THEORY

In antiquity one can find a certain awareness of the natural moral law, but some of the main ancient sources for modern natural law theory were unknown to the Middle Ages. The dramatic case of Antigone, for instance, who insisted that a higher law from God required her to violate the edict of Creon and bury her brother is often cited by natural law theorists today. The texts of ancient tragedy, however, were not available until the Renaissance. Aristotle provides a crucial piece of the puzzle by developing the concept of teleology as a central part of the concept of nature. But for Aristotle, the normative dimension of nature takes the form of an ethics of the virtues rather than the form of a natural law theory.[42] The ancient source for the idea of natural law is Stoicism, and medieval thinkers know this source largely through Cicero. Stoicism, however, tends to be fatalistic in ways that Christian authors found unacceptable. A third indispensable element in the picture comes from certain non-negotiable religious commitments, such as belief in a providential creator who orders creatures toward ends of divine design as well as a tremendous amount of emphasis on personal responsibility for one's deliberate actions.

The Aristotelian contribution to the medieval notion of natural law consists especially in an understanding of nature, including human nature, as having a deeply teleological structure. In general, a thing's nature for Aristotle is determined by the dominant ("substantial") form that is intrinsic to any natural object and that unfolds from within an entity according to the structures and patterns typical of the beings of a given kind or species. By virtue of this orientation toward a goal, there is a spontaneous inclination toward the full actualization of the potentialities within the being. As rational animals, human beings for Aristotle manifest the same basic goal-directed ("teleological") structure as other animals. But they differ in that the highest capabilities of this nature are rational. The rational control that humans have over their actions means that their inbuilt drives toward their ends needs to be mediated by many deliberate choices. Among the points that Aristotle emphasizes in this regard is our capacity for speech and for life in community with others (domestic life, political life, social life). At the summit of the inclinations that characterize our existence are the desires for knowledge and for fulfillment (for what he called *eudaimonia* or happiness).

There are occasional references to natural law in Aristotle, but his ethics as a whole is not an ethics organized around the idea of law. Rather, it is an ethics of virtue. He contributes at least as much as any other single source to the medieval idea of natural or acquired virtue. In the argument of *Nicomachean Ethics* I.7, we find Aristotle's argument that nature does have an important role to play in ethics. This passage serves as a springboard for medieval natural law theorists. In it, Aristotle argues that every species of animal has a "proper function," that is, a specific trait or ability that is its specific difference. Doing that function well constitutes virtue for beings of that nature. Reason is the function specifically characteristic of human beings, and reasoning well is the measure of virtue in general and for the particular virtue of justice that is indispensable for living within any forms of society. The further development of his reflections on virtue in general in book three of the *Ethics* and on specific virtues in subsequent books thus have a basis in nature. He does not tend to handle questions of morality or political philosophy under the category of natural law. Why he does not take the route that medieval Aristotelians would often take is a matter of scholarly speculation, but it seems likely that the reason has to do with the notion that law needs a law-giver. Even if one has reasons for one's legislation that are intellectually grounded on the nature of individual or social flourishing and that eschew any form of arbitrariness, the enactment of law presumably requires that it be the formal result of someone's decision.[43] Aristotle's idea of God is neither that of a creator nor of a legislator. Unlike the medieval understanding of God, the Aristotelian idea is that of a God who is pure mind, completely involved in endless contemplation but unrelated to the cosmos. Even though having a nature is intrinsic to all physical objects, the "natures" of Aristotelian physics are eternal, not created. They are not the result of any divine decision. With no divine author of the natures of things in view, there is simply no reason to be thinking in terms of a divine legislator of morality. Indeed, morality for Aristotle has an entirely different ground, namely, the proper function of reason in practical matters of doing and making.

It is the Stoics who provide to the Middle Ages this crucial second component of natural law ethics. Yet their view of natural law is also very different from medieval versions. The basic Stoic notion is that all of the universe (all of nature) is permeated by a *logos* ("reason") that gives the *nomos* ("law") by which everything exists and acts. Rational beings (especially human beings and gods) have a special share in this *logos*, and human beings can become conscious of this *nomos* by "right reasoning" (*orthos logos*). To live in accordance with this natural order is virtue. Not to do so is folly, for nature will invariably win out, and one will invariably suffer if one tries to go against nature. Thus, for the Stoics there is freedom of choice, but anything other than observing the natural law is ultimately futile.

The technical terminology of the Stoic view on natural law comes in many respects from Cicero. Cicero is a skeptic rather than a Stoic, but he accurately transmits the views of the Stoics to the Middle Ages. There is a law of the universe, he tells us, a *lex aeterna et perpetua* ("an eternal and perpetual law") that is the *summa ratio insita in natura* ("highest reason built into nature"). Human customs or decisions that contradict it may not legitimately claim the label "law." What is more, every human being has the seed of the knowledge of this law (the *lumen naturae* or "light of nature"). As a result, there are insights of a moral character that we simply cannot fail to know. These things constitute *ius naturae* (what is "right by nature"), and thereby provide the source of knowledge about what it is right and just to do in the legal and political order. Cicero also provides the terms *ius gentium* ("law of the nations," later "international law") and *ius civile* ("civil law").

Another important stimulus for scholastic reflection on natural law ethics comes from the sphere of jurisprudence. The monk Gratian produced a massive work entitled *Concordance of Discordant Canons*[44] in the 1140s, in the effort to bring some coherence to the mass of church law that had accumulated by that time. Gratian's collection encouraged philosophical reflection both by its method of resolving difficulties and by some explicit and thematic consideration of questions about the nature of law and justice. Gratian's method involved the juxtaposition of conflicting legal positions such as the canons issued by various ecclesiastical councils and various judicial opinions about the resolution of cases. He then attempted his own reconciliation of differences, often by the introduction of some decisive distinction. The influence of his method, not only on the legal education at Bologna but on philosophical and theological education at Paris and Oxford, is enormous. R. W. Southern argues that this highly formalized method is one important result of the pervasive medieval quest for a complete system of knowledge; it gives evidence of the reverent attitude to books and authorities typical of the entire period.[45] Scholastic explorations of natural law exhibit a similar pattern of analyzing such varied texts and authorities as the Bible, Church fathers, and Roman jurists.

As one particularly telling example, we might consider the reconciliation attempted between conflicting texts on the source of natural law from the tradition of Roman jurisprudence. As cited in the *Digests*, Ulpian held the view that natural law is what nature teaches all animals, including the human, in contrast to any form of human-made legislation. But other Roman jurists such as Gaius, apparently under Stoic influence,[46] treat natural law as virtually equivalent to the application of reason to human life. The resolution to the question that Aquinas suggests affirms both positions by means of a careful distinction. There is, he argues, a natural law that is common to humanity and other animals. God the author of all these natures, providentially directs each kind of creature to a useful course of conduct by implanting in every being an inclination toward what is good for beings of that kind. But human nature can be distinguished from every other form of animal nature precisely by the power of reason. The natural moral law, Aquinas insists, is the specifically human form of participation in the providence of God. Where other kinds of creature participate by instinctively responding to whatever appears to them as attractive or dangerous, human beings participate in it by subjecting whatever appears good or bad to the scrutiny of reason. Needless to say, the power of reason does not come fully formed in human children but needs to be trained. Thus our human participation in natural law is both like and unlike the way in which every other creature is governed by divine providence. Although the natural moral law governs all human beings, it is possible for a given human being to observe that law well or poorly, dependent not only on how well an individual is prepared to resolve questions requiring judgment and decision, but on how well or poorly a culture prepares its members to do so.

This position on natural law stresses the connection between the human and the divine. As Aquinas points out, natural law is our human participation in the providence of the eternal law. But there is also a connection to the animal world, of which we are such a distinctive part. What we cannot help but notice in medieval treatments of natural law is an organic unity between reason and the sub-rational aspects of human nature. Reason is different from our sensory powers in kind, yet never isolated from them. Except for those cases in which we are granted some special illumination from God, our reason needs the data provided by our bodily senses as input to reflect upon. The very way in which we receive any such sensory input can, and regularly does have, an emotional and appetitive coloration. We might feel spontaneously attracted or revulsed from something. We can readily feel inclined or fearful. Our human form of participation in the natural law involves our bringing those movements of desire and emotion under the judgment of reasoning. The individual must ask whether any perceived good is worth pursuing (or where a perceived evil is worth avoiding). We can likewise ask about the means that it will be necessary to employ in order to gain or avoid it, and the likely consequences of achieving any course we should decide upon.

Crucial then among the distinctions that reason must make in coming to some practical decision is the distinction between genuine and merely apparent goods, and the relative ranking of any good on the hierarchy of being. We need to be mindful of any relevant factors operative in the situation at the time. One might, for example, be deeply aware of the need to do one's work, even though it seems drudgery, in order to feed one's family, and have to forgo something as pleasant as contemplation of beautiful objects or even the study of philosophy. Later medieval moralists, troubled and sometimes amused by the possible complexity of the calculations that could easily be needed to sort these things out, develop a sophisticated casuistry for the resolution of a vast range of cases. But those efforts at the systematization of the process of moral inquiry should not overshadow the mainstream tradition here that yokes natural law reasoning within an individual to the cultivation of the virtue of prudence.

Prudence, as Aristotle suggests, is the moral habit or disposition by which one can readily and effectively see a situation in a realistic way, neither over-optimistically nor over-pessimistically. One will then be in a position to come to a rightly ordered decision that is neither paralyzed by endless deliberation nor overly hasty because of having been reached without enough deliberation. Intrigued by Aristotle's own remarks on the profound connection of this intellectual virtue and all the other more properly moral virtues, medieval moralists debate at length about whether one could have this virtue without the other cardinal virtues – justice, temperance, and courage. They wonder about whether there are many different virtues or really only one, seen under different aspects. They notice how difficult it would be to become truly courageous, for instance, without also having prudence. One needs to see a situation realistically so as to know what is truly dangerous, given one's own genuine strengths and weaknesses, and one needs to be able to bring oneself to decisions in a timely manner. Conversely, it is hard to conceive of knowing a situation realistically and bringing deliberation to a timely point of decision if one did not have some of the genuine disposition to meet real danger courageously. In short, one can readily see the case made by medieval thinkers for treating the virtues as distinct and yet for seeing virtue as ultimately one.

In medieval versions of natural law theory, there is considerable stress on the virtue of prudence as crucial for a well-developed conscience. An individual needs to be able to discern what is genuinely good from what is really harmful. Here, in discussing the question of knowledge, it is crucial to distinguish between the thematic sort of knowledge that a moral theorist seeks to gain (the *scientia* of ethics, natural law ethics as an academic discipline, perhaps as part of moral theology) and the sort of knowledge that any person whatsoever needs to gain in order to live well and make the right decisions in life. This sort of knowledge need not at all be thematic or explicitly stated in propositions in the way that would satisfy a theorist. Yet it is knowledge nonetheless, and some of it will take the form of propositions, even if much of morality is known through submitting one's inclinations to reflection and judgment.

What Aristotle calls the practical syllogism strikes medieval theorists as a useful formalization of the reasoning that often takes place much less formally or explicitly. The facility that human beings show in bringing the options that present themselves to us under the right general rule shows the importance of the virtue of prudence for observing the natural moral law. One might, for instance, feel the attraction of taking revenge for an insult or of satisfying some desire for food. But right reasoning (*recta ratio*) means knowing how to submit these apparent goods (the expected satisfaction of seeing a wrong-doer suffer consequences for his deed, or of having the good feeling of a full stomach) to the test of genuine goodness: is this a real case of injustice, or is it a quest for power or superiority? Is this good really good for me, or is it likely to unsettle the humors?

For the easier availability of sound general principles and sound practical reasoning, medieval natural law theorists articulate sophisticated models of conscience.[47] They emphasize the need for the formation of conscience by the development of such virtues as prudence, but they also stress the value of authoritative statements to record the principles that one needs to bring to bear. The commandments of the Decalogue are relevant in this regard, and many a medieval theorist sees them not as arbitrary assertions of divine will but as divine declarations about what is most in accord with human nature. Not only the commandments of the so-called "Second Tablet" dealing with human society (e.g., Honor thy father and thy mother, Do not kill, Do not commit adultery, and so on) but even the "First Tablet" commandments dealing with human relations to God (e.g., Thou shalt have no other gods, Keep holy the sabbath, etc.) strike these authors as truths parallel to the moral insights about the natural law that are in principle available to right reason. That is, a given person might know God's existence by faith or by reason; but however one comes to know about God, one ought to honor God as the supreme being, one ought to place nothing else before this God in one's affections, and one ought to do whatever God commands, including worship.

With his characteristic penchant for structures, Aquinas refers to these biblical precepts as "divine law," that is, the explicit specification of important precepts of the eternal law insofar as it specifically governs humanity. Human beings, he explains, could in principle come to discover much of the content of these precepts by natural law reasoning, that is, by their own reason reflecting on human nature as part of our participation in the eternal law that God has providentially inscribed within that nature. But precisely because not everyone has the same inclination to such intellectual labor, nor the same ability to do it, nor sufficient leisure, God has providentially revealed these precepts for the guidance of our consciences. Since we are responsible for what we have known or should have known, the demands of morality are higher for those to whom these precepts have been disclosed by revelation. Yet anyone who has reached a certain stage of reasoning bears responsibility under the natural law for observing the basic obligations of morality, at least to the extent that individual and cultural preparation has enabled, or at least not hindered, the development of right reasoning about the natural moral law.

One sees here a medieval way of being attentive to the problem of relativity of experience across times and cultures. That a given individual does not know the relevant general principle may mitigate or even remove responsibility altogether if there is no way that one could reasonably expect the individual to have known it. There might, for instance, be some cultural blindness or some factor in a given individual's history. But in no way does this allowance for factors that can genuinely restrict personal or culpability impugn the objectivity of the moral order. For Aquinas, the moral order is as universal as human nature, for there is a single author of that nature in God. It may, rather, provide a reason to judge that one culture is inferior or superior to another, just as it might give reason to judge that one person had made more progress in moral maturity or in the growth of some virtue than another.

Put in terms of conscience, there may even be a reason to hold that a given person is subjectively less blameworthy, or perhaps not culpable at all, for doing something that, considered in itself, is objectively immoral. In this moral theory one is trying to measure not only the reality of some act against the divine standard but also trying to ascertain the status of how much a given individual knew and how free the person was to act. In this respect, the status of moral truths and moral knowledge follows the general track of epistemological realism to be discussed in the following chapter on the soul. A knowledge-claim in the mind is thought true if it adequately represents the proper relationship of agent and object, and the act in turn is ultimately judged against the standards of God's intention. Even though we may have no direct access to the Divine Ideas, we have other routes available for moral insight. We may come to know God's intentions by the self-disclosure of revelation. Likewise, we might come to know it by reflection on the natures that God has created; we can discern certain things about God's intention for watching how they move toward their real fulfillment and determining what would frustrate them. This latter approach is the route of natural law reasoning. When treated in a speculative way, it can be the basis of a body of knowledge (a moral *scientia*), but it is more a matter of "connatural" knowledge when considered as found in an ordinary person's inclinations. But just as the propositions of ethics need to be subjected to the scrutiny of theoretical reasoning, one's inclinations need to be subjected to the scrutiny of right reasoning in the practical order.

For medieval theorists of natural law, the problem of correlating moral theory and ethical practice is intensified as the result of the damage done by original sin. The darker one's reading of this situation, of course, the less likely one may be willing to think that natural law is going to help. How darkened in the human intellect? How weak is the will? How disordered the inclinations? If the damage to any one of them is too severe, the very possibility of natural law reasoning is dampened or even extinguished. To pursue these questions is to ask if it is possible to know human nature sufficiently, not only in its principle but in its ends and goals,[48] so as to feel the compelling cogency that is a mark of truth. This sort of compelling cogency is a general feature of knowledge in the strong sense and distinguishes it from, say, a guess that happens by luck to be right, or an opinion without grounds from strong levels of knowledge-claims. In any discipline, one more truly "knows" anything to the extent that one has grounds for saying that it could not fail to be the case: whereas one had better humbly refrain from making claims as certain when one has less stable grounds. In matters of logic, mathematics, or metaphysics, one can more easily get to a point of an exhaustive dichotomy, rule out one of the alternatives, and then feel the cogency of the remaining alternative. But to get to this level of certainty is harder in human affairs. Nevertheless, medieval natural law, especially by making its important distinction between moral *scientia* and prudential knowledge, could still articulate claims about moral truth according to human nature. In things that proceed by nature (that are the same "always or for the most part," as Aristotle noted), one has genuine knowledge, but knowledge of a different kind than, say, in mathematics or logic. One has not ruled out every alternative, but one may – with enough hard work in observation, comparison, abstraction, and careful formulation – understand what it is that human nature requires, or what it is that would always and everywhere injure or offend. A number of medieval theorists, for precisely this reason, are more confident in holding that the negative universal principles of the natural law have greater prominence than the positive precepts. All of these considerations depend, of course, in important ways, on the basic concept of human nature, and medieval philosophers tend to consider this through the concept of the soul, to which we now turn.

NOTES

1   See Lewis (1964), pp. 17, 92–121.
2   On the history of the idea of the Milky Way, see Jaki (1972), esp. pp. 33–67 for his discussion of medieval contributions to this notion.
3   See Ptolemy (1998). Ptolemy's original text was translated into Latin from Greek in 1160 and from Arabic in 1175.

4   The popular perception of the Middle Ages as a period having no inter-
    est in empirical investigations neglects the vast efforts in both Europe
    and the Middle East to perfect astronomical tables and instruments such
    as the quadrant and the astrolabe that were needed to render the
    Ptolemaic model practical in the form of almanacs, horoscopes, and
    planetaria. Islamic astronomers especially labored to complete certain
    unfinished parts of Ptolemy's project, such as the long-term motions
    involved in the "precession" of the sphere of fixed stars. Europeans
    focused on improving the usefulness and accessibility of the material
    for travel and less worthily for astrology.

5   For an overview of the process by which the basic model changed, see
    Randles (1999).

6   Galileo's *De Revolutionibus orbium caelestium* (1543) was published
    only in the year of Copernicus' death. It contains six books that in many
    ways parallel the structure of Ptolemy's *Almagest* but with appropriate
    adaptations for the repositioning of the earth and the sun. Galileo's
    work set off the modern phase of the process of finding a suitable model
    for the universe by proposing a solar system in which the earth takes
    the place that had been occupied by the sun and resolves around the
    sun in a way that produces the motions that appear to anyone on the
    surface of the earth as the result of the earth's own daily rotation on
    its axis. See Koestler (1968) for a charming account of how the major
    discoveries in modern astronomy were invariably made by theorists
    intent on proving something other than what the data eventually forced
    them to propose.

7   Galilei (2001). For background, see Blackwell (1991) and Machamer
    (1998).

8   See the recent statements by Pope John Paul II (1979) and (1992). For
    Galileo's own affirmation that the truths of science and the truths of
    faith are in ultimate harmony, see his letter to Father Benedetto Castelli
    on 21 December 1613, in Blackwell (1991).

9   For example, consider the following comment by Aquinas made in the
    course of his treatise on the Trinity at *Summa of Theology* I.32.1 ad 2,
    in Aquinas (1945): "Reason may be employed in two ways to establish
    a point: firstly, for the purpose of furnishing sufficient proof of some
    principle, as in natural science, where sufficient proof can be brought
    to show that the movement of the heavens is always of uniform velocity.
    Reason is employed in another way, not as furnishing a sufficient proof
    of a principle, but as confirming an already established principle, by
    showing the congruity of its results, as in astronomy the theory of
    eccentrics and epicycles is considered as established, because thereby
    the sensible appearances of the heavenly movements can be explained;

not, however, as if this proof were sufficient, forasmuch as some other theory might explain them." For Aquinas' sense that other astronomical hypotheses are possible, see his commentary on Aristotle's *On the Heavens* II.l.17, in Aquinas (1963).

10 Galileo (2001) use the term "systems of the world," as in his *Dialogue concerning the Two Chief World Systems*, and this usage is evidence of awareness that different models were in question.

11 The *Timaeus* was one of the few works of Plato to receive Latin translation prior to the Renaissance. Among the best modern explications of the *Timaeus* is Cornford (1997). For a fine set of essays on the reception of the *Timaeus* in antiquity, the Middle Ages, and the early modern period, see Reydams-Schils (2003).

12 Capella (1977).

13 Macrobius (1990).

14 See Boethius (2000). For a fine study of the astronomical views of this period, see Danielson (2000) and Grant (1994).

15 *On the Heavens*, in Aristotle (1984), vol. 1, pp. 447–511.

16 One of the best accounts of the systematizing penchant on medieval thinkers is found in Southern (1995), pp. 30–9. See also Lewis (1964), pp. 11f.

17 See *On the Heavens*, parts 9 and 10, in Aristotle (1984).

18 Even the disciplined study of any one part of this world needs to confront the fact that things do not always happen in exactly the same way, with perfect invariance, but "on the whole and for the most part." See *On Generation and Corruption* 778a and *Politics* 1255b, both in Aristotle (1984).

19 Parmenides provokes the long-running concern of ancient philosophy with being and becoming by his maxim, "from nothing, nothing comes." Likewise, what changes could being (what is) experience except to become non-being (what it is not)? For an account of the way in which the paradoxes of Parmenides engaged but eventually paralyzed Greek natural philosophy, see Warren (2007). Aristotle's resolution of the problem involves distinguishing between the predicative meaning of being (e.g., "cocker spaniels *are* dogs") and its existential sense ("there *are* some cocker spaniels over there"). This distinction allows one to explain that being can change without becoming non-being. In a "substantial change" the matter that constituted the being or substance is given entirely different form, so it continues to exist even if the being that it constituted no longer does. In an "accidental change" the being continues to exist but some of its dependent features are altered, e.g., by the acquisition or loss of matter in what one eats or grows bald, the development or degeneration of some skill through

practicing a musical instrument or forgetting what one once knew, and so on.

20 See especially *Physics* II, in Aristotle (1984).

21 For example, *Republic* VI–VII, in Plato (1997) for the analogy of the sun, the divided line, and the parable of the cave. These texts promote a strong sense of the distinction between the intelligible realm as immutable and the mutability of the material world.

22 See Sorabji (1987).

23 See Thorndike (1949).

24 See Carmody (1960).

25 The Toledan Tables were generated by the eleventh-century al-Zarqāli; the Alphonsine Tables were compiled at the command of Alfonso X of Spain in the 1260s and remained in wide use into the sixteenth century.

26 See Björno et al. (1997).

27 See Southern (1986), esp. pp. 92–107 and pp. 142–9.

28 Eccentrics are the epicycles of various cycles and different angular velocities of rotation are still required in Copernicus' system, much as they were in Ptolemy's; the difference is that Copernicus needs only 34 instead of 55.

29 The history of these developments in well narrated in French and Cunningham (1996) and Lloyd (1979).

30 The philosophical defense of free choice of the will is a much larger project that deserves separate treatment beyond the scope of the present essay. For one of the earliest and most enduring contributions to a long debate, see *On Free Choice of the Will* in Augustine (1982b).

31 Some important early episodes in the long history of this argument during the Middle Ages can be found in passing within *Confessions*, esp. VII, in Augustine (1991b) and *Consolation of Philosophy* V, in Boethius (2000). There are many important treatments of the subject in later scholastic philosophy; by way of example, see *Summa of Theology* I–II.116.4, in Aquinas (1945) for a defense of the role of secondary causes. One can see certain developments in Greek and Roman thought on the subject by noticing the increasing identification of the decisions of Zeus (Jupiter) with Fate. Other gods and goddesses (Juno and Venus, for instance, in the *Aeneid* have a certain liberty to advance the causes of their dependents, but ultimately their destinies are determined. Even when the religious background shifts from paganism to Christianity, the gravity of the problem of fate remains. Boethius' *Consolation of Philosophy* provides an interesting example of how seriously fate and astral determinism were taken by a philosopher intent on demonstrating

the fundamental compatibility of human freedom with a strong doctrine of divine omniscience.

32 *Consolation of Philosophy* Bk. V, prose 3, in Boethius (2000).

33 The later history of this problem includes Aquinas' insightful development of the comparison between divine knowledge and the sort of knowledge had by human artists – see *Truth* 3.1 in Aquinas (1993a).

34 See Kent (1995).

35 This is one of the main themes in the work of Duhem (1985).

36 Although Aristotle does on rare occasions use the phrase "natural law," the main focus of his ethics is on virtue, not on law. It is also only fair to note that Aristotle's ethics does have a place for God, even if it does not recognize God as the providential author of nature but as purely contemplative. Returning to a theme originally sounded in Book I, Aristotle (1984) argues in Book X of the *Nicomachean Ethics* for the superiority of the contemplative life to the active life, for such a person will be most godlike as well as most thoroughly engaged in the activity that is the proper function distinctive of human life, reason.

37 For a fine overview of ancient, medieval, and modern views of natural law theory, see d'Entreves (1970).

38 The exceptions here are the radical Aristotelians, who were prepared to accept the idea of eternal natures, as Aristotle himself apparently did.

39 If modern proponents on traditional natural law morality have more often than not been Catholic, this may well be related to the predominance of Thomistic thought in the response to Protestantism that developed during the Counter-Reformation and the centuries since.

40 See Simon (1992), pp. 41–66 on the importance of the question of universals. See also Adler (1993) and (1940).

41 Theorists of the "new natural law" camp generally accept the view that the naturalistic fallacy is a genuine problem and have tried to revise the teleological views associated with such medieval figures as Aquinas in order to avoid the problem. See, for instance, Finnis (1998). Others have argued that a proper understanding of teleology as a fact within human nature allows one to argue for the fact of certain obligations; see, for instance, Lisska (1996).

42 Aristotle's most explicit argument for normativity in ethics is called the proper function argument and can be found at *Nicomachean Ethics* I.7, in Aristotle (1984).

43 See, e.g., Anscombe (1958).

44 Gratian (1993).

45 Southern (1995), esp. vol. 1, chs. 7–9, pp. 235–318.

46 Colish (1985).

47 See Potts (1980). It is important to note that modern philosophy tends
    to use the term "conscience" somewhat differently, as a moral faculty
    that autonomously and intuitively tells us the difference between right
    and wrong.

48 There is much discussion among Thomists about whether there is a
    single ultimate end (beatitude, the beatific vision of God) or a twofold
    ultimate end (not only this supernatural end but also a natural end
    akin to what Aristotle called *eudaimonia*, or happiness). See Bradley
    (1997).

7

SOUL

_____

To modern ears, "soul" sounds more poetic than scientific, or at least vaguely religious. Yet the medieval concept of soul has its origins in ancient Greek science, medicine, and philosophy, and medieval discussions of this topic are unintelligible apart from these considerations. In general, what the Latin tradition calls *anima* was known as *psyche* in Greek.

By contrast, there is no place for the notion of soul in modern science. Its empirical methodology attempts to provide, as far as possible, naturalistic explanations for everything, including the psychological, in terms of physical causes and mathematically calculable forces. The postulation of unseen forces (gravity, for instance) may be undertaken only insofar as one cannot explain the data without them. In the meantime, the practitioners of the discipline in effect accept the principle of sufficient reason and put themselves under the obligation of continuing to search for an adequate explanation of the sort that makes sense within the discipline. In a sense, to use this methodological principle of parsimony in refusing to postulate any entities unneeded for explanation is to accept a principle often associated with a figure from late in the history of medieval philosophy, William of Ockham, namely, Ockham's razor.

In an effort to observe the proper methodological constraints required in modern scientific disciplines, any recourse to the notion of an immaterial soul needs to be dismissed. Some contemporary philosophers of mind have accordingly sought to explain thought, choice, and other mental experiences as epiphenomenal upon matter, that is, as effects that occur by reason of the highly complex organization of matter. It is crucial for empirical disciplines to attempt to provide their explanations without postulating entities that are in principle inaccessible by empirical means. But the necessity of respecting the methodological discipline of not resorting to an immaterial principle in one's effort to explain as much as one can by means of material principles should not be thought to be equivalent to a metaphysical assertion that denies the existence of an immaterial entity. When medieval philosophers discussed the soul, they did so by using the same principle of parsimony. In order to explain such phenomena as the unity of a living substance over time, the immaterial character of thought and knowledge, and the freedom manifest in the exercise of choice by the human will, they found it necessary to use the notion of a soul considered as a form of being that is real but immaterial.

This chapter will first lay out the main philosophical options for the concept of soul as the medieval period inherited them from Greek philosophy. It will then consider the Augustinian view that was predominant for much of the Middle Ages, and finally the changes in the concept of soul that came about with the twelfth-century recovery of the texts of Aristotle and with them the outlines of Aristotelian natural philosophy.

1 THE GREEK BACKGROUND

In ancient philosophical writings, the term "soul" designates the life-principle in anything that is alive. Hence, not only human beings but also all other animals and even all plants are thought to have a soul precisely because this is a way to explain the difference between a living being and a corpse. Considered in this way, there would be rational human souls, various kinds of animal souls, and even plant souls, different in kind from one another, but each one a life-principle. By a sort of shorthand, many ancient and medieval authors restrict their use of the term "soul" (*psyche, anima*) to the specific kind of soul that is found in human beings. This type of soul is envisioned as qualitatively different from any other type of life-principle by virtue of the human capacities for rationality and free choice. But even when these thinkers use the term in this restricted way, the larger context of "soul" as the life-principle for anything alive is always in the background. To give the name "soul" to the principle of dynamic unity that distinguishes any living plant or animal from the heap of matter that remains when that plant or animal has died is to recognize that there is something real about life that needs to be accounted for in addition to the material constituents that make up anything's physical body.

The precise account of soul differs from school to school. Plato and those who follow his approach tend to regard the soul as a separate substance, as something other than the body that it animates and thus as something that lives on after bodily death.[1] Aristotle and his followers, on the other hand, treat the soul functionally as the dominant form (the "substantial form") and structuring principle of the material body; as a form rather than a substance in its own right, the soul is thought to be inseparable from that body in the way that a material structure does not exist separately from the matter that it is structuring even though it can be thought apart from that matter. One can think of a cube as a geometrical structure independently of any physical cube of wood or metal. When the soul is viewed as a structural principle and not as a substance in itself, it presumably no longer exists once whatever the being for which it is the structure is destroyed and the matter is reconstituted under other forms. It is only fair to note here that Aristotle neither affirms nor denies the immortality of the rational soul, and there remains a scholarly question about the proper interpretation of his texts on this question.[2] Other ancient natural philosophers, however, such as the atomists Democritus and Leucippus, and later the Epicurean Lucretius, develop a materialist view of soul as itself a purely material structure of highly refined sorts of atoms.[3]

Whatever the theoretical disagreements between these schools, they all hold that a sufficient explanation for the data needs to include the identification of a principle of unification, that is, something adequate to explain the unity of a living being over the course of time as a being that is identifiably the same despite the ingestion and excretion of matter. Each of these schools recognizes a need to posit something that can account for the unity that persists over the course of the organism's lifetime. Likewise, there is need for a principle to explain the coordination of operations that the being exhibits and the ways in which a healthy being's activities tend to contribute to the common good of the whole organism and not just to the specific good of some limb or organ. The name given to this life-principle is "soul."

If the notion of soul now sounds at least vaguely religious, this may be due to the extent to which the deeply religious thinkers of the medieval age adopted for their own use a notion that they received and adapted from Greek philosophers[4] who never claimed to be able to see or touch a soul. Ancient poets respected the ephemeral qualities of souls after death by calling them "shades" (umbrae). Philosophically, the idea of soul designated something posited in answer to questions about the source of unity and operations within living things. An organism's integrity over time requires there to be a sufficient cause. Seeing that things like trees and birds, let alone human beings, are all unified beings that have a beginning to their existence and have stable patterns of growth as well as typical operations, ancient thinkers speak of "soul" as the life-principle of such beings. The justification for so speaking thus involves reasoning back from the operations and activities that are exhibited by a given being to the powers that make possible such operations and activities. Reasoning that the observed coordination of these powers must imply that they are seated somewhere, ancient philosophers offered the concept of soul to designate what makes a living being genuinely one being with various powers and not merely an aggregate of smaller parts or elements. By contrast, a pail of water or a clod of earth has no such organic unity but only unity in place and homogeneity of composition. A pile of sand has only the unity of being in the same place. The reasoning invoked in this conceptualization shows a steady use of the principle of parsimony. While there is no reason to postulate a power unless one cannot otherwise explain an activity or operation, one may and even should postulate such a power when the observed activity or operation would otherwise be unexplainable. By this line of reasoning, Aristotle argued for the concept of psyche in his On the Soul[5] as a principle needed to unify the various powers whose existence may be inferred from the activities and operations empirically observed in a given type of living being.

This general philosophical procedure of moving from operation back to power and in turn back to a unifying seat of those powers readily lends itself to a classification scheme for souls based on the specific powers manifested by different groups of living beings. In this way the life-principle of plants of all types is thought of as "vegetative soul," while the life-principle of brute animals is thought of as "sensitive soul." This organizational schema also allows for subdivisions of these general types of soul insofar as they seem warranted by the evidence for genuinely different *kinds* within these larger groups. The operations typically observed in plants require, in general, the postulation of such powers as life, growth, and reproduction in the vegetative soul, but more specific powers are the basis for all subgroups. For animals, the list of basic traits that are regularly observed includes the activities of self-motion, sensation, memory, and various emotions; to explain these operations, the theorist hypothesizes the presence of powers sufficient to explain these activities, and the list of specific powers that need to be postulated to explain these activities once again serves as the justification for the identification of subgroups within the larger group of sensitive or animal souls. Methodologically, each type of soul is to be designated by the highest power that needs to be postulated in order to explain the bodily structures and activities found in a given type of being. Thus all animals are said to have "sensitive souls" that have sensory powers in addition to vegetative powers and all plants to have "vegetative souls" for that is the highest sort of powers that they have. The intention of this sort of designation system is to suggest not that sensation is the only power that animals have, but that it is their highest power. Sensitive souls also possess their own version of the powers typical of vegetative souls, for animals also take nutrition, grow, and reproduce, but in their own distinctive ways. The higher powers inform the manner in which the lower powers exist and operate, precisely because of the other function for which souls are postulated, namely, the unity that is to be explained by the dominant principle of organization called the "substantial form." The souls of human beings are called "rational souls," precisely because of the presence of such rational powers as intellect and will, in addition to a full set of lower powers. As a general rule, medieval philosophers imitated their Aristotelian and Neoplatonic predecessors in holding that higher forms of soul possess not only the specific powers distinctive of their own level of being but also the powers that lower-order souls possess, yet they possess them in their own distinctive way. Some theorists postulated a nested arrangement of plural souls within a given being.[6]

So, besides being the life-principle that animates the body, the soul has as one of its central tasks the unification of the composite entity. Explanation of plants and animals in terms of physiological structures and bodily organs presumes that there is a whole whose good is served by the operations of these organs and structures. This is the case whether a given operation be under conscious control, as in the case of human choice, or instinctual (when a hound, for instance, chases some fowl), or at an entirely involuntary level (the normal beating of an animal's heart or a plant's production of flower and fruit). What "soul" names, then, is the first principle of organization of a body having life within it, and all the philosophers in question took their cue from common-sense observations that there is a significant difference between the dynamic unity of a living being and the mere aggregation of dead matter in a corpse, a difference that they attributed to the presence or absence of that principle of organization and of life.

Philosophical conceptions of the soul in the medieval period tend to be clustered around two poles that are, in a general way, Platonic and Aristotelian. Yet in some important ways the main medieval versions of the soul are quite different from their classical sources, especially by reason of certain religious beliefs. The religious commitments relevant here include the conviction that human beings are made in the image and likeness of God, the belief in an eventual resurrection of the body after the pattern of the risen Christ, and the expectation that God will rectify in the next world whatever wrongs go unrequited in this. Any borrowed philosophical ideas had to be reconciled with considerations like these.

At the core of the Platonic position is the notion that the soul is a being that is in itself a spiritual and immaterial substance. According to Socrates as he appears in the texts of Plato, the embodiment that a human soul experiences during earthly life is a kind of imprisonment, from which death is a final liberation. Philosophizing during this life can anticipate this liberation by making us forgetful of our bodily condition through concentration on the timeless reality and true being of the Ideas.[7] By contrast, the Aristotelian understanding of the soul regards it as the organizing principle of suitably arranged matter that makes that matter a living organism. So considered, the soul is not an independent entity but a necessary component of a living being. The soul is a living body's structuring principle rather than a substance in its own right. For Aristotle, the relationship of body and soul falls under the same general principle of "hylemorphism" that he finds to apply without exception across the physical universe. As its etymology suggests (*hyle*, "timber," and then more broadly, "matter"; *morphe*, "form," "structure"), hylemorphism is the view that every physical object is a composite of one or another type of matter and some unifying substantial form.[8] In the case of a living being, the form refers not just to the shape and external appearance of the organism or to whatever internal structural features it may have (such as a skeleton or vertebrae); it also refers to the principle of vitality that makes the matter of the organism alive and active as this type of organism. Like any other soul, the rational soul of a human being is the substantial form that animates suitably disposed matter. Although there are a number of passages in Aristotle that still allow one to speculate on the question of immortality for the soul by virtue of its likeness to divinity, the text of *On the Soul* breaks off in the third book just before that question is to be treated.[9] In effect, this Aristotelian stance on the soul as the substantial form of the matter that constitutes a living being makes the soul a part of the material cosmos. In this way Aristotle's psychology is structurally a part of his physics, that is, his account of the physical world in terms of "natures." It is the recovery of the principles of Aristotelian natural philosophy in the twelfth century that so profoundly reshapes medieval philosophical thinking about the soul.

For all of his concentration on the distinctness of the soul from the body, Plato also returns a number of times to a consideration of the tripartite division of the soul into *logos* ("reason"), *thumos* ("spirit"), and *epithumia* ("appetite"). This distinction allows him to account for division and conflict within the individual. In the *Republic* Plato carefully correlates these three parts of the soul with parts of the body (head, breast, belly).[10] In fact, much of Plato's concern is with the education of appetites and the emotions by the formation of various virtues under reason's proper governance.[11]

Likewise, for all of Aristotle's naturalism, he finds that the problem of knowledge defies a naturalistic explanation. Despite his philosophical disposition to give explanations in terms of this-worldly physical factors without resort to other-worldly or immaterial factors wherever possible, Aristotle recurrently takes epistemological questions to require an explanatory principle of a spiritual or non-material character. In order to explain something that is as immaterial as knowledge, he recognizes the need to postulate an immaterial cause, the intellect. In knowing anything, we transcend the particularity of the material objects that we encounter through sense perceptions. We know what we know by the formation of universal concepts under which we can classify the various individual objects and features of objects that come into our ken. In this vision of knowledge, understanding anything is more than, say, a perceptual acquaintance with something. Understanding involves making the connections and distinctions that allow one to grasp what something is like by holding before the mind how something is the same or different in comparison with other things. For a sufficient explanation of this mental activity, Aristotle feels the need to posit an immaterial "agent intellect" as the efficient cause required for knowledge, namely, the ability to abstract the forms of things from the impressions that the sensory powers of the soul receive in all their particularity through the body's sense organs.[12]

The explanation of knowledge in third book of On the Soul follows the same pattern of analysis that Aristotle uses rigorously for the examination of the activities of plants and animals in the first two books. In each case he reviews the broad variety of explanations that other theorists had proposed (especially those offered by the pre-Socratic natural philosophers). But gradually he makes the case that only an analysis in terms of matter and form (that is, the type of stuff and the structure of that stuff) will be adequate to account for the phenomenon in question.

The phenomenon that especially needs to be explained by this hylemorphic approach in the third book is intellectual knowledge. Perception of sensory qualities can be accounted for by the operation of appropriate material organs that are receptive to a certain kind of phenomenon (ears for hearing sounds, for instance, and eyes for seeing colors). But the problem of knowledge presents a new sort of challenge: the spiritual (that is, non-material) character of mental activity. When we have intellectual knowledge of anything, what we have is not just the retention of an image or a remembered smell or an inner echo of the original sounds. Rather, knowledge is understood as somehow different in kind from sensory perception. It is a grasp of what something is and what it is like.

For Aristotle, this takes place by the operation of the "agent intellect." This term refers to the intellect acting in such a way as to abstract from the sensory impressions that it has received the forms that structure things. He includes here both the substantial form that makes something a unified being of a given type and the various accidental forms that constitute its qualitative and quantitative features. The knowledge that results through this acquisition of a thing's various forms has some sort of generality. By contrast, sensory cognition is always particular, for sensations are always particular. Knowing involves the use of concepts that can be applied to an entire set of individuals so as to name the kinds and the recurrent features of things. It involves judgments about significance and relationships that transcend the data presented through the senses. Further, by its linguistic powers the human mind can focus on absences as well as presences. It can group things together in various classifications and separate them by distinctions. It can propose explanations and question what is proposed. The great variety of mental activities that enter into the process of thinking and the knowledge that results can transcend the ever-changing world of material particulars and can approach the understanding of what things are in their essences.

One of hallmarks of this Aristotelian theory of knowledge is that there is nothing in the intellect that does not come through the senses. But this position brings Aristotle to a problem that strains the resources of hylemorphism as he envisions it. Nothing can give what it does not have. If the soul were merely the form that is the structure of matter and nothing more in its own right, how could it ever produce something immaterial as its result? The Platonist can more readily explain the immateriality of knowledge by thinking of the soul as an immaterial substance and so as not constricted to merely bodily activities. But the Platonist has trouble explaining how an immaterial substance can adequately unify a body, for a truly immaterial soul has no parts that can attach to the body in the way that one material part can attach to another. In addition, the Platonist has insufficient place for the contribution made by the senses in the generation of knowledge. If there really is such an experience as genuinely new learning, the senses must be doing more than merely triggering a recollection. In resolving the correlative problem of the unification of a living being's material parts as one entity, Aristotle's basic concept of the soul as a substantial form (rather than a substance in its own right) permits him to explain more about how the senses work. But the problem of the immateriality of knowledge remains.

In fact, it may have been to his perplexity in this general area that we owe the abrupt ending of Book III.[13] In addition to the scholarly suggestions that the final passage at III.13 is simply Aristotle's intended ending for the book, or that an early manuscript suffered the loss of its final pages, some scholars have wondered whether Aristotle may in all honesty have stopped writing at the point when he came to a question that he did not know how to answer. How could a material form such as the substantial form that animates a body be responsible for an immaterial effect like knowledge?

One of the main medieval answers to this difficulty is that provided by the Islamic thinker Averroes, one of the most careful and rigorous of Aristotle's commentators. He holds that it is not the individual soul that actually brings about its own knowledge, but rather a single intelligence that is separate from all human individuals. For Averroes, this single intellect serves as the agent intellect for every human mind. It impresses the knowledge of these forms upon what Aristotle calls their "passive" (or perhaps better, "receptive") intellects.[14]

What this solution tries to achieve is an explanation for knowledge as the immaterial effect of an immaterial cause without imperiling the role of the soul as the substantial form of matter. It presumes that the structural principle ("substantial form") sufficient to explain the unity of a being composed of material parts must itself be a material structure. But for other Aristotelians like Thomas Aquinas, this answer only resolves one problem by introducing others. In particular, it raises the problem of explaining the considerable difference between what one person knows and the next, and the obvious need for personal focus and industry for any learning to occur.[15] Mindful that it is individuals who expend themselves in learning whatever they come to know, Aquinas finds Averroes' answer inadequate and tries to resolve the problem by articulating an additional way in which forms can exist. There clearly are such things as forms that are purely material. In this case, the form has no existence apart from being an entity's physical structure. Likewise, there are beings that are purely forms (such as the angels) and thus purely immaterial. But there must also be forms of a third type. These forms must not only be capable of serving as the substantial forms for unified corporeal substances, but also capable of immaterial activities like knowing and making free choices. As subsistent (that is, capable of existing as substances in their own right once their role in the unification of matter is finished), they will presumably be immortal when separated by death from the bodies that they animated in their role as substantial forms.

As we noted above, it is important to consider the problem of knowledge as well as the problem of unity. To hold that the power of abstraction belongs to each individual rational soul will help to explain the differences in what various individuals know. The explanation that each individual has an intellect of its own is more satisfactory than when the immateriality of cognition had to be referred to some separate agent intellect; Averroes' account could explain the immateriality of knowledge but has difficulties accounting for differences in what specific individuals know. Aquinas' position, on the other hand, entails that the human soul that serves during earthly life as the substantial form of a body and as the seat of its rational powers will somehow need to become a spiritual substance at death when it ceases to be the form of a material being. Thus the rational soul must represent a third type of substantial form – one that is different in kind and not just in degree of power or complexity[16] in comparison with the animating principles of any other animal. As we will see when we return to this question in the third part of the present chapter, this solution will also prove to be helpful in discussions about the soul's immortality.

2 AUGUSTINE'S ADAPTATIONS OF THE PLATONIC POSITION

The basic polarity between the views of the soul derived from Plato and those derived from Aristotle persists throughout the whole of the medieval period. But there are certain differences that arise from the religious commitments of medieval thinkers. In particular, the scriptural notion that human beings are created in the image and likeness of God has a pervasive influence on all medieval theorizing on this subject. From the earliest efforts in philosophical anthropology that were made by patristic thinkers[17] through the nominalism of four-teenth-century scholasticism, there is an effort to follow the ancients wherever possible. This can be seen in the attention that medieval thinkers pay to both the subjective aspects of soul in terms of indi-vidual personality and its objective aspects in terms of its species-typical activity and manner of embodiment. But medieval thinkers are also clear about the limitations of those ancient theories of soul that disregard bodily experience or yield to materialist explanations that risk denying or leaving unexplained the immateriality of the soul, its immortality, and its freedom.

For Augustine, as for virtually every thinker who followed him, there is a soul animating everything that is alive, whether plant, animal, or human being. Soul is what gives life (*vita*) to the body. It is thus the source of activities such as nutrition, growth, and repro-duction in all life-forms, as well as of sensation and desire in animals, and of thinking and willing in human beings. Questions about the human soul become a special concern for Augustine during his post-conversion period at Cassiciacum (386–87), and remain so all his life. He regularly uses the term *anima* ("soul") for all kinds of living beings, but he restricts the term *animus* ("mind") to the rational souls of human beings.

The fundamental position that Augustine works out on questions of the soul can rightly be called a kind of Christian Platonism. He shows little to no acquaintance with the psychological texts of Aristotle.[18] It is especially through reading Latin translations of the *Enneads* of Plotinus and related Neoplatonic literature that Augus-tine breaks with a position that he had earlier found compelling. So long as he does not distinguish sharply between imagination and thought, he holds the view that everything real has to be corporeal, including the soul, but that some material things are more gross and some more refined.[19] In the course of the nine years that he spent with the Manicheans, he found himself increasingly dissatisfied with this view of things, but he saw no likely alternative.[20] Surprised to hear Bishop Ambrose of Milan preaching about both God and the soul as spiritual rather than corporeal,[21] Augustine comes to realize that there is a difference between imagination and thought. This distinction allows him to grasp that the human soul is something spiritual, not just a refined kind of matter, and that the soul is always present as a whole, not as something that has parts like bodies do. It is not something corporeal that is more present in larger bodies and less so in smaller ones, and it is without length or breadth or depth. In support of this position, Augustine argues in various books that the soul could not be conscious of what takes place in the different parts of the body unless the soul were present as a whole in each of the body's parts. As evidence that the mind or soul must be thought to have a non-bodily nature, Augustine repeatedly offers the very power to imagine bodily objects in their absence, as well as the fact of the mind's knowledge of itself, for that kind of reflection he thinks to be impossible for a corporeal object.[22]

Equally fundamental to Augustine's notion of the soul is his position that it must be a creature of God and not some part of God himself. This way of putting his views shows a concern to distance himself from the Manichean position that the souls of human beings are parts of the refined material that constitutes the divine force that have broken off during some great cosmic struggle between the ultimate principles of good and evil and then become enmeshed in the darker and grosser forms of matter.[23] The Manichean position had been consoling to Augustine for a long time as a way in which to maintain that the physical nature of the body in which he believed his soul to be entrapped could be blamed for his sins.[24] But in due time he comes to the conviction that it is unfair to claim the credit for one's virtuous deeds unless one also accepts responsibility for wicked choices as well. His recognition that personal responsibility lies in the choices that one freely makes rather than in the material nature of the body brings him to see that the soul is the seat of personal moral responsibility and not merely something that is, as it were, chipped off the good principle and imprisoned within the flesh. The soul is not a detached portion of the being of God but something other than God that God made. This admission also pushes him beyond any lingering sympathy for the Neoplatonic position that the soul itself is ultimately divine.[25] As further metaphysical support for a position that he finds that moral integrity requires him to hold, he calls upon the fact of the soul's mutability. That we can at one time be wise but later foolish, or now ready to choose something but later unwilling to do so, means to him that we are creatures and not God himself, for God must be recognized to be immutable.[26]

In affirming that the soul is a creature and not itself divine, Augustine nevertheless holds that nothing is dearer to God than human beings. The rational soul is created in God's image.[27] In opposition to the Manichees, who understand Genesis 1: 26 to imply that God must have bodily parts like ours, Augustine insists that it is in our souls that we bear the likeness of God. In his *Literal Commentary on Genesis*, Augustine advances the view that it is the Son of God in whose image Adam and all subsequent human beings are made.[28] Later, however, he corrects himself by insisting that every human soul is made in the image of the Trinity. The final eight books of his *De Trinitate* are given to meditating on various ways in which the soul offers us a model for conceiving the unity of the Divine Trinity, in whose image we are made.[29] As the seat of remembering, understanding, and loving, for instance, the soul exhibits a triadic unity, and in the rolling present of consciousness we have access to the past by memory and to the future by anticipation as a creaturely way of participating in the timeless eternity of God.

There is an abiding tension in Augustine's account of the unity of soul and body. He alternates between asserting that the human being is "a rational soul having a body" (in such a way that the resulting composite "does not make two persons, but only one") and the suggestion that the real person is to be identified with the rational soul,[30] for the *animus* is a "substance partaking of reason adapted to rule a body."[31] Despite the difficulties in explaining just how this union works, Augustine is persistently hostile to the view championed by such other prominent patristic thinkers as Origen, that souls come to be embodied as a penalty for previously committed sins. He knows of the reincarnation theories of Manicheism and pagan Neoplatonism but regards the view that human souls ever entered into animal bodies or into the bodies of other humans as contrary to Christian faith and to sound morality.[32] To imagine that souls would have to return to the evils faced during an earlier life (whether in happiness or misery) would render insecure the happiness with God promised to the blessed as the just reward of a good life. Hence, Augustine can preserve the basic Platonic view of the soul as a subsistent substance by recasting Platonic expectations of reincarnation through the transmigration of souls into a doctrine of immortality and the expectation of single once-and-for-all resurrection of the body.

In pondering the dual account of human creation found in Genesis (1: 26ff and 2: 7ff), Augustine finds the question of the origin of souls after Adam extremely problematic. In a mature work, *On Free Choice of the Will*, Augustine is especially alert to the need to defend the justice of God for having made a world in which it is possible for a creature freely to choose to do evil and to sin. Nonetheless, Augustine still finds four possible explanations for the origin of souls: (1) God may have created them individually for each new person; (2) new human souls might somehow draw their being from the one soul that God created (the view that would later be called traducianism); (3) souls may have already existed in some hidden place and are then sent by God to enliven and rule the bodies of individuals when ready; (4) these separated souls might not need to be sent by God but could decide of their own choice to inhabit bodies.[33]

What complicates this issue for Augustine is the set of problems associated with the theological doctrine of original sin[34] as well as his sense of scriptural passages such as Romans 9: 11.[35] He takes the Bible to eliminate the possibility that the souls of those newly born could have personally committed any sins in a previous life. He could discover no independent philosophical argument on this question, and no scriptural text for the position of immediate and direct creation of the soul by God. This position is held by other patristic thinkers such as Jerome, and it will be the position of various scholastic thinkers such as Aquinas.[36] In the fourth book of *De anima et eius origine* (*On the Soul and Its Origin*) he justifies his agnostic position on the question of precisely how God created souls by a detailed argument. While the traducian view might be able to explain the transmission of original sin,[37] this explanation seems incompatible with the soul's incorporeality. It implies that one's soul is generated by one's parents, like one's body is. To hold for immediate creation by God could explain the spirituality of the soul but not the transmission of original sin. Augustine flirts with the two options that involve existence for the soul prior to its embodiment. But whatever attraction he may have felt for these positions, his experiences in the controversy with the Pelagians[38] over grace and free will leave him convinced that the proper resolution of this question simply cannot include any view in which human souls "fall" into their earthly bodies because of some personal sin.[39]

Augustine's early treatises show his indebtedness to those Neoplatonic thinkers who rescued him from thinking of the soul corporeally. His early works also manifest a readiness to accept the reality of a world soul,[40] as Plato did in the *Timaeus* (at 30b ff), which structures and animates the whole world.[41] Augustine's late volume of retractations never amounts to a total repudiation of this concept, but only a qualification. If there is such a thing as a world soul, he explains, it cannot be God but only a creature. The abiding appeal of this view for Augustine is evident in passages such as the discussion of time in the eleventh book of the *Confessions*, where he defines time as a "distention" or "stretching" of soul.[42]

What is most important about the soul, for Augustine, is that it is made to desire a happiness that can only be realized fully and definitively by union with God.[43] For him this view entails that the soul is *capax Dei*, that is, truly capable of union with the God in whose image it is made. This insight yokes his concerns about the meaning of life and the proper contour of ethics with certain commitments of a metaphysical order in a vision that dominates medieval writings in the area of spirituality even after the new perspectives on soul that comes about in the thirteenth century with the recovery of the texts of Aristotle.[44]

3 THE CONCEPT OF SOUL IN SCHOLASTIC THOUGHT

Aristotle's writings did not come into the Latin-speaking world of the twelfth and thirteenth centuries alone. They were accompanied by numerous commentaries and treatises. Although these Greek and Islamic commentators and thinkers generally set out to explain the meaning of Aristotle's sometimes rather obscure texts, they occasionally alter his meaning to one degree or another in the course of pressing their own points. For Latin scholasticism, the comprehension of these newly received source texts invariably includes the project of trying to discern the difference between what Aristotle himself must mean and what other authorities have added, as well as assessing the validity of the new viewpoints. The most important of these authors is Averroes, whose enthusiasm for Aristotle contributes much to the tradition of regarding Aristotle as "*the* Philosopher" and whose own labors earn him the title "*the* Commentator."

The thirteenth-century controversies over the meaning of Aristotle's texts on the soul amount to a three-sided debate. The controversy pitted a group that later scholars have dubbed the "radical Aristotelians" (also known as the "Latin Averroists") against, on the one hand, figures such as Thomas Aquinas who wanted to defend traditional Christian views by means of a modified version of the new Aristotelian philosophy of nature. On the other side were various Augustinian thinkers such as Bonaventure, who found the Aristotelian approach suspect and unlikely to be capable of sufficient modification to be compatible with the Christian religion. Although Augustinian thinkers of the scholastic period regularly (but sometimes reluctantly) adopt some of the new Aristotelian terminology, they invariably voice the difficulties they see about the possibility of harmonizing the Aristotelian idea of the soul as the single substantial form of the body with their faith in such doctrines as the immortality of the soul.

The philosophical problems that thinkers of the Augustinian tradition find with Aristotelianism involve both metaphysics and epistemology. In order to guarantee the spirituality of knowledge, the radical Aristotelians, following Averroes, locate the agent intellect in a separate being. This separate agent intellect, as we have seen, is thought responsible for the abstractions required for knowledge. It cannot reside in the human soul so long as the soul needs to serve as the substantial form that structures and enlivens the material body of the individual human being. Hence, the agent intellect must reside in a separate spiritual being, a divine intelligence.[45] Further contributing to the doubt of the Augustinians that Aristotle's views could ever be reconciled with Christian religious commitments are his views on such subjects as God and the world. Aristotle's version of the proof of the existence of God as the unmoved mover,[46] for example, makes God seem so utterly self-sufficient and distant as to be uninterested in any knowledge of the world, let alone in the sort of providential care for the world to which the Christian understanding of God is deeply committed. But within Aristotle's framework, this position seems inescapable. For God to be fully actual, as the proof for God's existence requires, God must be in potency to nothing, not even in potency to gaining knowledge about the world. Hence, God must be conceived as thought thinking only about itself and not about the world. Aristotle's attack on the Platonic theory of Ideas seems, at least by implication, to involve an attack on another aspect of Plato's thought that Christian thinkers had readily borrowed and adapted when they revised the location of the archetypes and envisioned them as ideas in the mind of God (as we saw in chapter 3). While the Platonic version of the Ideas may stand above or at least independent of the divine demiurge in the *Timaeus*, Christian thinkers from Augustine on relocate these Ideas within the mind of God and assign them the role of exemplary causality in order to explain how God creates the world. No such doctrine of creation is part of the worldview of Aristotle, for whom the world is presumed to be eternal and in no need of a creator. Given their reservations about these issues, Augustinian thinkers saw little reason to adopt Aristotle's views on psychology.

The interpretation of Aristotle sponsored by his Averroist commentators gained ground in places like the Arts Faculty at the University of Paris. But rather than simply rejecting the new Aristotelian views that seemed to many of their contemporaries quite promising for progress in natural science, a number of the religious authorities tried to engage them head on. Pope Gregory IX commissioned a review of Aristotle's works that eventually brought figures like Thomas Aquinas to work on the problem at the court of Urban IV in Orvieto. In support of the project, figures like William of Moerbeke labored to produce more precise translations of Aristotle, so as to make his real meaning more accessible and thus to make it possible to determine whether they were irremediably antithetical to religion or perhaps could be suitably modified.

Aquinas' effort to understand and appreciate Aristotelian natural philosophy brings him to stake out his own position on Aristotle's ideas as both philosophically cogent and (ironically) even better suited than the Augustinian approach for defending Christian orthodoxy, especially in regard to questions about personal unity and moral responsibility. In criticizing Plato, Aquinas finds a way to reprove certain wayward tendencies among the thirteenth-century defenders of Augustine without having to criticize them or Augustine directly. What corrections he needs to make on Aristotelian views, he tends to make quietly, so as not to give the Augustinian enemies of Latin

Averroism the advantage that would come from any explicit statements of reservation about "the Philosopher" himself.[47]

Chief among the Franciscan defenders of Augustine as the most
authentic interpreter of Christian tradition and revelation in the thirteenth century is Bonaventure. Although over the course of his life
he increasingly uses the terminology of Aristotle that had become *de
rigueur* in these debates, Bonaventure regards the Scriptures as a
better source of wisdom and knowledge on many topics, and especially on questions of the soul. By careful attention to Augustine's
reading of the Scriptures, Bonaventure thinks that one can find sufficient arguments for regarding the soul as the locus of intelligence and
freedom.[48] It exists, for God created *ex nihilo*. It is made in the image
of God and thus it is capable of knowing the Creator by recalling its
own nature as a creature. Although it is now mired in the consequences of original sin, it is made for happiness and for the good use
of its freedom, a freedom that can be restored by the healing touch
of God's grace. In Bonaventure's analysis, the very capacity for divine
beatitude that God freely and generously shares with the soul implies
that the soul must be free in order to be able to cooperate with God's
will. It must be immortal and incorruptible so as to be capable of
enjoying endless beatitude. And it must have been divinely created,
for, if it were generated by its parents, it would in turn be subject to
corruption. Although Bonaventure employs the language of Aristotle
in many respects, he regularly stresses the non-Aristotelian view that
the soul is always a substance in its own right, separable from the
body at death.[49]

Bonaventure sees no particular problem in holding both that the
soul animates the material body as its substantial form and that the
soul itself is a substance with its own matter and form. But it is his
quite un-Aristotelian notion of the presence of a plurality of forms
within a substance that permits him to articulate an alternative vision
of how composite unities work. His account makes use of a modified
version of the ancient Stoic doctrine of seminal reasons.[50]

In his various treatments of the soul,[51] Bonaventure suggests that
it comes into existence directly by God's action and thus is "created
ex nihilo" rather than "made" out of any previously existing thing,
whether out of a divine substance or some other creaturely substance
by any corporeal process of generation through human parents.
For Bonaventure, it is the mutability of the soul that proves its

substantiality, for matter is the principle of potentiality for change within any being whose form gives it a fixed identity over time. By reason of free choice of the will, the soul is clearly able to change, even to the point of losing the eternal beatitude for which it is made. In order to account for the soul's mutability, he posits what he calls "spiritual matter" that is in itself entirely indeterminate.

On this spiritual matter God imposes the form of rationality in order to create a specific human soul as a substance that is fit to be joined to a corporeal body, which also has various levels of developing forms that organize it.[52] Now, while "material" and "corporeal" might seem to be synonyms, Bonaventure makes a distinction between them. In itself, matter is simply the ability to accept the form that will diversify it from any other creature. But as a complete lack of form, matter in itself is something more like "infinite possibility" rather than "extension in space and time." In short, for Bonaventure matter in itself is indifferent as to whether it receives a spiritual form or a corporeal form, and thus he can speak about spiritual matter as well as about corporeal matter. The divine gift of existence by the *ex nihilo* creation of a spiritual form is what brings into being a subsistent soul, with its own spiritual matter or capacity for change as well as its distinctly rational form. Thus, in considering the soul as a created substance, Bonaventure is not treating the soul as an Aristotelian substantial form that animates the body but is emphasizing its subsistence in its own right as a composite substance, and thus he must still explain the unity of the soul with the body.

One could well imagine the immediate Aristotelian objection to such a proposal. For the soul to be this complete a composite substance would mean that its connection to any corporeal body would be merely an accidental unity and not a genuine substantial unity. If one is going to explain how body and soul are truly united as one person, the soul must presumably be something less than an individual substance in its own right. Thomas Aquinas, for instance, holds that the separated soul is an incomplete substance, something that is capable of existing on its own after death while awaiting the resurrection of the body but not the complete person. During earthly life it serves as the substantial form of the body in such a way as to constitute one complete substance.[53]

Bonaventure meets this objection head-on by denying that a substance like the soul that is composed of its own form and matter cannot participate in composition at other levels of being. Rather, he insists, the crucial factor is whether the unified organization of the soul (or, for that matter, of the body) has exhausted its natural inclinations for union. On the basis of our experience of embodied life, Bonaventure contends that the human soul, though in itself a composite unity of matter and form, has a further natural desire for union with a physical body. He envisions the body as separately constituted by the organization imposed on corporeal matter by its own set of forms. Here, he explains, is the place where Plato and various of his successors (of whom Bonaventure had read in Macrobius' *Commentary on the Dream of Scipio*) went wrong, for they persisted in regarding the body as the prison and not the companion of the soul.[54]

An Aristotelian might accuse Bonaventure of holding that the body is then only accidentally united to the soul. But Bonaventure's acceptance of a plurality of forms in a composite allows him to say that the spiritual soul is a subsistent substance in its own right. It is integrally part of the unity that is a human being during earthly life by virtue of the satisfaction of natural desires. A number of later Franciscan thinkers hold positions closely related to Bonaventure on this question, including Matthew of Aquasparta, Walter de la Mare, John Peckham, Roger Marston, John Peter Olivi, and eventually John Duns Scotus,[55] who insists that there is no more problem about reconciling the unity of a being and the plurality of its forms than in asserting real unity of any composite. In this tradition ordinary matter is treated not as pure potentiality but as something that has received existence and so has the capacity of any real entity to be capable of development by the actualization of forms (the seminal ideas) latent within it.

In this explanation one sees something very different from the view taken by Bonaventure's contemporary, Thomas Aquinas. Aquinas argues at length for the Aristotelian doctrine that the unity of any material substance is provided by its having a single substantial form as its principle of organization.[56] He understands the potentiality of matter to consist in the passive ability to receive forms from a cause that actually possesses in its own nature the form to be communicated. Considered in its pure form, the principle of potentiality is called prime matter. But as matter is generally experienced in the world, it is highly determinate in its organization, whether at the macro-level in such forms as wood or rock, or at the elemental level as earth, air, fire, or water.[57] In taking this view, Aquinas is mindful of the limited range of forms that any particular material substance will be able to receive when it is subject to a substantial change.

In order to explain the limitations on what any actual bits of matter prove capable of receiving, Aquinas has recourse to the notion of the "virtual presence" of lower levels of form present in a substance. In this way he can protect the doctrine that a single substantial form is responsible for the genuine unity of a substance.[58] At the same time, he can explain how lower-level structures (such as water) can still be present and operative within the structures of higher-level unities. On Aristotelian principles, a plurality of substantial forms would render impossible the unity of a composite substance. A plurality of substantial forms implies a plurality of substances and no true unity.

The chief concern about the Aristotelian view of soul that a thinker like Aquinas has to overcome (without, on the other hand, yielding to the naturalism of the Latin Averroists) was the suspicion that making the soul into the form of the body would necessarily make it into merely a material form and thereby imperil the spirituality of the soul and its subsistence after bodily death. What Aquinas finds most unsatisfying about the Augustinian approach of the sort that Bonaventure and others held is the dangers latent in any form of Platonism. Such a model provides an insufficient account of human unity.

This worry is not simply a hypothetical concern, but an issue of great practical importance to Aquinas' religious order, the Dominicans, who had been charged by the Pope with combating the form of Manicheism that appeared in the Middle Ages under the form of Catharism and Albigensianism.[59] In its medieval as in its ancient versions, Manichean dualism understands the real self to be the soul, while the flesh belongs to the world of matter and evil.[60] Medieval Cathars are believed to have given license to the flesh while claiming to preserve their minds pure by a pure intention. But to their critics this policy seems hypocritical, not to mention a truly grave danger to salvation. In addition to much vigorous evangelization and to juridical use of the Inquisition, the Dominicans also mounted an intellectual campaign against what must have seemed to them to be a schizophrenic view of human psychology. Although most of campaign had already occurred before Aquinas' day, training was still being provided should further battles be necessary. This training took place in the Dominican *studium*, or house of studies, for which a number of Aquinas' treatises are written.

Aquinas' own recurrent attention to questions about the soul and human unity should be understood in light of this background as much as in the context of debating the Franciscan doctrine of the plurality of forms and showing the impossibility of more than one substantial form. Substantial form, he argues, refers to the dominant organizing principle that makes all of one's matter into one single substance (whatever residual structures are still operative at lower levels), and the notion of a plurality of such forms is contradictory to unity. From writings as early in his career as his *Commentary on the Sentences of Peter Lombard*, Aquinas adopts the insight of Boethius that in every creature there must necessarily be found some sort of composition, simply because its existence is distinct from its essence.[61] This is to say that only in God are existence and essence the same, but in everything else the same essence is shared by the many individuals of a species, each of which has come to exist in its own right, with all the accidental features and all the relationships that belong to this or that individual in the course of its history.

In fairness, it is not that Bonaventure, or Augustine before him, in any way wants to cast doubt on the unity of the human being. But the acceptance of a plurality of forms within substance raises serious questions about whether their explanation of unity is convincing, especially given their commitment to treating the soul as a substance in order to guarantee its immortality. To the extent that medieval Aristotelians are able to resolve questions about the immortality of the soul, they seem to have been in a better position to defend personal unity.

4 OVERVIEW

Philosophical treatments of the concept of soul during the medieval period tend to be religiously motivated variations on the main Platonic and Aristotelian alternatives proposed in antiquity. On the Platonic model adopted by Augustine and later championed especially by the Franciscan philosophers in the scholastic period, the human soul is envisioned as a being or substance in its own right, the seat of moral responsibility in this life and the bearer of personal identity after separation from the body at the time of one's bodily death. The proponents of this view steadily reject any hint of reincarnation as unwarranted by any evidence and as antithetical to morality. Among the apparent advantages of this model is its greater suitability for attempts to prove the immortality of the soul, but the difficulties of this model for explaining personal unity become increasingly apparent after the recovery of Aristotelian philosophy of nature in the twelfth century and the objections raised to the doctrine of the plurality of substantial forms.

Medieval thinkers who are more inclined to the general position of Aristotle are challenged to work out a defensible position on the soul. The "radical Aristotelians" tend to be willing to embrace doubt about personal immortality as a possible consequence of a strict hylemorphic position. But other interpreters, especially Thomas Aquinas, find reason to hold that the human soul does serve as the substantial form of suitably disposed matter, as Aristotle had held. They recognize that it cannot be regarded as simply a material structure because it does perform activities that are immaterial in nature such as acts of knowing and free choice of the will. Hence, it must be understood as something that is made to be the organizing principle of matter but that is capable of subsistence existence on its own after death.

NOTES

1   Plato's arguments for the immortality of the soul in the *Phaedo* include an account of the body as the "prison" from which the soul is liberated by death and of the soul as a simple substance, having no parts into which it might break up (see *Phaedo* 78b–81e). Other dialogues present as having three parts (reason, spirit, and appetite), but these more complex accounts still seem to presume that the soul is immortal and simple. See *Republic* X.611c–612b, in Plato (1997), where Plato argues that the soul is simple, despite what he has shown earlier; see also *Phaedrus* 246a–249d. For a general overview, see Guthrie (1978).

2   *On the Soul* (in Greek, *Peri psyches*; in Latin, *De anima*) in Aristotle
    (1984) is a work in three books, the first of which concerns the general
    notion of soul as a life-principle, the second the distinction between
    the souls of plants and those of animals on the basis of the additional
    kinds of powers found in animals, and the third the distinction between
    the human souls and the souls of other animals, again on the basis of
    the additional kinds of powers found in human existence. For a
    summary and analysis of Aristotle's views on soul, see Granger
    (1996).

3   See Taylor (1999).

4   In passing, we should also note that the Scriptures contain many ref-
    erences to "soul" and "spirit" even if they do not present a philo-
    sophical treatise on the subject. The Greek terms *psyche* (soul) and
    pneuma (spirit), for instance, are used in the Septuagint, the Greek
    translation of the Hebrew portions of the Bible, to represent the
    Hebrew terms *nephesh*, *ruah*, and *neshamah*. The first of these refers
    primarily to what Greek philosophy thought of as vegetative and
    sensitive powers of the soul, the second to the seat of moral respon-
    sibility, and the third to intelligence. Within Jewish circles there was
    considerable disagreement on the subject, for parties like the Saddu-
    cees were materialists who denied immortality, while the Pharisees
    affirmed it. The Jewish Platonist Philo of Alexandria argued for the
    divine origin of each soul and contrasts the *psyche* (the source of
    bodily life) with the *pneuma* (the spiritual seat of intelligence). See
    Runia (1986).

5   The Latin-speaking world of the Middle Ages came to know this book
    as *De Anima*. The Greek text was first translated about 1215 (anony-
    mous), then from Arabic by Michael Scotus sometime before 1235, and
    again from the Greek between 1265 and 1268 by William of Moerbeke.
    Many scholastic philosophers wrote commentaries on it as well as
    treatises *De Anima* in their own name.

6   A nested arrangement of plural souls would presumably involve
    some sort of host within which other souls would dwell, perhaps on
    the model of parasites that dwell in the body of other animals. See
    Henry of Ghent (1993) and Matthew of Aquasparta (1961), pp. 65,
    168.

7   See, for instance, *Phaedo* 66e5–67b2, in Plato (1997).

8   For a more complete account of this, see chapter 6 on cosmos and
    nature.

9   For a text in Aristotle that allows the possibility of immortality, see *On
    the Soul* III.5.430a22; there are also hints of this position at II.1.403a4–
    7 and II.2.413b24–7, in Aristotle (1984).

10 *Republic* IV.435d, in Plato (1997). In the *Phaedrus* at 246c we find the image of three parts of the soul likened to a team of two horses and a charioteer. See also *Timaeus* 69c ff. for a discussion of how specific parts of the body correlate with the powers of the soul.

11 For a current account of how this moral formation works, see Rist (2002), esp. chs. 3 and 4.

12 *On the Soul* III, chs. 5–7, in Aristotle (1984).

13 For a review of scholarly opinions on the question of the apparent incompleteness of book three, see van Steenberghen (1980).

14 See Leaman (1998).

15 Aquinas' critique of Averroes' reading of Aristotle on this point as well as the alternative interpretation can be found in Aquinas (1993b).

16 The distinction between a difference of degree and a difference in kind turns on whether or not there is continuity or discontinuity in regard to some property that is the focus of the comparison. Within a given kind, there can be considerable differences in the amount or intensity to which some property is present, but every member of the kind needs to possess the property in question to some degree. Something that totally lacks a property that is constitutive of a certain group (admittedly, found in varying amounts within individuals of that group) is said to be different in kind. For a recent treatment of this question in the Aristotelian-Thomistic tradition, see Adler (1993).

17 Although the works of Greek patristic authors of the third and fourth century fall outside the scope of this book, one can see in their treatises a sensitivity to the changes that their faith requires them to make in the philosophical notions that they received from antiquity. See, for instance, Ladner (1958).

18 One of Augustine's rare discussions of a text by Aristotle comes in the fourth book of the *Confessions*, where he notes the relative ease with which he grasped Aristotle's *Categories*. See *Confessions* IV.xvi.28, in Augustine (1991b).

19 *Confessions*, V.10.19, in Augustine (1991b).

20 See *Confessions* 7.1.1, in Augustine (1991b).

21 See *On the Happy Life* 1.4, in Augustine (1944).

22 See *Confessions* 7.1.2, in Augustine (1991b); *De Trinitate* 10.4.6, in Augustine (1991a).

23 Augustine has various anti-Gnostic writings, including *On True Religion* from the year 390; see 9.16, in Augustine (1979).

24 *Confessions* 5.10.18, in Augustine (1991b).

25 See *On Order* 2.17.46, in Augustine (2007).

26 *Confessions* 7.1.1, in Augustine (1991b).

27 See, e.g., *The City of God* XI.26, in Augustine (1984).

28 *The Literal Meaning of Genesis* 16.57–8, in Augustine (1982a).

29 Augustine (1991a).

30 For instance, "I, I the soul" of *Confessions* 10.9.6, in Augustine (199b).

31 *De quantitate animae* 13.22, in Augustine (1933).

32 See *The Literal Meaning of Genesis* 7.9.13, 7.11.17, in Augustine (1982a) and *The City of God* X.30, in Augustine (1984).

33 *On Free Choice of the Will*, 3.20.56–7, in Augustine (1982b).

34 A full-scale treatment of original sin is beyond the scope of this book. For a fine recent treatment of the subject, see Quay (1995), chs. 1–6. For Augustine's views, see, for instance, *On Marriage and Desire* II.xxvi.43: "The deliberate sin of the first man is the cause of original sin" in Augustine (1998) See also *Answer to the Pelagians* I.2.4; V.10; III.9.25; IV.3, in Augustine (1998). The classic text within Scripture that Augustine sees as teaching the doctrine of original sin is *Romans* 5: 12ff.

35 *Romans* 9: 10–12 in Bible (1965): "when Rebecca had conceived children by one man, our forefather Isaac, though they were not yet born and had done nothing either good or bad, in order that God's purpose of election might continue, not because of works but because of his call, she was told."

36 See Kelly (1998).

37 This position was often taken on the strength of the biblical notion that all were in Adam when he sinned; see 1 Corinthians 15: 22: "For as in Adam all die, so also in Christ shall all be made alive" in Bible (1965).

38 Like Augustine in his struggle against the Manichees, the Pelagians laid great stress on free choice of the will, but to such an extent that it was possible for human beings to save themselves by right use of free will. Augustine objected to the Pelagian view that divine grace is only an extrinsic sort of assistance, such as the good example of Christ and his saints or the clear directives of the Scriptures.

39 One of the most lively controversies in recent Augustinian scholarship has concerned this question. For the view that Augustine did long hold this position, see the works of O'Connell (1968) and (1987). For the contrary position, see O'Daly (1987). There is a thorough examination of this entire question in Rombs (2006).

40 See *On the Immortality of the Soul* 15.24, in Augustine (1947).

41 For more detailed discussion of the concept of "world soul," see chapter 6 on cosmos and nature.

42 In addition to *Confessions* XI, there are also important discussions on the concept of time and creation in his *City of God* XI and XII.

43 *On the Happy Life* 2.12, in Augustine (1944); *The Trinity* 14.4.6 and 8.11, in Augustine (1991a).

44 Most medieval theories of morality, for instance, will regularly insist on considerations of virtue as well as law, of the Beatitudes and the gifts of the Holy Spirit if one intends to present a holistic account of moral theory. See Pinckaers (1995), esp. pp. 141–67. See also Wilken (2003), esp. ch. 11, "Likeness to God."

45 Although this position risks removing the grounds for claiming that human souls are spiritual and immortal, some theorists found this a price worth paying in return for the other advantages gained by adopting Aristotelian natural philosophy. See van Steenberghen (1980) and Dodd (1998).

46 *Metaphysics* XII. 6–7, in Aristotle (1984).

47 See van Steenberghen (1980).

48 *On Free Choice of the Will* II.3.7–8, 10, in Augustine (1982b).

49 For a more detailed study of Bonaventure's views on the human soul, see Gilson (1965), pp. 285–307.

50 Augustine explains his theory of the "seminal reasons" in his *Literal Commentary on Genesis*, esp. V and VI; see also IX.17.32, in Augustine (1982a) and *The Trinity* III.2.13, in Augustine (1991a). His theory of certain infinitesimal "seeds" (in addition to the "eternal reasons" in God, the divine ideas) as the causes of the patterns of change, growth, reproduction, and other biological activities is in some respects an incipient but relatively undeveloped theory of secondary natural causes. It follows from his view of the simultaneous creation of all things by God. See McKeough (1984). For the Stoic theory of seminal reasons, see Lapidge (1978), pp. 178–9.

51 See his commentary on the *Sentences* of Peter Lombard, esp. distinctions 17–18, in Bonaventure (1902); his *Breviloquium*, esp. II.9, in Bonaventure (1992), and his mystical treatise, *The Soul's Journey into God*, in Bonaventure (1978).

52 See his commentary on the *Sentences* of Peter Lombard, 17.1.2, 18.2.3 in Bonaventure (1902), and his *Breviloquium* II.9.5, in Bonaventure (1992).

53 See *Summa of Theology* I.75–6, esp. 75.2 ("whether the soul is something subsistent"), 75.5 ("whether the soul is composed of matter and form"), 76.1 ("whether the intellectual principle is united to the body as its form"), and 76.4 ("whether in man there is another form besides the intellectual soul") in Aquinas (1945).

54 See Bonaventure's commentary on the *Sentences* of Peter Lombard, 18.2.2: "ad suum sodalem, non sicut ad carcerem," in Bonaventure (1902).

55 For a survey of the Franciscan tradition on this question, see French and Cunningham (1996). Scotus' position is discussed at length in Ingham and Dreyer (2004), pp. 101–16.

56 For instance, in his treatises *De spiritualibus creaturis* ("On Spiritual Creatures") and *De substantiis separatis* ("On Separate Substances").

57 See *On Being and Essence*, esp. chs. 3, 5 in Aquinas (1983); his *On the Principles of Nature*, esp. chs. 1, 2; and his *On the Mixture of the Elements*, both in Bobik (1998).

58 For Thomas's opposition to seminal reasons, see *Truth* 11.1 in Aquinas (1993a).

59 A classic account of the history of this subject can be found in Mandonnet (1944), esp. ch. 3.

60 See Lansing (1998) and Sumption (1999).

61 *Commentary on the Sentences of Peter Lombard*, d.8, q.5, a.1–3 in Aquinas (1947), Boethius, *On the Trinity*, ch. 2.

8

CONCLUSION

This survey of some of the basic concepts of medieval philosophy permits a number of important generalizations. First, despite the tendency in some quarters to doubt whether there is such a thing as medieval philosophy and to see in medieval thought only religion or theology, there is ample evidence of distinctively philosophical currents that were operative throughout the period. Second, in contrast to the notion that medieval thought is monolithic, there is clearly a genuine diversity of opinion on many of the topics that were recurrently addressed in the various philosophical movements of the Middle Ages. This diversity is reflected by the stances taken on the problems chosen for study in this volume. The medieval awareness of disagreement on these issues recurrently proves a stimulus for philosophizing that led to progress in a number of areas. But the diversity of philosophical approaches in the medieval period is not so great as to have prevented real philosophical engagement. One of the conditions for philosophical disagreement in any age is the presence of sufficient agreement to make discussion possible. Despite the fact of significant differences in philosophical commitments, the philosophers of the Middle Ages share enough common ground to engage in productive dialogue. The basic concepts discussed in this book suggest important areas of agreement as well as places for airing their disagreements. Finally, just as the creative philosophizing in the Middle Ages invariably involved the adoption of some philosophical concepts from antiquity, the rejection of others, and the adaptation of yet others, so too the philosophical movements of the Renaissance and modernity would involve the adoption, the rejection, and the adaptation of medieval notions. Our own efforts at philosophizing today will be better for understanding more deeply the medieval contribution to these areas of concern.

The ideas examined in the course of this volume again and again show thinkers with considerable religious commitments turning to philosophical arguments and distinctions so as to make progress in understanding better what they believe. Not only on basic questions such as the existence of God, but on related topics like God's relation to the world and the divine nature, there is a thoroughgoing use of philosophical methods as well as the insights of ancient philosophers.

The recourse to philosophy for examining religious language about God is highly significant. While religions often convey their experiences of God in the form of stories and thus make use of human languages and images from ordinary experience, these practices came under sophisticated scrutiny in the Latin-speaking Middle Ages. Perhaps it was the expansion of Christian religion into the philosophically literate culture of the Mediterranean that provided the opportunity and the sense of need for this sort of philosophical reflection. Each of the main philosophies of the ancient world had a significant impact on the way in which Christian thinkers presented and understood their faith commitments.

For long centuries the preferred philosophical form for Christian ideas was Platonic, owing especially to its affirmation of the immortality of the soul and the presence of a creator-like figure in the demiurge of the *Timaeus*. But admiration for the moral stance of Stoicism also shaped some of the patterns used in articulating Christian positions. Later, a recovery of Aristotelian texts on ethics and natural philosophy in the high Middle Ages provided a kind of "second spring" for the Christian use of philosophy, and the impact was wide-ranging, including the development of natural law ethics and a renewed interest in the nature of things that eventually blossomed into modern science.

In each of the chapters of this book we have had reason to return to the relation between faith and reason that was the special focus of the opening chapter. While the history of medieval thought does include a number of figures who rejected philosophy altogether, the mainstream of philosophers in this period accepted as their task the project to which Augustine and Anselm gave a name when they spoke of *fides quaerens intellectum* – faith seeking understanding.

The directionality implied in this phrase is crucial. Most of these thinkers are not trying to give a religious orientation to a philosophical position but to use philosophical insights and ways of proceeding to deepen understanding and appreciation of their religious faith. Some individual thinkers, of course, give hints of doing the reverse. Eriugena, for instance, and Eckhart have positions that approach pantheism; the radical Aristotelians like Siger of Brabant become so enamored of Aristotelian hylomorphism as to call into question personal immortality; and fourteenth-century nominalists like William of Ockham nearly make logic into the rule that would be normative for reality rather than taking it as instrument for investigating being as what we do not create, control, or alter but what simply is. But where any of these figures venture toward holding philosophy to become normative for faith rather than properly autonomous in its methodology and useful for the project of faith seeking deeper understanding, there are medieval contemporaries who promptly engage them in debate.

We see this same readiness for dealing with questions about the relation of faith and reason in the discussions about the validity of various proofs offered for the existence of God and in the debates over whether any human language can express God's nature. There is considerable disagreement about which proofs, if any, are successful as philosophical demonstrations. In trying to talk about God's nature, some medieval philosophers clearly prefer the route of "negative theology" in which it is better to emphasize the limits of our human powers of expression by denying that there are any limits upon the divine nature rather than to risk confining the infinite in terminology that cannot escape delimiting what it tries to express. Others insist that the inevitable limits of human language do not imply an inability to say true things about God, so long as one is careful not to think that one comprehends the infinite in finite terminology. These thinkers urge that there is merit in pointing out the direction in which to find the infinite by means of a "super-eminent theology" that has a philosophically nuanced theory of analogous predication. That same debate is played out today in the debate between the critics of ontotheology and the defenders of analogical language in regard to God.

The medieval authors studied here give evidence of their appreciation for the connection between metaphysics, epistemology, and philosophy of nature in the stances that they take on universals, transcendentals, the divine ideas, and the natures of created things. In their positions on universals, for instance, we find a plurality of approaches in support of a basic metaphysical realism about kinds. With this stance they combine a philosophical appreciation of the difficulties in articulating how any human knowledge of natural kinds needs to work. In the course of developing their various positions on the divine ideas, they try to do so in a way that will escape the basic Aristotelian objections to the Platonic doctrine of Ideas by envisioning them as divine ideas within the mind of God. The adaptations that they make in the received tradition result in a philosophically sophisticated metaphysics not so much focused on eternal essences as on created things seen as participating in the divine ideas. This approach proves useful to them for describing a cosmos of created beings that have distinct natures, and it makes possible a renewal of the philosophy of nature. The development of a doctrine of the transcendental properties of being serves to support the claim that these natures are objective, intelligible, and universally present in each of the beings of a given kind, but it also provides a connection to certain religious doctrines. The transcendental property of being called "goodness" (*bonum*), for instance, is correlated with their religious conviction that a benevolent God created everything that exists, and thus anything that is evil (morally wicked or metaphysically deficient) is a privation of the due goodness within some being rather than a positive reality in its own right.

All considered, the medieval philosophers under study here offer rich resources for our contemporary philosophizing. To appreciate the contributions that these thinkers can make to perennial philosophical problems, it is crucial to know the background that is the field for their work, and then to appreciate the concepts that they developed, the distinctions that they made, and the arguments that they offered for their positions. It is the hope of the author of this volume to have assisted in that project.

GLOSSARY

accident, accidental form   in the Aristotelian tradition, the general name for any of the various dependent features of a being, namely: *quality, quantity, relation, action, passion, time, place, habit, posture*

accidental change   any of the types of modification that a being can undergo without ceasing to be the type of being that it is; hence, a change in any of its *accidents*; see also *substantial change*

acquired habit   a disposition of character that comes about by repetition, as in the case of a *virtue* that one achieves by making the same choice over and over again

act   often used in the phrase "in act" as a kind of shorthand for "actual" or "real"; the term can also be used to mean "an action," and some authors distinguish between "the act of a human being" (what physically occurs) and "a human act" (an action for which one bears responsibility because it was deliberately undertaken)

action   one of the Aristotelian *accidents*; it is the term for the *category* of terms that designate what a being does

actuality   what something is, how it is; this term is often juxtaposed with *potentiality* (what something can become, how it might be)

agent intellect   for Aristotle, the power of the mind to abstract the forms of things from the sensory impressions that a person has received

angel, angelic intelligence   incorporeal, thinking beings

analogy   an extended comparison of the properties of objects thought to be similar; analogical predication involves the use of a given term to convey meanings that are in some ways the same but in some ways different (e.g., the use of "healthy" to describe certain kinds of diet, exercise, and facial complexion) *see equivocity and univocity*

anima Latin term for *soul*

animus Latin term for *mind*

apology a type of oration designed to provide a reasonable and persuasive defense.

apophatic theology the approach to language about God that stresses what we cannot know and hence prefers to use negations and denials rather than positive assertions (e.g., "immaterial")

Apostolic Age the earliest period of Christian history, so named for the Apostles who knew Jesus Christ and their immediate disciples; see *patristic*

Arianism the theological position named after Arius, its founder, that Christ was a being superior to humans but inferior to God

becoming an English way to render *fieri* ("to become, to be made") so as to indicate process, including coming into existence, changing in any way, and even passing away.

being in Latin *ens* (the present participle) refers to "a being" while *esse* (the infinitive) means "to be, to exist." The conjugated forms of *esse* (*sum, es, est . . .*, I am, you are, he/she/it is . . .), whatever the verb tense, can be used existentially or predicatively, e.g., *deus est* ("God is, God exists") and *deus potens est* ("God is powerful"). Because *being* can refer to *essence* as well as to *existence*, one can use the verb "to be" predicatively to talk about features that belong to an essence, regardless of whether there are any existing instances of that essence, e.g., "unicorns are white."

biblical wisdom literature the sapiential books of the Bible, including Psalms, Proverbs, Job, Ecclesiastes (Qoheleth), Ecclesiasticus (Sirach), Song of Songs, Daniel, and Wisdom of Solomon.

category the general Aristotelian term for the types of possible predicates and the types of being; according to Aristotle's book *Categories*, there are ten categories: *substance* and the nine *accidents*, namely, quality, quantity, relation, action, passion (the undergoing of action), time, place, habit, and posture.

causality the principle that for those beings whose *sufficient reason* is not found in themselves, there must be in another an adequate explanation for this existence or activity; see *material cause, formal cause, efficient cause, final cause*

cognition a general term for knowledge; one may speak, e.g., of sensory cognition and intellectual cognition

conceptual distinction a distinction that is the product of reason

conceptualism   the philosophical position that takes universals to exist only in the mind but to have some basis in extra-mental reality

contingent being   a being that has been caused to exist, but that could not have existed; see *necessary being*

cosmology   the study of the universe, from the Greek term *kosmos*, which refers to any beautifully or well-ordered whole, including the world

creation ex nihilo   the doctrine that there was no pre-existent material out of which God fashioned the universe, but that God created the matter as well as the forms of everything that is

creature   a general term for any of God's creations considered in its status as existing because of the divine gift of existence; the term does not deny that this-worldly causes were operative in its coming to be, but it stresses the status of this being as ultimately dependent on a divine source

demiurge   from the Greek word for "craftsman," this term is used in Plato's *Timaeus* for the god who shapes the material world in imitation of the Forms

dialectic   a synonym for logic

discursive reasoning   cognition that comes about through a step-by-step process

divine ideas   the patterns or forms for things, in the mind of God

divine illumination   the view that God brings the human mind to know certain truths by shining an incorporeal light upon the intellect

efficient cause   the agent of change; that which is responsible for actuating a potency, for communicating a perfection

emanation   for Neoplatonism, the outpouring of being from the divine source, the progressive movement from the one to the many

empiricism   in the broad sense, any view appealing to experience, and especially sensory experience, as the source of knowledge; in modern philosophy, a theory of knowledge associated with figures like Locke, Berkeley, and Hume and contrasted with *rationalism*

epistemology   the theory of knowledge

equivocity   the use of a given term with entirely different meanings (e.g., the "bark" of a tree and the "bark" of a dog); see *analogy* and *univocity*

essence what a thing is; often the Latin term *essentia* is used to render the Greek term *ousia*

eternal, everlasting although sometimes synonyms, there is a technical difference between these terms, in that *eternal* is used to refer to the simultaneous presence of all times to God, whereas *everlasting* refers to temporal endurance without end

exemplary causality a term for God's use of the divine ideas as the prototypes of all things in the act of creation

existence that a thing is, its actuality, its presence

fideism a theological position that regards religious faith as a reliable source of knowledge but tends to be skeptical about the possibility of gaining much knowledge about God or morality by unaided reason

fides quaerens intellectum faith seeking understanding

final cause the end or goal; that for the sake of which something is done

form in general, a being's structural principle, that which provides not only shape (Greek *morphe*) and external appearance (Greek *idea*) but also internal structures that make possible a being's activities and functions; see *substantial form* and *accidental form*.

Form capitalized in order to indicate a reference to the exemplars for all things, according to Plato; also known as *Ideas*. The Greek words being rendered here are *eidos* and *idea*.

formal cause the structural principle that makes something what it is

formal distinction for Duns Scotus, a way to distinguish things that are never found separately but whose difference from one another is not merely the product of reason (e.g., the distinction between a thing's existence and its essence)

Genesis the first book of the Bible; its opening chapters contain the story of God's creation of the world

genus/species according to Aristotle, a hierarchical system of classification used for defining things by indicating the group to which something belongs and the difference that distinguishes that thing within a larger group

goodness as a transcendental property of being, the perfection of a being that makes it suitable for being desired; as a term in morality, the rectitude in the order of a person's loves (that is, an inclination to love the right object in the right way)

habit   one of the Aristotelian *accidents*; it is the *category* for terms that describe how a being usually or customarily acts or appears; a disposition. When writing of the *habits* involved in the *virtues*, scholastic writers often distinguish between *acquired* and *infused* habits

hermeneutics   the study of theories about the interpretation and understanding of texts and systems of meaning

hylemorphism (sometimes spelled as **hylomorphism**)   the Aristotelian doctrine that physical substances are unities of matter and form

idea   that by which something is known, a concept

Idea   capitalized in order to indicate a reference to the exemplars for all things, according to Plato; also known as *Forms*

immanence   the notion that God is present to the world; see *transcendence*

Incarnation   the Christian Belief that the second person of the Trinity, the eternal Son of God the Father, assumed a human nature (etymologically, the term *incarnation* suggests "took flesh") as Jesus Christ in the womb of Mary. "Christ" is not a family name but a title, from the Greek translation *Christos* of the Hebrew term *Messiah* ("anointed one").

infused habit   the introduction of a state or disposition by divine gift, e.g., the bestowal of faith or charity

intellect   the power of cognition in a rational being; the capacity to understand, to abstract, to make judgments, to reason

intuition   an immediate type of cognition – see *discursive reasoning*

kataphatic theology   the view that stresses the infinite nature of divine perfections and hence tends to use terminology that stresses the lack of any limitation in the attribute being predicated of God (e.g., God is said to be "good" and "wise" but not in the limited ways in which goodness and wisdom are commonly experienced directly in creatures)

knowledge   see *scientia, cognition*

logos   a Greek term with a wide range of meaning, including "word," "reason," "account"; in Christian theology, this term is often used for the Second Person of the Trinity ("the Word of God")

Manicheism   the dualist school of thought that originated from the eclectic Persian thinker Mani; this school of thought emphasizes a pair of principles (Light and Darkness) as an explanation for good and evil in the world

material cause in the Aristotelian system, one of the four causes; that out of which something is made; more technically, the principle of potentiality within any finite being

matter a general term for whatever is physical; more broadly, a general term for anything that has potential for change

memory the capacity to remember, the faculty for retaining what one has experienced and what one can come to know

metaphysics the study of being as being, taken by medieval thinkers to include the study of reality as such, the study of the source of all being (God), the study of the types of being (the *categories* studied in *ontology*), and the study of the *transcendentals* (the cross-categorical principles).

mind a general term for the power to know and to will, including not just the capacity to perform mental activities but also the development of mental habits; the seat of consciousness

monophysitism the doctrine that Jesus had only a single nature, rather than the position taken by orthodox forms of Christianity, that he was a divine person (the Son of God) who assumed a human nature at the time of the Incarnation.

naturalism the philosophical disposition to give explanations in terms of this-worldly physical factors without resort to other-worldly or immaterial factors wherever possible; this position should be distinguished from *metaphysical naturalism*, the position that there is nothing other than the physical

natural philosophy the study of the principles of *nature*, with a special focus on the *causes* and the kinds of things

nature the English for *natura* (Latin) and *physis* (Greek), terms with a wide range of meanings, including something's innermost qualities, powers, dispositions but also something's outward appearance, the kind or type something is, because of its inner constitution. Its technical meaning in Aristotelian philosophy is the internal principle of a thing's growth and operations

necessary being a being for whom it is impossible not to exist; see *contingent being*

Neoplatonism the philosophy of Plotinus and Platonically influenced philosophers; in general, this school of thought stressed the inapplicability of Aristotle's *categories* for the intelligible realm

and followed a Platonic approach to the higher realms of being by
developing a theory of emanation of all things from the One

nominalism   the philosophical approach that proceeds from holding
that *universals* do not exist in their own right but are simply
terms

Ockham's razor   see *parsimony*

omniscience   the quality of being all-knowing; when said of God, it
is generally taken to be a claim that there is nothing that God does
not know, rather than a claim to understand exactly how God
knows everything, or how God can know everything, including
human free choices, without compromising the freedom of those
choices.

ontology   often a synonym for *metaphysics*, but (strictly speaking)
the study of the kinds of beings according to their *categories*

Organon   literally, "a tool"; the name for the set of Aristotle's
logical works

original sin   in Christian doctrine, the sin of Adam for which God
expelled Adam and Eve from the Garden of Eden and that is
inherited by all their descendants, not as an actual sin in the way
it was for Adam (for which a person must knowingly and deliberately choose to do wrong) but as an inherited punishment (morality) and as a kind of defect (usually described in terms of darkness
of mind, weakness of will, and disorder in desires). Theologians
have often speculated on just how original sin is transmitted from
one generation to the next.

pantheism   on the question of the relation of God and the world,
the view that sees all being as ultimately the being of God

parsimony   the principle of explanation, according to which one
may not postulate unnecessary hypothetical entities when simpler
explanations are sufficient; correlatively, one may postulate hypothetical entities when simpler explanation cannot account for a
given phenomenon; sometimes known as *Ockham's Razor*

participation   in metaphysics, a term by which to describe the way
in which individuals share in a universal, a common essence

passion   (1) one of the Aristotelian *accidents*; it is the *category* for
terms that describe how something is affected or what it is undergoing, experiencing, suffering; (2) within philosophical psychology, a general name for the emotions considered as movements of
soul, such as joy, hatred, or fear

passive intellect see *potential intellect*

patristic a term for the period of early Christian history, from the close of the Apostolic age until the medieval period, so named for the "Church Fathers" (mostly bishops and monks) who wrote scriptural commentaries and spiritual treatises, often making use of philosophical categories and arguments

peripatetic the term often applied to the followers of Aristotle by reason of their empirical approach; the Greek word from which this term derives means "walking around"

place one of the Aristotelian *accidents*; in general, it is the *category* for location-terms, considered as a sub-type of *relation*

pneuma Greek term for "wind, air, breath, spirit, life"

possibility the absence of logical contradiction

posture one of the Aristotelian *accidents*; in general, it is the *category* for terms that describe the internal *relation* of a being's parts to one another

potential intellect for Aristotle, the power of the mind to understand things by means of the forms abstracted by the *agent intellect* from whatever sensory impressions a person has received

potentiality the capacity to be or to become actual; see *possibility*

powers of the soul the capacities of a living being to act according to the patterns typical of its nature

predicables according to Porphyry, the five types of super-categories: genus, species, difference, property, and accident

predication the attribution of a property to something

pre-Socratic the general name for Greek philosophers and naturalists who worked before the time of Socrates, including Thales, Anaximenes, Anaximander, Heraclitus, Parmenides, Empedocles, Anaxagoras, and atomists like Democritus and Leucippus

providence divine care for the created world

psyche Greek term for "soul"

quality one of the Aristotelian *accidents*; in general, the category for terms describing what sort of properties something has

quantity one of the Aristotelian *accidents*; in general, the category for terms describing how much of something there is

rational soul the life principle of a human being, the seat of a person's powers of life, including the powers of digestion, growth, reproduction, sensory-perception, *memory*, locomotion, *intellect*, and *will*

rationalism   in the broadest sense, any view that appeals to reason as a source of knowledge or justification; in a pejorative sense, a term to express the criticism that a thinker is trying to impose a subjective order upon things and failing to respect objective reality; in modern philosophy, the name of a school of thought associated with figures like Descartes, Spinoza, and Leibniz and contrasted with *empiricism*

realism   the philosophical approach that affirms that universals somehow genuinely exist

recollection   the act of remembering again, e.g., when one is trying to bring back to mind what one has forgotten; for Plato, learning proceeds through recollection of the Forms that one encountered prior to embodiment.

reincarnation   the doctrine that souls become enfleshed in a series of bodies

scholasticism   the new approach to philosophy and theology prominent in the universities beginning in the thirteenth century and characterized by a rigorous method of making distinctions, defining terms, defending theses, and raising and answering objections, often conducted in public disputations

scientia   the Latin term for an organized body of knowledge that can trace conclusions back to first principles; often translated as "science" (despite the tendency in standard English to restrict the term "science" to empirical, experimentally based bodies of knowledge such as physics or chemistry)

semantics   the theory of meaning

seminal reasons   according to Stoicism and Augustine, the microscopic seeds in matter that are the formative source for forms of macroscopic objects

sensitive soul   the life principle in any animal, the seat of an animal's powers of life, including the powers of digestion, growth, reproduction, sensory-perception, memory, and locomotion

simplicity   the state of not having component parts; when said of God, it generally names not a distinct attribute but a kind of rule for human speech about God, namely, the rule that the various perfections one attributes to God are named by distinct terms but are not actually separate in God.

soul   the life-principle in any living thing; hence medieval thinkers speak of the *vegetative soul* of plants, the *sensitive soul* in animals, and the *rational soul* in human beings

species   etymologically related to the Latin words for "appearance," a *sensible species* refers to the sensory impression received by a knower; metaphysically, *species* refers to a group within a *genus* that can be identified by a distinguishing difference

subsistent existence   to exist as a substance in one's own right

substance   in general, a unified being; a particular instance of a natural kind (but the term *substance* can also be used for the species or kind); the name for the first of Aristotle's *categories*

substantial change   the kind of change that a being undergoes when it ceases to be organized by the *substantial form* that had been its principle of organization; in the course of a radical change of this sort, the *matter* that this *substantial form* had been organizing comes to be organized by some other *substantial forms(s).*

substantial form   the dominant principle of organization in a unified being

sufficient reason   the principle that for everything that exists there is an adequate explanation, either in itself or in another; see *causality*

super-eminent theology   the view that one does well to proceed in discussions about the nature of God by pointing toward the infinite in what one attributes to God (e.g., "omniscient" or "omnipotent")

supposition   the reference of a given term within a sentence

syllogism   an argument in which two premises (each with two terms, one of them common to both premises) lead to a conclusion

terminist logic   the doctrine of those logicians who emphasized the theory of the properties of terms and stressed the classification of the various kinds of *supposition*

Thomism   the school of thought that follows Thomas Aquinas

time   (1) one of the Aristotelian *accidents*; in general, the category for terms that describe the relation of one being in terms of the measurement of motion of other beings, especially celestial bodies with highly regular patterns of motion such as the moon and the sun; (2) Plato described *time* as "the moving image of eternity"; (3) Augustine recognizes the Aristotelian notion but prefers to regard time as the "distention" or "stretching" of the *soul*, in such a way that at the "present" moment we may also be conscious of the "past" by memory and we may anticipate the "future" by desire or expectation

traducianism   the theory that holds that souls are not directly created by God but are generated from the souls of one's parents

transcendentals   the cross-categorical properties of being, including *unity, truth,* and *goodness*; the terms that express these properties

transcendence   the notion that God is entirely distinct from the world; see *immanence*

truth   when said about propositions or about positions that someone is holding, the conformity between thought and reality; when used as a *transcendental* term, it is co-extensive with *being* and names the property of a being by which it is intelligible, i.e., able to be understood

unity   the state of being whole, not divided (whether divisible or indivisible); when used as a *transcendental* term, it is coextensive with *being* and indicates that the being under discussion is undivided

universal   a term is universal if it is of the sort that can be said of every member of a class; for some theorists, there were not only universal terms and concepts but the separately existing essences that are the common source for all members of a given class

univocity   the use of a given term in exactly the same sense; see *analogy* and *equivocity*

vegetative soul   the life principle in any plant, the seat of a plant's powers of life, including the powers of nutrition, growth, and reproduction

virtue   a well-developed disposition, an excellence; for medieval thinkers, there are intellectual virtues (such as wisdom, science, prudence) as well as moral virtues (such as justice, courage, moderation).

will   rational appetite; the mental capacity to feel attraction from what is perceived as good and aversion to what is perceived as evil; also, the capacity to take delight in a perceived good and to feel revulsion toward a perceived evil, and the capacity for making a free choice

world soul   according to Plato's *Timaeus,* that which is responsible for the regularity of the movements of the universe

HISTORICAL FIGURES

Unless other wise specified, the dates given are AD. Some dates are approximations, as indicated by the abbreviation "*c.*" For some individuals, it is hard to provide any dates other than what is called their *floruit* (a peak moment of their maturity), indicated here by the abbreviation "*fl.*"

Abelard (1079–1142) theologian known for developing a voluntarist ethics and for submitting theological propositions to the tests of grammar and logic; seducer of Héloïse.

Adelard of Bath (*c.*1080–*c.*1160) English scholar, interested in astronomy and philosophy of nature.

Albert the Great (*c.*1193–1284) Dominican friar and later bishop, a Neoplatonic thinker influenced by the recovery of Aristotle, the mentor of Aquinas.

Alexander of Hales (*c.*1185–1245) English Franciscan who taught at Paris and wrote an early commentary on the *Sentences* of Peter Lombard.

Ambrose (340–97) bishop in Milan, influential upon Augustine.

Anselm (1033–09) abbot of Bec and later archbishop of Canterbury, who developed a philosophical proof for the existence of God now called the ontological argument.

Aquinas, Thomas (*c.*1224–74) Dominican friar who created a Christian form of Aristotelianism.

Aristotle (387–321 BC) Greek philosopher with an empirical approach who studied under Plato and then founded his own school, the Lyceum.

Augustine (354–430) bishop of Hippo, among the greatest of medieval philosophers and theologians.

Averroes (1126–98)   Islamic philosopher from Spain in the Aristotelian tradition.

Avicenna (980–1037)   Islamic philosopher from Persia in the Platonist tradition.

Bernard of Clairvaux (1090–1153)   a Cistercian abbot concerned with the reform of monastic life; he was suspicious of the tendency of thinkers like Abelard to subordinate theology to logic.

Boethius (c.480–524)   Roman senator and philosopher who tried to reconcile Plato and Aristotle.

Boethius of Dacia (c.1240–c.1285)   Scandinavian philosopher at Paris associated with the radical Aristotelianism of Siger of Brabant.

Bonaventure (c.1217–74)   Franciscan friar and later cardinal, a scholastic thinker in the tradition of Augustine.

Buridan, Jean (c.1300–64)   French cleric whose works on impetus and inertia prepared the way for the heliocentric view of the cosmos; also known for contributions on the problem of free choice.

Cicero (106–43 BC)   Roman statesman and philosopher in the period of the late Republic.

Clarembald of Arras (1110–87)   French theologian of the school of Chartres who commented at length on the works of Boethius.

Clement of Alexandria (c.150–c.216)   patristic theologian in Christian Egypt.

Copernicus, Nicholaus (1473–1543)   Polish astronomer responsible for the idea of the heliocentric cosmos.

Democritus (c.450 BC –c.370 BC)   Greek natural philosopher in the tradition of atomism.

Dionysius the Areopagite (sometimes called Pseudo-Dionysius (fl. 6th century)   a Syrian monk who developed the tradition of negative theology under this pseudonym.

Eckhart, Meister (c.1260–1327)   Dominican friar and mystic who developed a form of negative theology that some suspected of pantheism.

Eriugena, John Scotus (c.810–c.877)   mystical philosopher who developed the thought of Dionysius into a system that some have charged with pantheism.

Galileo Galilei (1564–1642)   Italian astronomer whose use of the telescope provided important evidence for the heliocentric view of the cosmos.

Gaunilo of Marmoutiers (*fl.* 11th century) monk who voiced objections to Anselm's proof for the existence of God and thereby elicited a valuable philosophical response from Anselm.

Gilbert of Poitiers (1076–1154) scholastic theologian with heterodox views on various theological points.

Gratian (*fl.* 12th c.) canon lawyer from Bologna who used the scholastic method on the body of ecclesiastical law to produce the massive *Concordance of Discordant Canons*.

Gregory IX (*c.*1145–1241) canon lawyer and later an influential pope in the scholastic period.

Gregory of Nyssa (330–95) theologian in Asia Minor who made great use of Platonic thought.

Grosseteste, Robert (1170–1253) English statesman and philosopher, later bishop of Lincoln, known especially for his work in science and the philosophy of nature.

Héloïse (1101–62) bright female student seduced by Abelard; later prioress at Argenteuil.

Heraclitus (*c.*535 BC–*c.*475 BC) Greek philosopher famous for his doctrine of universal change.

Jerome (331–420) responsible for the first thorough translation of the Bible into Latin.

John of Sacrobosco (1195–1256) English astronomer and astrologer.

Justin I (490–527) Eastern Roman Emperor at Byzantium at the time of Boethius.

Leucippus (*c.*490 BC–???) Greek philosopher in the atomist tradition.

Lombard, Peter (*c.*1100–*c.*1164) compiler of an important collection of texts (especially drawn from Augustine) that served as the standard textbook in theology for centuries.

Lucretius (*c.*99–55 BC) Epicurean philosopher at Rome, author of *On the Nature of Things*.

Macrobius (*fl.* 395–423) Roman grammarian and Neoplatonic philosopher.

Maimonides (1135–1204) Jewish philosopher in the Aristotelian tradition.

Mani (216–76) eclectic thinker from Mesopotamia, founder of Manicheanism.

Marston, Roger (1235–1303) Franciscan friar who studied under Peckham and promoted Augustinianism over in response to the Aristotelian revival associated with Aquinas.

Matthew of Aquasparta (1240–1302) Franciscan friar who became a Master at Paris in the Augustinian tradition favored by Bonaventure.

Maximus the Confessor (580–682) mystical theologian who made great use of Neoplatonic thought.

Nicholas of Cusa (1401–64) German cardinal and mystic who made significant contributions to the area of negative theology on the possibilities and limits of human knowledge of God.

Olivi, John Peter (1248–98) Franciscan friar and theologian with controversial views on poverty.

Origen (*c.*185–253) Christian theologian at Alexandria who made much use of neoplatonic thought.

Parmenides (*c.*530 BC–*c.*480 BC) philosopher from Elea, famous for his monism.

Peckham, John (1230–92) Franciscan friar and later Archbishop of Canterbury, disciple of Bonaventure and opponent of Aquinas.

Philip the Chancellor (*c.*1160–1236) French theologian and archdeacon of Paris who was very hostile to the increasing influence of the new mendicant orders like the Franciscans and the Dominicans.

Philo (20 BC–AD 50) Jewish philosopher at Alexandria.

Plato (*c.*428–347 BC) Greek philosopher who studied under Socrates and then founded his own school, the Academy, and developed the theory of the Forms or Ideas.

Plotinus (207–70) founder of Neoplatonism, author of the *Enneads*.

Porphyry (232–305) Neoplatonist in the tradition of Plotinus, whose works he edited.

Ptolemy, Claudius (85–165) astronomer and philosopher responsible for the geocentric model of the cosmos.

Scheibler, Christoph (1598–1653) Lutheran scholastic thinker famous for his view on the transcendentals.

Scotus, John Duns (1265–1308) Franciscan friar noted for his position on individuation.

Siger of Brabant (*c.*1240–*c.*1284) member of the Arts Faculty at Paris who championed a radical interpretation of Aristotle that seemed to some at odds with Christian thought.

Socrates (469–399 BC)   stonemason who practiced philosophy in Athens.

Suárez, Francisco (1548–1617)   Jesuit philosopher and theologian in Spain who produced his own version of Thomism, especially influential in law and in metaphysics.

Tertullian (c.155–230)   theologian from North Africa who doubted the utility of philosophy.

Thābit ibn Qurra (836–901)   Islamic astronomer, mathematician, and physician from Baghdad.

Theodoric (454–536)   king of the Ostrogoths at Ravenna in the time of Boethius.

Urban IV (c.1195–1264)   an especially influential pope during the scholastic period.

Victorinus (fl. 361)   Neoplatonist philosopher influential on Augustine.

William of Champeaux (c.1070–c.1121)   staunch realist on the question of universals.

William of Moerbeke (1215–86)   translator of many Aristotelian works from Greek into Latin.

William of Ockham (1288–1347)   English Franciscan famous for his position on universals.

REFERENCES

Abelard, Peter (1971). *Scito te ipsum.* Translated by D. E. Luscombe as *Ethics, or Know Thyself,* in *Peter Abelard's Ethics.* Oxford: Clarendon Press.

Adler, Mortimer (1993). *The Difference of Man and the Difference It Makes.* Bronx, NY: Fordham University Press.

Adler, Mortimer (1940). *Problems for Thomists: The Problem of Species.* New York: Sheed & Ward.

Aertsen, Jan A. (1999). "Is There a Medieval Philosophy?" *International Philosophical Quarterly* 39/4 (1999): 385–412.

Aertsen, Jan A. (1996). *Medieval Philosophy and the Transcendentals: The Case of Thomas Aquinas.* Leiden and New York: E. J. Brill.

Aertsen, Jan A. (1988). *Nature and Creature: Thomas Aquinas's Way of Thought.* Translated by Herbert Donald Morton. Leiden: E. J. Brill.

Alexander of Hales (1951). *Glossa in quatuor libros sententiarum Petri Lombardi.* Quaracchi: Bibliotheca Franciscana.

Alighieri, Dante (1318). "Letter to Can Grande della Scalla." Available online by the Princeton Dante Project at: http://etcweb.princeton.edu/dante/index.html.

Allison, Henry E. (2004). *Kant's Transcendental Idealism.* Revised and enlarged edition. New Haven, CT: Yale University Press.

Ameriks, Karl, ed. (2000). *The Cambridge Companion to German Idealism.* New York: Cambridge University Press.

Ando, Clifford, ed. (2003). *Roman Religion.* Edinburgh: Edinburgh University Press.

Anscombe, G. E. M. (1958). "Modern Moral Philosophy." *Philosophy* 33: 1–19.

Anselm (1998). *Anselm of Canterbury: The Major Works.* Edited by Brian Davies and G. R. Evans. Oxford and New York: Oxford University Press.

Aquinas, Thomas (1995). *In duodecim libros Metaphysicorum Aristotelis expositio*. Translated by John Patrick Rowan as *Commentary on Aristotle's Metaphysics*. Notre Dame, IN: Dumb Ox Books.

Aquinas, Thomas (1993b). *De unitate intellectus contra Averroistas*. Translated with commentary and interpretive essays by Ralph McInerny as *Aquinas Against the Averroists: On There Being Only One Intellect*. West Lafayette, IN: Purdue University Press.

Aquinas, Thomas (1993a). *De veritate*. Translated by Robert W. Mulligan, S.J. as *Truth*, vol. 1. Albany, NY: Preserving Christian Publications.

Aquinas, Thomas (1983). *De ente et essentia*. Translated by Armand A. Maurer as *On Being and Essence*. Toronto: Pontifical Institute of Medieval Studies. 2nd revised edition.

Aquinas, Thomas (1975). *Summa contra Gentiles*, 4 vols. Translated by Anton C. Pegis, Vernon J. Bourke, J. F. Anderson, and C. J. O'Neil. Notre Dame, IN: University of Notre Dame Press.

Aquinas, Thomas (1963). *In Aristotelis libro de Caelo et Mundo*. Translated by R. F. Larcher as *Exposition of Aristotle's Treatise on the Heavens*. Columbus, OH: College of St Mary.

Aquinas, Thomas (1952). *Quaestiones disputate de potentia Dei*. Translated by the English Dominican Fathers as *On the Power of God*. Westminster, MD: Newman Press.

Aquinas, Thomas (1947). *Scriptum super sententiis magistri Petri Lombardi*. Edited by Marie Fabien Moos. Paris: P. Lethellieux (1947–56).

Aquinas, Thomas (1945). *Summa theologiae*. Translated as *Summa of Theology* in *Basic Writings of Saint Thomas Aquinas*, 2 vols., edited by Anton C. Pegis. New York: Random House.

Ariès, Philippe and Georges Duby, eds. (1987). *A History of Private Life*. Cambridge, MA: Belknap Press of Harvard University; vol. 2: *Revelations of the Medieval World*.

Aristotle (1984). *The Complete Works of Aristotle: The Revised Oxford Translation*. Translated by Jonathan Barnes. Princeton: Princeton University Press.

Armstrong, A. H. (1967). *The Cambridge History of Later Greek and Earl Medieval Philosophy*. Cambridge: Cambridge University Press.

Augustine (2007). *De Ordine*. Translated by Silvano Borruso as *On Order*. South Bend, IN: St Augustine's Press.

Augustine (1998). *Contra duas epistolas Pelagianorum* and *De nuptiis et concupiscentiae*. Translated by Roland E. Teske and John E. Rotelle as *Answer to the Pelagians II and Marriage and Desire*. Hyde Park, NY: New City Press.

Augustine (1995b). *Contra Academicos*. Translated by Peter King as *Against the Academicians*. Indianapolis, IN: Hackett.

Augustine (1995a). *De Doctrina Christiana*. Translated by R. P. H. Green as *On Christian Doctrine*. Oxford: Clarendon Press.

Augustine (1991b). *Confessions*. Translated by Henry Chadwick. New York: Oxford University Press.

Augustine (1991a). *De Trinitate*. Translated with introduction and notes by Edmund Hill, O.P., as *Augustine: The Trinity*; introduction, translation, and notes by Edmund Hill, O.P. Brooklyn, NY: New City Press.

Augustine (1990). *Soliloquiae* and *De immortalitate animae*. Translated by Gerard Watson as *Soliloquies and Immortality of the Soul*. Warminster, UK: Aris & Philips.

Augustine (1984). *De civitate Dei*. Translated by Henry Bettenson as *Concerning the City of God Against the Pagans*. Harmondsworth, Middlesex: Penguin Books, 1984.

Augustine (1982c). *De diversis quaestionibus LXXXVI*. Translated by David L. Mosher as *Eighty-Three Different Questions*. Washington, DC: The Catholic University of America Press.

Augustine (1982b). *De libero arbitrio voluntatis*. Translated by Anna S. Benjamin and L. H. Hackstaff as *On Free Choice of the Will*. Indianapolis, IN: Bobbs-Merrill.

Augustine (1982a). *De Genesi ad litteram*. Translated by John Hammond Taylor, S.J., as *The Literal Meaning of Genesis*, 2 vols. Ramsey, NJ: Newman Press.

Augustine (1979). *De vera religione* and *De magistro*. Translated by John H. S. Burleigh in *Augustine: Earlier Writings*. Philadelphia, PA: Westminster Press.

Augustine (1961). *Enchiridion de fide, spe et caritate*. Translated by Henry Paolucci as *The Enchiridion on Faith, Hope, and Love*. South Bend, IN: Regnery Gateway.

Augustine (1947). *De immortalitate animae*. Translated by Ludwig Schopp as *Augustine: On the Immortality of the Soul*. Washington, DC: The Catholic University of America Press.

Augustine (1944). *De beata vita*. Translated by Ruth Allison Brown as *The Happy Life*. Washington, DC: The Catholic University of America.

Augustine (1933). *De quantitate animae*. Translated by Francis E. Tourscher as *The Measure of the Soul*. Philadelphia, PA: Peter Reilly.

Bearman, P. J., ed. (2002). *The Encyclopedia of Islam*. Leiden: E. J. Brill.

Bible (1965). *The Oxford Annotated Bible, with the Apocrypha*. Revised Standard Version (RSV). Edited by Herbt G. May and Bruce Manning Metzger. New York: Oxford University Press.

Björno, Azel A., R. O. Besthorn, and H. Sufer, eds. (1997). *Die astrono-mischen Tafeln des Muhammed ibn Musa al-Kwarizmi (The Astrono-mical Tables of Muhammed ibn Musa al-Khwarizmi, fl. 813–846).* Frankfurt-am-Main, Germany: Institute for the History of Arabic-Islamic Science at the Johann Wolfgang Goethe University.

Blackwell, Richard (1991). *Galileo, Bellarmine, and the Bible, including a translation of Foscarini's Letter on the motion of the earth.* Notre Dame, IN: University of Notre Dame Press.

Bobik, Joseph (1998). *Aquinas on Matter and Form and the Elements.* Notre Dame, IN: University of Notre Dame Press.

Bobik, Joseph (1965). *Aquinas: On Being and Essence. A Translation and Interpretation.* Notre Dame, IN: University of Notre Dame Press.

Boethius (2000), *Consolationes Philosophiae.* Translated by Victor E. Watts. *Consolation of Philosophy.* London: Penguin.

Boethius (1978). *De Trinitate* and *Quomodo Substantiae (De Hebdomadi-bus).* Edited and translated by H. F. Stewart, E. K. Rand, and S. J. Tester in *Boethius: The Theological Tractates.* Cambridge, MA: Harvard University Press. Loeb Classical Library.

Boland, Vivian (1996). *Ideas in God According to Saint Thomas Aquinas: Sources and Synthesis.* Leiden: E. J. Brill.

Bonaventure (1992). *Breviloquium.* Translated by Erwin Esser Nemmers. St Louis, MO: Herder.

Bonaventure (1978). *Itinerarium mentis in Deum.* Translated by Ewert Cousins, in *Bonaventure: The Soul's Journey into God, The Tree of Life, and The Life of St Francis.* Mahwah, NJ: Paulist Press, pp. 51–116.

Bonaventure (1902). *In Sententiae Petri Lombardi,* in vol. 2 of *Opera Omnia Doctoris seraphici S. Bonaventurae,* 10 vols. Quaracchi: Ad Aquas Claras (1882–1902).

Bonaventure (1970). *Collationes in Hexaemeron.* Translated by José de Vinck as *Collations on the Six Days.* Vol. 5 of *The Works of Bonaventure.* Paterson, NJ: St Anthony's Guild.

Bourke, Vernon J., ed. (1978). *The Essential Augustine.* Indianapolis, IN: Hackett.

Bradley, Denis (1997). *Aquinas on the Twofold Human Good: Reason and Human Happiness in Aquinas's Moral Science.* Washington, DC: The Catholic University of America Press.

Broadie, Alexander (1993). *Introduction to Medieval Logic,* 2nd edition. New York: Oxford University Press.

Brown, Stephen (2007). *Historical Dictionary of Medieval Philosophy and Theology.* Lanham, MD: Scarecrow Press.

Buckley, Michael J. (1987). *At the Origins of Modern Atheism*. New Haven, CT: Yale University Press.

Buridan, John (2001). *Summulae de Dialectica*. Annotated translation with philosophical introduction by Gyula Klima. New Haven, CT: Yale University Press.

Burnell, Peter (2005). *The Augustinian Person*. Washington, DC: The Catholic University of America Press.

Burrell, David (1993). *Freedom and Creation in Three Traditions*. Notre Dame, IN: University of Notre Dame Press.

Capella, Martianus (1977). *De Nuptiis Philologiae et Mercurii*. Translated as *The Marriage of Philology and Mercury* in *Martianus Capella and the Seven Liberal Arts*, 2 vols. Edited and translated by William Harris Stahl and Richard Johnson, with E. L. Burge. New York: Columbia University Press.

Carabine, Deirdre. (2000). *John Scottus Eriugena*. New York: Oxford University Press.

Carmody, Francis J. (1960). *The Astronomical Works of Thabit b. Qurra*. Berkeley, CA: University of California Press.

Casarella, Peter J. (2006). *Cusanus: The Theory of Learned Ignorance*. Washington, DC: The Catholic University of America Press.

Chadwick, Henry (1981). *Boethius: The Consolation of Music, Logic, Theology, and Philosophy*. Oxford: Clarendon Press.

Chenu, M.-D. (1968). *Nature, Man, and Society in the Twelfth Century: Essays on New Theological Perspectives in the Latin West*. Translated and edited by Jerome Taylor and Lester K. Little. Chicago, IL: University of Chicago Press.

Clanchy, M. T. (1997). *Abelard: A Medieval Life*. Malden, MA: Blackwell.

Clarembald of Arras (2002). *The Boethian Commentaries of Clarembald of Arras*. Edited and translated by David B. George, John R. Fortin, et al. Notre Dame, IN: University of Notre Dame Press.

Clement of Alexandria (1991). Translated by John Ferguson as *Stromateis*. Washington, DC: The Catholic University of America Press.

Clement of Alexandria (1960). Translated by G. W. Butterworth as *Clement of Alexandria*. Cambridge, MA: Harvard University Press. Loeb Classical Library.

Cochrane, Charles Norris (2003). *Christianity and Classical Culture: A Study of Thought and Action from Augustus to Augustine*. Indianapolis, IN: Liberty Fund.

Cogan, Marc (1999). *The Design in the Wax: The Structure of the Divine Comedy and Its Meaning*. Notre Dame, IN: University of Notre Dame Press.

Colish, Marcia L. (1985). *The Stoic Tradition from Antiquity to the Early Middle Ages*. Leiden: E. J. Brill.

Collins, James D. (1984). *The Emergence of Philosophy of Religion*. New Haven, CT: Yale University Press.

Collins, James D. (1978). *God in Modern Philosophy*. Westport, CT: Greenwood Press.

Cornford, Francis Macdonald (1997). *Plato's Cosmology: The Timaeus of Plato, translated with a running commentary*. Indianapolis: Hackett.

Cousins, Ewert (1978). *Bonaventure and the Coincidence of Opposites*. Chicago, IL: Franciscan Herald Press.

Cullen, Christopher M. (2006). *Bonaventure*. New York: Oxford University Press.

Danielou, Jean (1973). *Gospel Message and Hellenistic Culture: A History of Early Christian Doctrine before the Council of Nicea*. Philadelphia, PA: Westminster.

Danielson, Dennis Richard (2000). *The Book of the Cosmos: Imagining the Universe from Heraclitus to Hawking*. Cambridge, MA: Perseus, 2000).

Davies, Brian, ed. (1998). *Philosophy of Religion: A Guide to the Subject*. London: Cassell.

Davies, Brian (1992). *The Thought of Thomas Aquinas*. Oxford: Clarendon Press.

Deely, John (2001). *Four Ages of Understanding*. Toronto, ONT: University of Toronto Press.

de Libera, Alain (1993). *La Philosophie médiévale*. Paris: Presses Universitaires de France.

de Lubac, Henri (1959). *Exégèse médiéval*, 4 vols. Paris: Aubier. English version: *Medieval Exegesis: The Four Senses of Scripture*, vol. 1, translated by Mark Sebanc (1998); vol. 2, translated by E. M. Macierowski (2000). Grand Rapids, MI: William B. Eerdmans.

d'Entreves, A. P. (1970). *Natural Law: An Introduction to Legal Philosophy*, revised edition. London: Hutchinson.

Descartes, René (1996). *Discourse on the Method and Meditations on First Philosophy*. Translated by David Weissman and William Theodore Bluhm. New Haven, CT: Yale University Press.

DiLascia, Daniel A., Eckhard Kessler, and Charlotte Methuen, eds. (1997). *Method and Order in Renaissance Philosophy of Nature*. Brookfield, VT: Ashgate.

Dillon, John M. (1990). *The Golden Chain: Studies in the Development of Platonism and Christianity*. Brookfield, VT: Gower.

Dillon, John M. (1996) *The Middle Platonists: A Study of Platonism 80 BC to AD 220*. London: Duckworth.

Dionysius the Areopagite (1987). Translated by Colm Luibheid and Paul Rorem as *Pseudo-Dionysius: The Complete Works*. Mahwah, NJ: Paulist Press.

Dobie, Robert J. (2003). "Reason and Revelation in the Thought of Meister Eckhart," *The Thomist* 67: 407–38.

Dodd, Tony (1998). *The Life and Thought of Siger of Brabant*. Lewiston, ME: Edward Mellen Press.

Dronke, Peter (1988). *A History of Twelfth-Century Western Philosophy*. New York: Cambridge University Press.

Duhem, Pierre (1985). *Medieval Cosmology: Theories of Infinite, Place, Time, Void, and the Plurality of Worlds*. Edited and translated by Roger Ariew. Chicago, IL: University of Chicago Press.

Dulles, Avery (1987). *The Catholicity of the Church*. New York: Oxford University Press.

Dulles, Avery (1994). *The Assurance of Things Hoped For: A Theology of Christian Faith*. New York: Oxford University Press.

Dumont, Stephen D. (1992). "Transcendental Being: Scotus and Scotists," *Topoi* 11: 135–48.

Dunn, Geoffrey D. (2004). *Tertullian*. New York: Routledge.

Eckhart, Meister (1974). *Quaestiones parisienses*. Translated with an introduction and notes by Armand Maurer as *Parisian Questions and Prologues*. Toronto, ONT: Pontifical Institute of Mediaeval Studies.

Epictetus (1998). *Discourses*. Translated by Robert F. Dobbin. Oxford: Clarendon Press.

Eriugena, John Scotus (1995). *Periphyseon*, Book IV. Edited and translated as *Liber quartus*, with English and Latin texts on facing pages, with English commentary. Dublin: Dublin Institute for Advanced Studies.

Eriugena, John Scotus (1987). *Periphyseon*, Books I–III. Translated by I. P. Sheldon-Williams and revised by John J. O'Meara as *Eriugena: Periphyseon (Division of Nature)*. Montreal: Bellarmin and Washington: Dumbarton Oaks.

Evans, G. R. (2000). *Bernard of Clairvaux*. New York: Oxford University Press.

Finnis, John (1998). *Aquinas*. New York: Oxford University Press.

Frank, William A. and Allan B. Wolter (1995). *Duns Scotus, Metaphysician*. West Lafayette, IN: Purdue University Press.

Frankfort, Henri (1977). *The Intellectual Adventure of Ancient Man: An Essay on Speculative Thought in the Ancient Near East*. Chicago, IL: University of Chicago Press.

French, R. K. and Andrew Cunningham. (1996). *Before Science: The Invention of the Friars' Natural Philosophy*. Brookfield, VT: Scolar Press.

Galen (1963). *On the Passions and Errors of the Soul.* Translated by Paul W. Harkins. Columbus: Ohio State University Press.

Galilei, Galileo (2001). *Dialogue Concerning the Two Chief World Systems, Ptolemaic and Copernican.* Translated by Stillman Drake. New York: Modern Library.

Gerson, Lloyd P. (1990). *God and Greek Philosophy: Studies in the Early History of Natural Theology.* New York: Routledge.

Gill, Mary Louise (1989). *Aristotle on Substance: The Paradox of Unity.* Princeton, NJ: Princeton University Press.

Gilson, Étienne (1969). *Reason and Revelation in the Middle Ages.* New York: Charles Scribner's Sons.

Gilson, Étienne (1965). *The Philosophy of St Bonaventure.* Translated by Dom Illtyd Trethowan and Frank H. Sheed. Paterson, NJ: St Anthony Guild Press.

Gilson, Étienne (1955). *History of Christian Philosophy in the Middle Ages.* London: Sheed and Ward.

Goodman, Lenn E. (2003). *Islamic Humanism.* Oxford: Oxford University Press.

Gracia, Jorge J. E. (1994). *Individuation in Scholasticism: The Late Middle Ages and the Counter-Reformation (1150–1650).* Albany, NY: SUNY Press.

Gracia, Jorge J. E. (1992). "Suárez and the Doctrine of the Transcendentals," *Topoi* 11: 121–33.

Granger, Herbert (1996). *Aristotle's Idea of the Soul.* Dordrecht: Kluwer.

Grant, Edward (1994). *Planets, Stars, and Orbs: The Medieval Cosmos 1200–1687.* New York: Cambridge University Press.

Gratian (1993). *Decretum Gratiani emendatum et notationibus illustratum una cum glossis.* Translated by Augustine Thompson and James Gordley as *Gratian: The Treatise on Laws (Decretum DD 1–20), with The Ordinary Gloss.* Washington, DC: The Catholic University of America Press.

Gregory of Nyssa (2000). *Homilies on the Beatitudes: An English Version with Commentary and Supporting Studies.* Edited by Hubertus R. Drobner and Alberto Viciano. Leiden: E. J. Brill.

Gregory of Nyssa (1972). *Dogmatic Treatises.* Translated by Henry Wace and Philip Schaff. Grand Rapids, MI: Eerdmans.

Gurr, John R. (1959). *The Principle of Sufficient Reason and Some Scholastic Systems, 1750–1900.* Milwaukee, WI: Marquette University Press.

Guthrie, W. K. C. (1978). "Plato's Views on the Nature of the Soul," in *Plato: A Collection of Critical Essays*, vol. 2: *Ethics, Politics, and Philosophy of Art and Religion.* Edited by Gregory Vlastos. Notre Dame, IN: University of Notre Dame Press, pp. 230–43.

Hadot, Pierre (2002). *What is Ancient Philosophy?* Translated by Michael Chase. Cambridge, MA: Belknap Press of Harvard University.

Henry of Ghent (2005). *Quaestiones quodlibetales.* Translated in part by Roland J. Teske as *Quodlibetal Questions on Moral Problems.* Milwaukee, WI: Marquette University Press.

Henry of Ghent (1993). *Quaestiones quodlibetales.* Translated in part by Roland H. Teske as *Quodlibetal Questions on Free Will.* Milwaukee, WI: Marquette University Press.

Hilduin of Saint-Denis (1994). *Passio sanctissimi Dionysii.* Edited by Philippe Chevallier in *The Works of Pseudo-Dionysius the Areopagite.* Turnhout: Brepols.

Hopkins, Jasper (1986). *A Concise Introduction to the Philosophy of Nicholas of Cusa,* 3rd edition. Minneapolis, MN: Arthur J. Banning Press.

Ingham, Mary Beth and Mechthild Dreyer (2004). *The Philosophical Vision of John Duns Scotus.* Washington, DC: The Catholic University of America Press.

Jaki, Stanley (1972). *The Milky Way: An Elusive Road for Science.* New York: Science History Publications.

John Paul II (1992). "Lessons of the Galileo Case." Address to the Pontifical Academy of Sciences on October 31, 1992, in *Origins* 22/22 (November 12): 371.

John Paul II (1979). "Address to the Pontifical Academy of Sciences" on November 10, 1979, in *Origins* 9/24 (November 29): 391.

Kant, Immanuel (2003). *Critique of Pure Reason.* Translated by Norman Kemp Smith. Revised 2nd edition. New York: Palgrave Macmillan.

Kelly, J. N. D. (1998). *Jerome: His Life, Writings, and Controversies.* Peabody, MA: Hendrickson.

Kelly, J. N. D. (1981). *Early Christian Creeds,* 3rd edition. New York: Longmans.

Kent, Bonnie D. (1995). *Virtues of the Will: The Transformation of Ethics in the Late Thirteenth Century.* Washington, DC: The Catholic University of America Press.

Klima, Gyula (2004). "The Medieval Problem of Universals," *The Stanford Encyclopedia of Philosophy,* accessible at: http://plato.stanford.edu/archives/2004/entries/universals-medieval/.

Kneale, William and Martha Kneale (1962). *The Development of Logic.* Oxford: Clarendon Press.

Koestler, Arthur (1968). *The Sleepwalkers.* New York: Macmillan.

Koterski, Joseph W. (2004). "Boethius and the Theological Origins on the Concept of Person," *American Catholic Philosophical Quarterly* 78/2: 203–24.

Koterski, Joseph W. (2003). "*Fides et ratio* and Biblical Wisdom Literature," in *The Two Wings of Catholic Thought: Essays on Fides et Ratio*. Edited by David Ruel Foster and Joseph W. Koterski, S.J. Washington, DC: Catholic University of America Press, pp. 129–62.

Koterski, Joseph W. (1998). "History of the Philosophy of Religion: From the Thirteenth Century to the Twentieth Century," in Davies (1998), pp. 12–21.

Kretzmann, Norman (1988). *The Cambridge History of Later Medieval Philosophy: From the Rediscovery of Aristotle to the Distintegration of Scholasticism, 1100–1600*. New York: Cambridge University Press.

Ladner, Gerhart B. (1959). *The Idea of Reform: Its Impact on Christian Thought and Action in the Age of the Fathers*. Cambridge, MA: Harvard University Press.

Ladner, Gerhart B. (1958). *The Philosophical Anthropology of Saint Gregory of Nyssa*. Cambridge, MA: Harvard University Press.

Lansing, Carol (1998). *Power and Purity: Cathar Heresy in Medieval Italy*. New York: Oxford University Press.

Lapidge, Michael (1978). "Stoic Cosmology," in *The Stoics*, Edited by John Rist. Berkeley, CA: University of California Press, pp. 161–85.

Leaman, Oliver (1998). *Averroes and His Philosophy*. Revised edition. Richmond, Surrey: Curzon.

Lewis, C. S. (1964). *The Discarded Image: An Introduction to Medieval and Renaissance Literature*. Cambridge: Cambridge University Press.

Lisska, Anthony (1996). *Aquinas's Theory of Natural Law, An Analytic Reconstruction*. Oxford: Oxford University Press.

Lombard, Peter (1971). *Magistri Petri Lombardi Parisiensis episcopi Sententiae in IV libros distinctae*. Grottaferrata: Editiones Collegii S. Bonaventurae ad Claras Aquas, 1971–81.

Lloyd, G. E. R. (1979). *Magic, Reason, and Experience: Studies in the Origin and Development of Greek Science*. New York: Cambridge University Press.

MacDonald, Scott (1992). "Goodness as Transcendental: The Early Thirteenth Century Recovery of an Aristotelian Idea," *Topoi* 11: 173–86.

Machamer, Peter, ed. (1998) *Cambridge Companion to Galileo*. New York: Cambridge University Press.

Macrobius, Ambrosius Aurelius Theodosius (1990). *In Somnium Scipionis commentarium*. Edited and translated by William Harris Stahl as *Commentary on the Dream of Scipio*. New York: Columbia University Press.

Maimonides, Moses (1963). *The Guide for the Perplexed*. Translated by Shlomo Pines. Chicago, IL: University of Chicago Press.

Mandonnet, Pierre (1944). *St Dominic and His Work*. Translated by Sr Mary Benedicta Larkin, O.P. St Louis, MO: B. Herder.

Mansini, Guy (2005). *Promising and the Good*. Ann Arbor, MI: Sapientia Press of Ave Maria University.

Marenbon, Jon, ed. (2003b). *Medieval Philosophy*. Vol. 3 of the Routledge History of Philosophy. New York: Routledge.

Marenbon, Jon (2003a). *Boethius*. Oxford: Oxford University Press.

Marrone, Steven P. (1985). *Truth and Scientific Knowledge in the Thought of Henry of Ghent*. Cambridge, MA: Medieval Academy of America.

Matthew of Aquasparta (1961). *Quaestiones disputatae de Anima*. Edited by A. J. Gondras. Paris: Vrin.

Matthews, Gareth B. (2001). "Knowledge and Illumination," in Stump and Kreztmann (2001), pp. 171–85.

McGinn, Bernard (2001). *The Mystical Thought of Meister Eckhart: The Man from Whom God Hid Nothing*. New York: Crossroads.

McInerny, Ralph (2006). *Praeambula Fidei: Thomism and the God of the Philosophers*. Washington, DC: The Catholic University of America Press.

McKeough, Michael John (1984). *The Meaning of the Rationes Seminales in St. Augustine*. Ann Arbor, MI: University Microfilms.

McKirahan, Robert D. (1992). *Principles and Proofs: Aristotle's Theory of Demonstrative Science*. Princeton, NJ: Princeton University Press.

Mews, C. J. (2005). *Abelard and Heloise*. New York: Oxford University Press.

Miller, Barry (1996). *A Most Unlikely God: A Philosophical Enquiry*. Notre Dame, IN: University of Notre Dame Press.

Morewedge, Parviz (1973). *The Metaphysica of Avicenna (ibn Sīnā): A Critical Translation-Commentary and Analysis of the Fundamental Arguments in Avicenna's Metaphysica*. New York: Columbia University Press.

Nash, Ronald H. (1969). *The Light of the Mind: St Augustine's Theory of Knowledge*. Lexington, KY: University Press of Kentucky.

Nash-Marshall, Siobhan (2000). *Participation and the Good: A Study in Boethian Metaphysics*. New York: Crossroad.

Noone, Timothy (2003). "Universals and Individuation" in Williams (2003), pp. 100–28.

O'Connell, Robert (1987). *The Origin of the Soul in St Augustine's Later Works*. Bronx, NY: Fordham University Press.

O'Connell, Robert (1968). *St Augustine's Early Theory of Man, AD 386–391*. Cambridge, MA: Harvard University Press.

O'Daly, Gerard (1987). *Augustine's Philosophy of Mind*. Berkeley, CA: University of California.

Origen (1973). *De Principiis*. Translated by G. W. Butterworth as *On First Principles, being Koetschau's text of the De Principiis*. New York: Harper & Row.

Panaccio, Claude (1999). "Semantics and Mental Language" in Spade (1999b). pp. 53–75.

Pecham, John (1993). *Questions Concerning the Eternity of the World*. Translated by Vincent G. Potter, S.J. Bronx, NY: Fordham University Press.

Pelikan, Jaroslav (2003). *Creeds and Confession of Faith in the Christian Tradition*. Vol. 1: *Rules of Faith in the Early Church*. New Haven, CT: Yale Univ. Press.

Perl, Eric D. (2007). *Theophany: The Neoplatonic Philosophy of Dionysius the Areopagite*. Albany, NY: SUNY Press.

Philip the Chancellor (1985). *Summa de bono*, 2 vols. Edited by Nikolaus Wicki. Bern, Switzerland: Francke.

Philo of Alexandria (2001). *On the Creation of the Cosmos According to Moses*. Translated by David T. Runia. Leiden: E. J. Brill.

Pieper, Josef (1989). *The Truth of All Things and Reality and the Good*. San Francisco, CA: Ignatius Press.

Pinckaers, Servais (1995). *The Sources of Christian Ethics*. Translated by Sr. Mary Thomas Noble, O.P. Washington, DC: The Catholic University of America Press.

Plato (1997). Translated by John M. Cooper and D. S. Hutchinson as *Plato: Complete Works*. Indianapolis, IN: Hackett.

Plantinga, Alvin (1996). "On Being Evidentially Challenged," in *The Evidential Argument from Evil*. Edited by Daniel Howard-Snyder. Bloomington, IN: Indiana University Press, pp. 244–61.

Plotinus (1966–88). Translated by A. H. Armstrong, Paul Henry, and Hans-Rudolph Schwyzer. Cambridge MA: Harvard University Press. Loeb Classical Library. 7 vols.

Porphyry (1887). *Isagoge et in Aristotelis Categorias Commentarium*. Edited by A. Busse in *Commentaria in Aristotelica Graeca*, vol. 4(1). Berolini: G. Reimarus.

Potts, Timothy (1980). *Conscience in Medieval Philosophy*. New York: Cambridge University Press.

Pruss, Alexander R. (2006). *The Principle of Sufficient Reason: A Reassessment*. New York: Cambridge University Press.

Ptolemy, Claudius (1998). *Ptolemy's Almagest*. Translated by G. J. Toomer. Princeton, NJ: Princeton University Press.

Quay, Paul M. (1995). *The Mystery Hidden for Ages in God*. New York: Peter Lang.

Randles, W. G. L. (1999). *The Unmasking of the Medieval Christian Cosmos, 1500–1760: From Solid Heavens to Boundless Aether*. Aldershott: Ashgate.

Ratzinger, Joseph (1990). *Introduction to Christianity*, trans. J. R. Foster. San Francisco, CA: Ignatius Press.

Régis, Louis M. (1949). *L'Odyssée de la Metaphysique*. Montreal: Institut d'Études Médiévales.

Reichberg, Gregory M. (1998). "Ancient and Early Medieval Thinking," in Davies (1998). pp. 5–11.

Relihan, Joel C. (2007). *The Prisoner's Philosophy: Life and Death in Boethius's Consolation*. Notre Dame, IN: University of Notre Dame Press.

Reydams-Schils, Gretch J. (2003). *Plato's Timaeus as Cultural Icon*. Notre Dame, IN: University of Notre Dame Press.

Rist, John (2002). *Real Ethics*. New York: Cambridge University Press.

Rist, John M. (1985). *Platonism and its Christian Heritage*. London: Variorum.

Rogerson, John et al. (1988). *The History of Christian Theology*. Vol. 2: *The Study and Uses of the Bible*. Grand Rapids, MI: Eerdmans.

Rombs, Ronnie J. (2006). *Saint Augustine and the Fall of the Soul: Beyond O'Connell and His Critics*. Washington, DC: The Catholic University of America Press.

Runia, David T. (1986). *Philo of Alexandria and the Timaeus of Plato*. Leiden: E. J. Brill.

Russman, Thomas (1987). *A Prospectus for the Triumph of Realism*. Macon, GA: Mercer University Press.

Scheibler, Christoph (1617). *Opus metaphysicum*. Giessae Hessorum: N. Hampellii.

Schönborn, Christoph (1994). *God's Human Face: The Christ-Icon*. Translated by Lothar Krauth. San Francisco, CA: Ignatius Press.

Scotus, John Duns (1997). *Quaestiones in Aristotelis Metaphysicam*. Translated by Girard J. Etzkorn and Allan B. Wolter as *Questions on the Metaphysics of Aristotle*. St Bonaventure, NY: Franciscan Institute Publications.

Scotus, John Duns (1950). *Doctoris subtilis et Mariani Ioannis Duns Scoti Ordinis Fratrum Minorum Opera Omnia*. Rome: Typis Polyglottis Vaticanae.

Seneca (1996). *Epistulae*. Translated by Richard M. Gammere as *Seneca: Epistles*. 3 vols. Cambridge, MA: Harvard University Press. Loeb Classical Library.

Simon, Yves (1992). *The Tradition of Natural Law*. Bronx, NY: Fordham University Press.

Sirat, Colette (1985). *A History of Jewish Philosophy in the Middle Ages.* New York: Cambridge University Press.

Smalley, Beryl (1964). *The Study of the Bible in the Middle Ages.* Notre Dame, IN: University of Notre Dame Press.

Solomon, Robert C. (2003). *The Age of German Idealism.* New York: Routledge.

Sorabji, Richard (1987). *Philoponus and the Rejection of Aristotelian Science.* Ithaca, NY: Cornell University Press.

Southern, Richard W. (1995, 2001). *Scholastic Humanism and the Unification of Europe,* 2 vols. Vol. 1: *Foundations.* Vol. 2: *The Heroic Age.* Oxford: Blackwell.

Southern, Richard W. (1990). *Saint Anselm: A Portrait in a Landscape.* Cambridge: Cambridge University Press.

Southern, Richard W. (1986). *Robert Grosseteste: The Growth of an English Mind in Medieval Europe.* Oxford: Clarendon Press.

Spade, Paul Vincent, ed. (1999b). *The Cambridge Companion to Ockham.* New York: Cambridge University Press.

Spade, Paul Vincent (1999a). "Ockham's Nominalist Metaphysics: Some Main Themes," in Spade (1999b), pp. 100–17.

Spade, Paul Vincent, ed. and trans. (1994). *Five Texts on the Mediaeval Problem of Universals: Porphyry, Boethius, Abelard, Duns Scotus, Ockham.* Indianapolis, IN: Hackett.

Stump, Eleonore and Norman Kretzmann, eds. (2001). *The Cambridge Companion to Augustine.* New York: Cambridge University Press.

Suárez, Francisco (1998). *Disputationes Metaphysicae,* in *Opera omnia,* vols. 25–6. Hildesheim, Germany: G. Olms.

Suárez, Francisco (1995). *De entibus rationis.* Translated from *Disputatio 54* of Suarez (1998) by John P. Doyle as *On Beings of Reason.* Milwaukee, WI: Marquette University Press.

Sumption, Jonathan (1999). *The Albigensian Crusade.* Boston, MA: Faber.

Taylor, C. C. W., ed. and trans. (1999). *The Atomists, Leucippus and Democritus, Fragments: A Text and Translation with a Commentary.* Toronto, ONT: University of Toronto Press.

Tertullian (1994). *De Praescripto.* Edited and translated by Alexander Roberts, James Donaldson, A. Cleveland Coxe, and Allan Menzies in *Ante-Nicene Fathers,* vol. 4. Originally published, 1885.

Thom, Paul (2003). *Medieval Modal Systems.* Burlington, VT: Ashgate.

Thorndike, Lynn, ed. (1949). *The Sphere of Sacrobosco and its Commentators.* Chicago, IL: University of Chicago Press.

Torrell, Jean-Pierre (2005). *Aquinas's Summa: Background, Structure, and Reception.* Translated by Benedict M. Guevin. Washington, DC: The Catholic University of America Press.

van Inwagen, Peter (1998). "Ontological Arguments," in Davies (1998), pp. 54–8.

van Steenberghen, Fernand (1980). *Thomas Aquinas and Radical Aristotelianism.* Washington, DC: Catholic University of America Press.

Warren, James (2007). *Presocratics: Natural Philosophy Before Socrates.* Berkeley, CA: University of California, Berkeley.

Weiss, Paul (1983). *Privacy.* Cardondale, IL: Southern Illinois University Press.

Wilken, Robert Louis (2003). *The Spirit of Early Christian Thought: Seeking the Face of God.* New Haven, CT: Yale University Press.

William of Ockham (1998). *Summa Logicae,* pt. 1. Translated by Michael J. Loux as *Ockham's Theory of Terms: Part I of the Summa Logicae.* Notre Dame, IN: University of Notre Dame Press.

William of Ockham (1980). *Summa Logicae,* pt. 2. Translated by Alfred J. Freddoso and Henry Schuurman as *Ockham's Theory of Propositions: Part II of the Summa Logicae.* Notre Dame, IN: University of Notre Dame Press.

Wilken, Robert Louis (2003). *The Spirit of Early Christian Thought: Seeking the Face of God.* New Haven, CT: Yale University Press.

Williams, Thomas, ed. (2003). *The Cambridge Companion to Duns Scotus.* Cambridge: Cambridge University Press.

Wippel, John F. (2000). *The Metaphysical Thought of Thomas Aquinas: From Finite Being to Uncreated Being.* Washington, DC: The Catholic University of America Press.

Zupko, Jack (2003). *John Buridan: Portrait of a Fourteenth-Century Arts Master.* Notre Dame, IN: University of Notre Dame Press.

INDEX OF NAMES

Historical Figures entries appear in *italics*

INDEX OF TERMS

Glossary entries appear in **bold**